Praxis 0200 0201 0202

Reading
Teacher Certification Exam

By: Sharon Wynne, M.S.
Southern Connecticut State University

"And, while there's no reason yet to panic, I think it's only prudent that we make preparations to panic."

XAMonline, INC.
Boston

Copyright © 2009 XAMonline, Inc.

All rights reserved. No part of the material protected by this copyright notice may be reproduced or utilized in any form or by any means, electronic or mechanical, including photocopying, recording or by any information storage and retrievable system, without written permission from the copyright holder.

To obtain permission(s) to use the material from this work for any purpose including workshops or seminars, please submit a written request to:

XAMonline, Inc.
21 Orient Ave.
Melrose, MA 02176
Toll Free 1-800-509-4128
Email: info@xamonline.com
Web www.xamonline.com
Fax: 1-781-662-9268

Library of Congress Cataloging-in-Publication Data

Wynne, Sharon A.
    Reading 0200, 0201,0202 : Teacher Certification/
    Sharon A. Wynne. -2nd ed. ISBN 978-1-58197-034-0
    1. Reading 0200, 0201, 0202.   2. Study Guides.   3. Praxis
    4. Teachers' Certification & Licensure.   5. Careers

Disclaimer:

The opinions expressed in this publication are the sole works of XAMonline and were created independently from the National Education Association, Educational Testing Service, or any State Department of Education, National Evaluation Systems or other testing affiliates.

Between the time of publication and printing, state specific standards as well as testing formats and website information may change that is not included in part or in whole within this product. Sample test questions are developed by XAMonline and reflect similar content as on real tests; however, they are not former tests. XAMonline assembles content that aligns with state standards but makes no claims nor guarantees teacher candidates a passing score. Numerical scores are determined by testing companies such as NES or ETS and then are compared with individual state standards. A passing score varies from state to state.

Printed in the United States of America   œ-1

PPST: Reading 0200, 0201, 0202
ISBN: 978-1-58197-034-0

TEACHER CERTIFICATION STUDY GUIDE

Table of Contents

COMPETENCY 1.0 THEORETICAL BASIS OF READING AS A PROCESS AND EARLY LITERACY 1

Skill 1.1   Demonstrate an understanding of, recognize and support cultural, linguistic, ethnic and linguistic differences in language and literacy learning as they are related to the socio-economic environment of students. 1

Skill 1.2   Demonstrate knowledge of the role of readers' prior knowledge and social/cultural/linguistic background, and of the role of social interaction in constructing meaning 4

Skill 1.3   Demonstrate knowledge of the role of fluency in constructing meaning 5

Skill 1.4   Demonstrate an understanding of the major theories of language development, cognition, and learning, including acquisition of language, social interaction, use of language for communication, relationship between oral and written language, activation of prior knowledge, construction of schemata, use of text structure, use of cueing systems, and development of reader response 6

Skill 1.5   Recognize the effects of emotional, social, physical, cultural, environmental and intellectual factors on language acquisition, language development and reading 10

Skill 1.6   Demonstrate an understanding of the relationships between and among reading, writing, listening, speaking, viewing, and thinking for all learners 11

Skill 1.7   Demonstrate an understanding that all languages have rules for grammar and are used for communication through semantics, syntax, orthography, morphology and phonological components 12

Skill 1.8   Demonstrate knowledge of phonemic awareness (e.g. rhyming, segmenting, blending sounds) and the alphabetic principle in reading acquisition 25

Skill 1.9   Demonstrate an understanding of genre patterns, and the influences of purpose, context and genre in constructing meaning 40

READING   i

Skill 1.10	Recognize and demonstrate understanding of the factors that influence early literacy and language acquisition and the different stages at which literacy occurs 45
Skill 1.11	Demonstrate an understanding of ways adults support and facilitate language acquisition 48

COMPETENCY 2.0   APPLICATION OF THEORETICAL AND KNOWLEDGE BASES OF READING IN INSTRUCTION 49

Skill 2.1	Demonstrate an understanding of the relationship between reading and writing instruction and of how writing and reading support each other at different developmental levels. 49
Skill 2.2	Demonstrate knowledge of how to construct instructional plans in which assessment, goals, instruction and reassessment are connected and continuous 51
Skill 2.3	Demonstrate knowledge of explicit instructional strategies to teach students how to monitor their own word identification strategies, comprehension, and comprehension strategies 53
Skill 2.4	Demonstrate knowledge of instructional approaches to foster higher-order, critical, reflective thinking about text 62
Skill 2.5	Demonstrate an understanding of different decoding strategies and of instructional approaches to teach students how to use them 64
Skill 2.6	Demonstrate an understanding of the instruction of comprehension strategies, including modeling when and how to orchestrate multiple comprehension strategies and their scaffolding 70
Skill 2.7	Demonstrate knowledge of explicit instruction and scaffolding for learning study skills and strategies 71
Skill 2.8	Demonstrate knowledge of how to evaluate the level of text difficulty and appropriateness of reading materials and programs for a variety of instructional purposes and learning situations 73
Skill 2.9	Demonstrate an understanding of how literacy needs differ across content areas (e.g. science, math, art) 76
Skill 2.10	Demonstrate an understanding of how to appropriately use texts within diverse genres for multiple purposes and lifelong learning 76

TEACHER CERTIFICATION STUDY GUIDE

Skill 2.11 Demonstrate knowledge of a variety of children's/adolescent literature, including multicultural literature, and how to mediate it to enhance instruction 78

Skill 2.12 Demonstrate an understanding of how technology can be used to enhance instruction 81

Skill 2.13 Demonstrate an understanding of how to teach students to recursively apply strategies for planning, drafting, revising, and editing texts to different genres for a variety of purposes and audiences 86

Skill 2.14 Demonstrate an understanding of the purpose of publication of student writing in literacy acquisition 90

Skill 2.15 Demonstrate an understanding of deliberate vocabulary instruction across grades and content areas 90

Skill 2.16 Demonstrate knowledge of how to plan and implement instruction that addresses the strengths and needs of all students 90

Skill 2.17 Demonstrate an understanding of instructional decisions to accommodate learners with social, cultural, linguistic and cognitive differences 90

Skill 2.18 Demonstrate knowledge of various instructional grouping strategies to motivate and engage all students (e.g. flexible, whole class, small group, individual, ability/achievement) and the issues associated with each 90

Skill 2.19 Demonstrate an understanding of how to create a safe and respectful environment for all students 91

Skill 2.20 Demonstrate an understanding of how to organize programmatic activities to encourage reading (e.g. book clubs, read-a-thons) with an understanding of differences between extrinsic and intrinsic motivation 91

COMPETENCY 3.0 READING MATERIALS AND INSTRUCTION AND READING ENVIRONMENT 93

Skill 3.1 Identify and use texts, trade books, and other print and non-print materials to foster appreciation of reading for students who are at various levels and from various cultures 93

Skill 3.2	Identify strategies appropriate for a variety of printed materials and identify texts that are appropriate for a specific reading purpose	93
Skill 3.3	Identify strategies for recognizing and evaluating students' attitudes and needs, and suggest books/materials in a variety of genres at appropriate difficulty levels to meet those needs	93
Skill 3.4	Identify techniques for providing opportunities for creative and personal responses to reading	94
Skill 3.5	Demonstrate an understanding of a variety of approaches to teaching reading and of methods to organize instruction effectively	95
Skill 3.6	Identify strategies for exposing students to a variety of genres and help them understand the characteristics of each genre	95
Skill 3.7	Identify various purposes for reading	95
Skill 3.8	Demonstrate an understanding of how to use a variety of non-print sources, how to use study aids and how to interpret graphics	95
Skill 3.9	Identify strategies to purposefully integrate the language arts into all content areas, including the use of technology	96
Skill 3.10	Identify components of a balanced literacy program, (word study, reading aloud, shared reading, guided reading, independent reading, writing, speaking, viewing and listening) and sensitivity to a developmental continuum	97
Skill 3.11	Identify ways to use flexible grouping to accommodate students' needs	98
Skill 3.12	Identify the influences of family and peers as well as ethnic, socioeconomic, regional, and cultural factors as they relate to reading development	99
Skill 3.13	Identify ways to include parents as partners in the literacy development of their children	99
Skill 3.14	Identify techniques for creating a literate environment in which students can connect purposes of reading to their personal lives	100

Skill 3.15	Identify ways to increase learners' motivation to read independently for information and pleasure	106
Skill 3.16	Identify ways to use the connection between reading and writing to foster and enhance communication skills in all students	110

COMPETENCY 4.0 READING COMPREHENSION 111

Skill 4.1	Demonstrate an understanding of instructional techniques such as modeling, scaffolding, and appropriate questioning strategies to enhance students' understanding of text	111
Skill 4.2	Demonstrate an understanding of appropriate and effective uses of oral and silent reading	112
Skill 4.3	Identify strategies for using context to define words and strategies to learn and extend word meanings	113
Skill 4.4	Demonstrate an understanding of techniques for teaching understanding and learning skills, such as Directed Reading/Thinking Activities (DR-TA); What we know, What we want to know, what we learned (KWL); Survey, Question, Read, Recite, (SQ3R); graphic organizers; test-taking strategies; varying reading Rate	113
Skill 4.5	Identify techniques that enable students to connect prior knowledge with new information	113
Skill 4.6	Identify techniques to develop comprehension strategies in the content areas	113
Skill 4.7	Demonstrate an understanding of ways to develop fluency in students' reading and its link to comprehension	113

COMPETENCY 5.0 VOCABULARY, SPELLING AND WORD STUDY 116

Skill 5.1	Demonstrate an understanding of strategies and skills (phonemic awareness, print concepts, conceptual vocabulary, experience with print, and stories) contributing to the development of reading	114

Skill 5.2	Demonstrate an understanding of word study strategies, as well as effective use of phonics (graphophonic cues), context (syntactic and semantic cues), and sight words (instant recognition)	114
Skill 5.3	Demonstrate an understanding of the use of phonics, along with other awareness and cues in text, e.g. phonemes, morphemes, endings, prefixes, suffixes, to analyze and decode words that are not recognized instantly	114
Skill 5.4	Demonstrate an understanding of the role that spelling plays in enhancing and informing instruction	114
Skill 5.5	Demonstrate strategies for teaching vocabulary (roots, affixes, context, word origins) and helping students use these strategies to enhance their reading comprehension	115

COMPETENCY 6.0 APPLICATION OF THEORETICAL KNOWLEDGE BASES OF READING IN DIAGNOSIS AND ASSESSMENT 116

Skill 6.1	Identify appropriate strategies to assess students' awareness of letter-sound correspondences, of vocabulary, and of reading comprehension	116
Skill 6.2	Understand formal and informal assessments such as criterion and norm referenced tests, running records, anecdotal records, work samples, Informal Reading Inventories (IRI's), portfolios, and self-assessment	116
Skill 6.3	Demonstrate an understanding of basic measurement concepts (e.g., reliability, validity)	124
Skill 6.4	Demonstrate an understanding of how to collaborate with classroom teachers to use assessment results to evaluate and modify reading instruction	125
Skill 6.5	Demonstrate an understanding of how to communicate the findings of reading assessment data with all stakeholders effectively (e.g., students, parents, classroom teachers, guidance counselors, speech teachers and other personnel.)	126
Skill 6.6	Demonstrate an understanding of how to communicate and collaborate children's reading development with families effectively	126

COMPETENCY 7.0 READING LEADERSHIP 127

Skill 7.1 Demonstrate an understanding of how to develop and adapt reading programs to meet student needs within the framework of guidelines and regulations at the classroom, building, district, state and federal levels 127

Skill 7.2 Demonstrate an awareness of how to access literacy research and disseminate it across the grade levels 128

Skill 7.3 Demonstrate an understanding of how to use school-wide initiatives and other services to students to improve instruction 128

Skill 7.4 Demonstrate an understanding of culturally relevant curricular approaches to improve instruction 129

Skill 7.5 Demonstrate an understanding of how standards and their assessment define curriculum, impact the reading program and influence instruction 129

Skill 7.6 Demonstrate an understanding of how to critically analyze school-wide reading programs and initiatives in relation to reading goals and student needs 131

Skill 7.7 Demonstrate an understanding of how to serve as a resource within a school 131

Skill 7.8 Demonstrate an understanding of how to promote collaboration among colleagues (e.g., classroom teachers, paraprofessionals, volunteers) for the literacy development of all students 132

Skill 7.9 Demonstrate an understanding of how to engage in, promote and provide professional development opportunities 132

Skill 7.10 Demonstrate an understanding of the importance of school and community when promoting home-school connections 133

Skill 7.11 Demonstrate an understanding of how to promote positive and effective literacy connections between the home and the school and between the school and the community 133

TEACHER CERTIFICATION STUDY GUIDE

Glossary 134

Directory of Theorists and Researchers 145

Bibliography of Print Resources 152

Tools for teaching and testing 167

Sample Test 171

Answer Key 201

Rigor Table 202

Rationales for Sample Questions 203

Constructed Response Questions 269

Tips and Reflections 274

Additional Citations 275

TEACHER CERTIFICATION STUDY GUIDE

Great Study and Testing Tips!

What to study in order to prepare for the subject assessments is the focus of this study guide but equally important is *how* you study.

You can increase your chances of truly mastering the information by taking some simple, but effective steps.

Study Tips:

1. Some foods aid the learning process. Foods such as milk, nuts, seeds, rice, and oats help your study efforts by releasing natural memory enhancers called CCKs (*cholecystokinin*) composed of *tryptophan*, *choline*, and *phenylalanine*. All of these chemicals enhance the neurotransmitters associated with memory. Before studying, try a light, protein-rich meal of eggs, turkey, and fish. All of these foods release the memory enhancing chemicals. The better the connections, the more you comprehend.

Likewise, before you take a test, stick to a light snack of energy boosting and relaxing foods. A glass of milk, a piece of fruit, or some peanuts all release various memory-boosting chemicals and help you to relax and focus on the subject at hand.

2. Learn to take great notes. A by-product of our modern culture is that we have grown accustomed to getting our information in short doses (i.e. TV news sound bites or USA Today style newspaper articles.)

Consequently, we've subconsciously trained ourselves to assimilate information better in neat little packages. If your notes are scrawled all over the paper, it fragments the flow of the information. Strive for clarity. Newspapers use a standard format to achieve clarity. Your notes can be much clearer through use of proper formatting. A very effective format is called the *"Cornell Method."*

> Take a sheet of loose-leaf lined notebook paper and draw a line all the way down the paper about 1-2" from the left-hand edge.
>
> Draw another line across the width of the paper about 1-2" up from the bottom. Repeat this process on the reverse side of the page.

Look at the highly effective result. You have ample room for notes, a left hand margin for special emphasis items or inserting supplementary data from the textbook, a large area at the bottom for a brief summary, and a little rectangular space for just about anything you want.

READING

3. Get the concept then the details. Too often we focus on the details and don't gather an understanding of the concept. However, if you simply memorize only dates, places, or names, you may well miss the whole point of the subject.

A key way to understand things is to put them in your own words. If you are working from a textbook, automatically summarize each paragraph in your mind. If you are outlining text, don't simply copy the author's words.

Rephrase them in your own words. You remember your own thoughts and words much better than someone else's, and subconsciously tend to associate the important details to the core concepts.

4. Ask Why? Pull apart written material paragraph by paragraph and don't forget the captions under the illustrations.

Example: If the heading is "Stream Erosion", invert it to read "Why do streams erode?" Then answer the questions.

If you train your mind to think in a series of questions and answers, not only will you learn more, but it also helps to lessen the test anxiety because you are used to answering questions.

5. Read for reinforcement and future needs. Even if you only have 10 minutes, put your notes or a book in your hand. Your mind is similar to a computer; you have to input data in order to have it processed. *By reading, you are creating the neural connections for future retrieval.* The more times you read something, the more you reinforce the learning of ideas.

Even if you don't fully understand something on the first pass, *your mind stores much of the material for later recall.*

6. Relax to learn so go into exile. Our bodies respond to an inner clock called biorhythms. Burning the midnight oil works well for some people, but not everyone.

If possible, set aside a particular place to study that is free of distractions. Shut off the television, cell phone, and pager and exile your friends and family during your study period.

If you really are bothered by silence, try background music. Light classical music at a low volume has been shown to aid in concentration over other types. Music that evokes pleasant emotions without lyrics is highly suggested. Try just about anything by Mozart. It relaxes you.

7. **Use arrows not highlighters.** At best, it's difficult to read a page full of yellow, pink, blue, and green streaks. Try staring at a neon sign for a while and you'll soon see that the horde of colors obscure the message.

A quick note, a brief dash of color, an underline, and an arrow pointing to a particular passage is much clearer than a horde of highlighted words.

8. **Budget your study time.** Although you shouldn't ignore any of the material, *allocate your available study time in the same ratio that topics may appear on the test.*

Testing Tips:

1. <u>Get smart, play dumb</u>. Don't read anything into the question. Don't make an assumption that the test writer is looking for something else than what is asked. Stick to the question as written and don't read extra things into it.

2. <u>Read the question and all the choices *twice* before answering the question</u>. You may miss something by not carefully reading, and then re-reading both the question and the answers.

If you really don't have a clue as to the right answer, leave it blank on the first time through. Go on to the other questions, as they may provide a clue as to how to answer the skipped questions.

If later on, you still can't answer the skipped ones . . . ***Guess.*** The only penalty for guessing is that you *might* get it wrong. Only one thing is certain; if you don't put anything down, you will get it wrong!

3. <u>Turn the question into a statement</u>. Look at the way the questions are worded. The syntax of the question usually provides a clue. Does it seem more familiar as a statement rather than as a question? Does it sound strange?

By turning a question into a statement, you may be able to spot if an answer sounds right, and it may also trigger memories of material you have read.

4. <u>Look for hidden clues</u>. It's actually very difficult to compose multiple-foil (choice) questions without giving away part of the answer in the options presented.

In most multiple-choice questions you can often readily eliminate one or two of the potential answers. This leaves you with only two real possibilities and automatically your odds go to 50/50 for very little work.

5. <u>Trust your instincts</u>. For every fact that you have read, you subconsciously retain something of that knowledge. On questions that you aren't really certain about, go with your basic instincts. **Your first impression on how to answer a question is usually correct.**

6. <u>Mark your answers directly on the test booklet</u>. Don't bother trying to fill in the optical scan sheet on the first pass through the test.

Just be very careful not to miss-mark your answers when you eventually transcribe them to the scan sheet.

7. <u>Watch the clock</u>! You have a set amount of time to answer the questions. Don't get bogged down trying to answer a single question at the expense of 10 questions you can more readily answer.

READING

Foundations of Reading

"Any child who doesn't learn how to read early and well will not easily master other skills and knowledge and is unlikely to ever flourish in school or in life."
Reading Is Rocket Science, American Federation of Teachers

"If our teaching of reading is to be an art, we need to draw from all we know, think and believe in order to create something beautiful."
Lucy Calkins

This guide was developed to serve the needs of test-takers on the PreK-6 level who are preparing for the Foundations of Reading certification test. The quotes which introduce this work point to the crucial nature and significance of effective teaching of reading for our children and our nation's future.

The competencies and skills shared in this guide are also intended to support the educator new to reading certification in ongoing teaching and learning in Reading. Therefore, sample strategies, web resources, student trade books, picture book citations, and explanations of ready-to-use practices are included.

This guide has a specified page limit and is designed for immediate use. The web resources and bibliographies provided will allow the reader to keep up with new research or investigate a particular strategy, referenced theorist, or term in a deeper, more detailed fashion. In addition, an Appendix, a dictionary of words and terms essential to one's knowledge base as a reading teacher, is included. Yet another study guide, a directory of key reading theorists, is included for your use as well.

It is my hope that this study guide will merit placement in your home or on your classroom professional library shelf for use as you begin your teaching career. Enjoy and share with your colleagues and parents, as we work together to nurture lifelong readers and writers.

Please let XAMonline know how you are able to use this guide to help you in your teacher certification experience and in your ongoing or future teaching and learning.

THIS PAGE BLANK

TEACHER CERTIFICATION STUDY GUIDE

COMPETENCY 1.0 THEORETICAL BASIS OF READING AS A PROCESS AND EARLY LITERACY

Skill 1.1 Demonstrate an understanding of, recognize and support cultural, linguistic, ethnic and linguistic differences in language and literacy learning as they are related to the socio-economic environment of students

A positive self-concept is a very important element of a student's ability to learn and to be an integral member of society. If students think poorly of themselves or have sustained feelings of inferiority, they are not able to optimize their potential for learning. It is therefore part of the teacher's task to ensure that each student develops a positive self-concept.

A positive self-concept does not imply feelings of superiority, perfection, or competence. Instead, a positive self-concept involves self-acceptance and self-respect. Encouraging these factors contributes to the development of a positive self-concept in students.

Teachers may take a number of approaches to enhancing self-concept among students. One such scheme is the process approach, which proposes a three-phase model for teaching. This model includes a sensing function, a transforming function, and an acting function. These three factors can be simplified into the words by which the model is usually given: reach, touch, and teach. The sensing or perceptual function incorporates information or stimuli in an intuitive manner. The transforming function conceptualizes, abstracts, evaluates, and provides meaning and value to perceived information. The acting function chooses actions from several different alternatives to be set forth overtly. The process model may be applied to almost any curricular field.

An approach that aims to directly enhance self-concept is called *Invitational Education*. According to this approach, teachers and their behaviors are classified as inviting or disinviting. Inviting behaviors enhance self-concept among students, while disinviting behaviors diminish self-concept.

Disinviting behaviors include those that demean students, as well as those that may be chauvinistic, sexist, condescending, thoughtless, or insensitive to student feelings. Inviting behaviors are the opposite of these and display consistency and sensitivity. Inviting teacher behaviors reflect an attitude of "doing with" rather than "doing to." Students are "invited" or "disinvited" depending on teachers' behavior.

Invitational teachers exhibit the following skills (Biehler and Snowman, 394):

- reaching each student (e.g., learning names, having one-to-one contact)
- listening with care (e.g., picking up subtle cues)
- being real with students (e.g., providing only realistic praise, "coming on straight")
- being real with oneself (e.g., honestly appraising your own feelings and disappointments)
- inviting good discipline (e.g., showing students you have respect in personal ways)
- handling rejection (e.g., not taking lack of student response in personal ways)
- inviting oneself (e.g., thinking positively about oneself)

Cooperative learning situations as practiced in today's classrooms grew out of research conducted by several groups in the early 1970s. Cooperative learning situations can range from very formal applications such as Student Teams-Achievement Divisions (STAD) and Cooperative Integrated Reading and Composition (CIRC) to less formal groupings sometimes called "group investigation," "learning together," or "discovery groups."

Cooperative learning is now firmly recognized and established as a teaching and learning technique in American schools. Since cooperative learning techniques are so widely diffused in the schools, it is necessary to orient students in the skills by which cooperative learning groups can operate smoothly and thereby enhance learning. Students who cannot interact constructively with other students will not be able to take advantage of the learning opportunities provided by the cooperative learning situations and will further deprive their fellow students of the opportunity for cooperative learning.

These skills form the hierarchy of cooperation in which students first learn to work together, so that they may proceed to levels at which they can engage in simulated conflict situations. This cooperative setting allows different points of view to be constructively entertained.

Effective teaching and learning for students begins with teachers who demonstrate sensitivity for diversity in teaching and relationships within school communities. Student portfolios include work that has a multicultural perspective and inclusion in which students share cultural and ethnic life experiences in their learning. Teachers are responsible for including cultural and diverse resources in their curriculum and instructional practices.

Exposing students to culturally sensitive room decorations and posters that show positive and inclusive messages is one way to demonstrate inclusion of multiple cultures. Teachers should also continuously make cultural connections that are relevant and empowering for all students. Cultural sensitivity should be communicated beyond the classroom with parents and community members to establish and maintain relationships.

Diversity can be further defined as the following:

- Differences among learners, classroom settings and academic outcomes
- Biology, sociology, ethnicity, socioeconomic status, psychological needs, learning modalities and styles among learners
- Differences in classroom settings that promote learning opportunities such as collaborative, participatory, and individualized learning groupings
- Expected learning outcomes that are theoretical, affective and cognitive

Teachers should establish a classroom climate that is culturally respectful and engaging for students. In a culturally sensitive classroom, teachers maintain equity and fairness in student interactions and curriculum implementation. Assessments include cultural responses and perspectives that provide further learning opportunities for students.

Some methods of displaying sensitivity to diversity include:

- Student portfolios reflecting multicultural/multiethnic perspectives
- Journals and reflections from field trips/ guest speakers from diverse cultural backgrounds
- Printed materials and wall displays from multicultural perspectives
- Parent/guardian letters in a variety of languages reflecting cultural diversity
- Projects that include cultural history and diverse inclusions
- Disaggregated student data reflecting cultural groups
- Classroom climate of professionalism that fosters diversity and cultural inclusion

Aiming for diversity allows teachers to expand their experiences with students, staff, community members and parents from culturally diverse backgrounds, so that their experiences can be proactively applied in promoting cultural diversity in the classroom. Teachers can engage and challenge students to develop and incorporate their own diversity skills in building character and relationships with cultures beyond their own. By encouraging students to become culturally inclusive, teachers are addressing the globalization of our world.

Skill 1.2 **Demonstrate knowledge of the role of readers' prior knowledge, social/cultural/linguistic background, and social interaction in constructing meaning**

Prior Knowledge

Prior knowledge can be defined as the entirety of an individual's experiences, learning, and development which precede his or her entering a specific learning situation or attempting to comprehend a specific text. Sometimes prior knowledge can be erroneous or incomplete. Obviously, if there are misconceptions in a child's prior knowledge, these must be corrected so that his or her overall comprehension skills can continue to progress. Even for kindergarteners, prior knowledge includes accumulated positive and negative experiences both in and out of school.

These experiences might range from wonderful family travels, watching television, visiting museums and libraries, to visiting hospitals, prisons or surviving poverty. Whatever prior knowledge the child brings to the school setting, the independent reading and writing the child does in school immeasurably expands his or her knowledge and hence broadens reading comprehension capabilities. As they prepare any imaginative/literary text, teachers must consider the following about students' level of prior knowledge:

- What prior knowledge needs to be activated for the text, theme or for the writing to be done successfully?
- How independent are the children in using strategies to activate their prior knowledge? Holes and Roser (1987) have suggested five techniques for activating prior knowledge before starting an imaginative/literary text:

FREE RECALL: Tell us what you know about . . .

UNSTRUCTURED DISCUSSION: Let's talk about . . .

STRUCTURED QUESTION: Who exactly was Jane Aviles in the life of the hero of the story?

WORD ASSOCIATION: When you hear these words—"hatch," "elephant," "who," "think"—what author do you think of?

RECOGNITION: "Mulberry Street"—what author comes to mind?

Previewing and predicting and story mapping are excellent strategies for activating prior knowledge.

Schemata

Schemata are structures which represent generic concepts stored in our memory (Rumelhart, l980). Young children develop their schemata through experiences. The more closely the reader's experiences and schemata approximate those of the writer, the more likely the reader is to comprehend the text. Prior knowledge and lack of experience can influence comprehension. It is obvious that for many children from non-native English-Language-speaking backgrounds, and perhaps for those from struggling socioeconomic family structures, schemata deficits indicate the need for intense teacher support as these children become emergent and early readers.

Often the teacher will have to model and scaffold for the child the steps to form a schemata from the information provided in a text.

Comprehension

Cooper (citation missing here) defines comprehension as "a strategic process by which readers construct or assign meaning to a text by using the clues in the text and their own prior knowledge." We view comprehension as a process in which the reader transacts with the text to construct or assign meaning. Reading and writing are both interconnected and mutually supportive. Comprehension is a strategic process in which readers adjust their reading to suit their reading purpose and the type or genre of text they are reading. Narrative and expository texts require different reading approaches because of their different text structures.

Strategic readers also call into play metacognitive capacities as they analyze texts so that they are aware of the skills needed to construct meaning from the text structure.

Skill 1.3 Demonstrate knowledge of the role of fluency in constructing meaning

Fluency is the ability to read a text quickly and accurately. In silent reading, readers can recognize words automatically and they fully comprehend what they read. If comprehension is not immediate, these readers can use context clues to grasp the meaning of the sentence or paragraph. When reading aloud, fluent readers display confidence and read effortlessly and with expression (prosody). Readers who are not fluent read slowly, often one word at a time. By focusing on reading accurately, meaning is lost.

Fluency is an important skill because it helps readers develop from word recognition to comprehension. When readers don't have to spend time focusing on reading individual words, they can group words together to form ideas, which leads to comprehension. Not only can they grasp the main idea of the text, but they can make connections between the text and their prior knowledge and events in their own lives.

Fluency is a skill that is developed over time with repeated practice, exposure to literature and opportunities to read for various purposes. Early readers read words rather than phrases and sentences and the act of reading often appears to be laborious rather than enjoyable. Fluency changes over time as readers are exposed to more difficult texts. The most fluent readers at one level may read slowly when they are first introduced to a more difficult text because they need time for comprehension.

Fluency requires more than just a repertoire of recognizable words, however; expression is also part of fluency. To read fluently with expression a reader must be able to break the text into meaningful phrases and clauses. Some techniques to use when teaching students to read fluently include:

- repeated reading of the same text
- oral reading practice using audiotapes
- providing models of what fluent reading looks and sounds like
- reading to students
- choral reading
- partner reading
- Readers' Theatre

Skill 1.4   Demonstrate an understanding of the major theories of language development, cognition, and learning, including acquisition of language, social interaction, using language for communication, understanding the relationship between oral and written language, activating prior knowledge, constructing schemata, using text structure and cueing systems, and developing reader response

Decoding

In the late l960s and the l970s, many reading specialists, most prominently Fries (1962), believed that successful decoding resulted in reading comprehension. This meant that if children could sound out words, they would then automatically be able to comprehend those words. Many teachers of reading and many reading texts still subscribe to this theory.

Asking Questions

Another theory or approach to teaching reading that gained currency in the late 1960s and the early 1970s was the importance of asking inferential and critical thinking questions which would challenge and engage children in the text. This approach to reading went beyond the literal level of what was stated in the text to an inferential level of using text clues to make predictions and to a critical level of involving the child in evaluating the text. While asking engaging and thought-provoking questions is still viewed as part of teaching reading, it is viewed currently as only one component of that process.

Comprehension Skills

As various reading theories, practices, and approaches percolated during the 1970s and 1980s, many educators and researchers in the field came to believe that the teacher of reading had to teach a set of discrete comprehension skills (Otto et al, 1977). The reading teacher thus became a teacher of individual comprehension skills. Children in such classrooms gleaned such concepts as main idea, sequence, and cause and effect that were supposed to make them better comprehenders. But did acquiring such skills make them lifelong readers?

Transactional Approach

During the late 1970s and early 1980s, researchers in the field of education, psychology and linguistics began to examine the ways in which a reader comprehends. Among them was Louise Rosenblatt, who posited that reading is a transaction between the reader and the text. It is Rosenblatt (1978) who explained successful reading as a process in which the reader constructed meaning from a text in such a way that reflected both the reader and the text. She described two general purposes for reading: *efferent* and *aesthetic*. Efferent reading is looking for and remembering information to use functionally. Examples would be filling out a job application, reading a story in preparation for a test, or reading a newspaper article to find out who won the state basketball championship. Aesthetic reading connects one's own life to the text; the aesthetic reader is swept away by the beauty of a poem or responds emotionally to a book such as *Bridge to Terabithia*.

These differing purposes call for somewhat different reading strategies: one might skim the newspaper article for basketball information but read a poem closely ten times and create mental images of different passages. When children are asked to read all fiction differently (What's the setting? What's the main conflict in the plot? There will be a test on Thursday!), it can thwart a child's joy in the written word and work against his or her desire to be a lifelong reader.

Bottom-up, Top-Down Interactional Theories of Reading

Bottom-up theories of reading assume that children learn from part to whole, starting with the smallest segments possible. Instruction begins with a strong phonics approach, learning letter-sound relationships and often using basal readers or *decodable books*. Decodable books are vocabulary-controlled using language from word families with high predictability. Thus we get sentences like "Nan has a tan fan." Reading is seen as skills-based and the skills are taught one at a time.

Top-down theories of reading suggest that reading begins with the reader's knowledge, not the print. Children are seen as having a drive to construct meaning. This stance views reading as moving from the whole to the parts. An early top-down theory was the *whole word* approach. Children memorized high-frequency words to assist them in reading the Dick and Jane books of the 1930s. Then teachers helped children discover letter-sound correspondences in what they read.

A more recent top-down theory is the *whole language* approach. This approach was influenced by research on how young children learned language. It was thought that children could learn to read as naturally as they learned to talk. Children were surrounded by print in their classrooms, reading quality literature often printed in Big Books, and were viewed as writers from the start. Hence, even kindergarten children were encouraged to keep journals. Advocates of whole language viewed the "skill'em-drill'em-and kill'em" approach based on bottom-up theories as a deadly dull introduction to the world of reading.

Interactive theories of reading combine the strengths of both bottom-up and top-down approaches. Teachers need to be able to teach decoding, vocabulary, and comprehension skills to support children's drive for meaning and desire for a stimulating exchange with high-quality literary texts from their earliest days in school. Strategies include shared, guided, and independent reading, Big Books, reading and writing workshops, and the like. Today this approach is called the *balanced literacy approach*. It is considered to be a synthesis of the best from bottom-up and top-down methods.

Literacy and Literacy Learning

To be literate in a twenty-first-century world means more than being able to read and write. To live well and happily in today's society an individual has to be able to read not only newspapers and books, but emails, blogs, directions for how to use one's cell phone, and the like. A disconnect has evolved between the isolated reading comprehension skills schools were teaching and the literacy skills, including listening and speaking, that are crucial for employment and personal and academic success. Thornburg (1992, 2003) has also noted that technology capacities and the ability to communicate online are now integral parts of our sense of literacy.

Cooper (2004) views literacy as reading, writing, thinking, listening, viewing, and discussing. These are not viewed as separate activities or components of instruction, but rather as ways of developing and being nurtured simultaneously and interactively. Children learn these abilities by engaging in authentic explorations, readings, projects and experiences.

Just as in learning how to ride a bike the learner goes through various approximations before actually learning how to ride, so too does the reader with the scaffold (support) of a teacher go through various approximations before developing his or her own independent literacy skills and capacities.

Emergent Literacy is the concept that young children are emerging into reading and writing with no real beginning or ending point. Children are introduced into the world of print as soon as their parents read board books to them at the age of one or two. When children scribble-write or use invented spelling during the preschool years, they reveal themselves as detectives of the written word, having watched parents and teachers make lists, write thank-you notes, or leave messages. This view of the reader assumes that all children have a drive to make meaning in print and will begin doing it almost on their own if surrounded by a print-rich environment.

Reading Readiness is an approach which is antithetical to emergent literacy in that it assumes that all children must have mastered a sequence of reading skills before they can begin to read.

Language Acquisition is continuous and never-ending. From the perspective of this theory and research, all children come to school with a language base which the school must build on. As a consequence of the connection between oral language and reading, it is important that schools build literacy experiences around the language the child brings to the school.

The Role of Literature in Developing Literacy

The balanced literacy approach advocates the use of "real literature"—recognized works of the best of children's fiction and non-fiction trade books and winners of such awards as the Newberry and Caldecott medals—for helping children develop literacy. Balanced literacy advocates argue that:

- Real literature engages young readers and assures that they will become lifelong readers.
- Real literature also offers readers a language base that can help them expand their expressiveness as readers and as writers.
- Real literature is easier to read and understand than grade-level texts

In some US districts a phonics-only approach is heavily embedded. However, the majority of school districts would describe their approach to reading as the balanced literacy approach, which includes phonics work as well as the use of real literature texts. To contrast the phonics and balanced literacy approaches as opposite is inaccurate, since a balanced approach includes both.

It is important to go online and to visit the key resources of the National Council of Teachers of English (NCTE) and the International Reading Association (IRA) to keep abreast of the latest research in the field.

Activation of Prior Knowledge and Schemata is covered in Skill 1.2

Skill 1.5   **Recognize the effects of emotional, social, physical, cultural, environmental and intellectual factors on language acquisition, language development and reading**

Adolescent literature, because of the age range of readers, is extremely diverse. Fiction for the middle group, usually ages ten/eleven to fourteen/fifteen, deals with issues of coping with internal and external changes in their lives. Because children's writers in the twentieth century have produced increasingly realistic fiction, adolescents can now find problems dealt with honestly in novels.

Teachers of middle/junior high school students see the greatest change in interests and reading abilities. Fifth and sixth graders, included in elementary grades in many schools, are viewed as older children while seventh and eighth graders are preadolescent. Ninth graders included sometimes as top dogs in junior high school and sometimes as underlings in high school, definitely view themselves as teenagers. Their literature choices will often be governed more by interest than by ability; thus, the wealth of high-interest, low readability books that have flooded the market in recent years. Tenth through twelfth graders will still select high-interest books for pleasure reading but are also easily encouraged to stretch their literature muscles by reading more classics.

Because of the rapid social changes, topics that once did not interest young people until they reached their teens - suicide, gangs, homosexuality - are now subjects of books for even younger readers. The plethora of high-interest books reveals how desperately schools have failed to produce on-level readers and how the market has adapted to that need. However, these high-interest books are now readable for younger children whose reading levels are at or above normal. No matter how tastefully written, some content is inappropriate for younger readers. The problem becomes not so much steering them toward books that they have the reading ability to handle but encouraging them toward books whose content is appropriate to their levels of cognitive and social development. A fifth-grader may be able to read V.C. Andrews book *Flowers in the Attic* but not possess the social/moral development to handle the deviant behavior of the characters. At the same time, because of the complex changes affecting adolescents, the teacher must be well versed in learning theory and child development as well as competent to teach the subject matter of language and literature.

Skill 1.6   Demonstrate an understanding of the relationships between and among reading, writing, listening, speaking, viewing, and thinking for all learners

Reading, writing, listening and speaking are the four main components of language arts at any grade level. They are interrelated and they complement each other. By ensuring that all four of these strands are woven into your language arts classes, you can ensure a balance of experiences to give students the instruction and support they need. With such a balance, students are able to integrate all of the English language processes and build on their prior knowledge and experiences.

Speaking and listening are the foundation for many other language skills and teachers should provide ample opportunities for students to speak and listen in class as part of the daily routine. Classrooms are places where talk flows freely. Teachers can take advantage of this talk to assess how students are thinking about topics and themes and responding to literature. When students can express ideas in their own words, it helps them to make meaning of their experiences with reading.

Although speaking in class may seem natural for some students, listening is something that has to be nurtured and taught. Good listeners will respond emotionally, imaginatively and intellectually to what they hear. Students need to be taught how to respond to presentations by their classmates in ways that are not harmful or derogatory in any way. There are different types of listening that the teacher can develop in the students:

- Appreciative listening to enjoy an experience
- Attentive listening to gain knowledge
- Critical listening to evaluate arguments and ideas

Skill 1.7 **Demonstrate an understanding that all languages have rules for grammar and are used for communication through semantics, syntax, orthography, morphology and phonological components**

Development of Word Analysis Skills and Strategies, Including Structural Analysis

Structural analysis is a process of examining the words in the text for meaningful word units (affixes, base words, inflected endings). There are six types of word types which are formed and therefore can be analyzed using structural analysis strategies. They include:

- Common prefixes or suffixes added to a known word ending with a consonant
- Adding the suffix "ed" to words that end with consonants
- Compound words
- Adding endings to words that end with the letter e
- Adding endings to words that end with the letter y
- Adding affixes to multisyllabic words

When teaching and using structural analysis procedures in the primary grades, teachers should remember to make sound decisions on which to introduce and teach. Keeping in mind the number of primary words in which each affix appears and how similar they are will help the teacher make the instructional process smoother and more valuable to the students.

Adding affixes to words can be started when students are able to read a list of one-syllable words by sight at a rate of approximately twenty words correct per minute. At the primary level, there is a recommended sequence for introducing affixes. The steps in this process are:

- Start by introducing the affix in the letter-sound correspondence format
- Practice the affix in isolation for a few days
- Provide words for practice which contain the affix (word lists, flash cards, etc.)
- Move from word lists to including passage reading, which include words with the affix (and some from the word lists/flash cards).

Word Study Group

This involves the teacher taking time to meet with children from Grades 3-6 in a small group of no more than six children for a word study session. Taberski (2000) suggests that this meeting take place next to the Word Wall. The children selected for this group are those who need to focus more on the relationship between spelling patterns and consonant sounds.

It is important that this not be a formalized traditional reading group that meets at a set time each week or biweekly. Rather the group should be spontaneously formed by the teacher based on his or her quick inventory of the selected children's needs at the start of the week. Taberski has templates in her book of *Guided Reading Planning Sheets.* These sheets are essentially targeted word and other skills sheets with her written dated observations of children who are in need of support to develop a given skill.

The teacher should try to meet with this group for at least two consecutive 20-minute periods daily. Over those two meetings, the teacher can model a Making Words Activity. Once the teacher has modeled making words the first day, the children would then make their own words. On the second day, the children would sort their words.

Other topics for a word study group within the framework of the Balanced Literacy Approach that Taberski advocates are inflectional endings, prefixes and suffixes, and/or common spelling patterns. These are covered later in this chapter. It should be noted that this activity would be classified by theorists as a structural analysis activity because the structural components (i.e. prefixes, suffixes, and spelling patterns) of the words are being studied.

Discussion Circles

Cooper (2004) believes that children should not be taught vocabulary and structural analysis skills. Flesch and E.D. Hirsch, who are key theorists of the phonics approach and advocates of Cultural Literacy (a term coined and associated with E. D. Hirsch), believe that specific vocabulary words at various grade and age levels need to be mastered and must be explicitly taught in schools. As far as J. David Cooper is concerned, however, all the necessary and meaningful (for the child and ultimately adult reader) vocabulary can't possibly be taught in schools (no apologies to Hirsch). To Cooper it is far more important that the children be made aware of and become interested in learning words by themselves. Cooper feels that through a child's reading and writing, he or she develops a love for and a sense of ownership of words. All of Cooper's suggested structural analysis word strategies are therefore designed to foster the child's love of words and a desire to "own" more of them through reading and writing.

Discussion Circles is an activity which fits nicely into the balanced literacy lesson format. After the children conclude a particular text, Cooper suggests that they respond to the book in discussion circles. Among the prompts, the teacher-coach might suggest that the children focus on words of interest they encountered in the text. These can also be words that they heard if the text was read aloud. Children can be asked to share something funny or upsetting or unusual about the words they have read. Through this focus on children's response to words as the center of the discussion circle, peers become more interested in word study.

Banking, Booking, and Filing It: Making Words My Own

Children can literally realize the goal of making words their own and exploring word structures through creating concrete objects or displays that demonstrate the words they own. Children can create and maintain their own files of words they have learned or are interested in learning.

The files can be categorized by the children according to their own interests. They should be encouraged to develop files using science, history, physical education, fine arts, dance, and technology content. Newspapers and web resources, which the teacher has approved, are excellent sources for such words. In addition, this provides the teacher with the opportunity to instruct the child in appropriate age- and grade-level research skills. Even children in grades two and three can begin simplified bibliographies and webliographies for their "found" words. Children can learn how to annotate and note the page of a newspaper, book, or URL for a particular word.

They can also copy down the word as it appears in the text (print or electronic). If appropriate, the child can place the particular words found for a given topic or content in an actual bank of the child's own making. The words can be printed on cards. This allows for differentiated word study and appeals to those children who are kinesthetic and spatial learners. Of course, children can also choose to create their own word books which include their specialized vocabulary and descriptions of how they identified or hunted down their words.

Write Out Your Words, Write With Your Words

Ownership of words can be demonstrated by having the children use them as part of their writings. The children can author a procedural narrative (a step by step description) of how they went about their searches to compile the words they found for any of the activities. If the children are in Grades K-1, or if the children are struggling readers and writers, their procedural narratives can be dictated and then posted by the teacher.

ELL students can share their accounts in their native language first and then translate (with the help of the teacher) these accounts into English with both the native language and the English language versions of the word exploration posted.

Children with special needs may model a word box on a specific holiday theme, genre or science/social studies topic with the teacher. Initially, this can be done as a whole class. As the children become more confident, they can work with peers or with a paraprofessional to create their own individual or small team/pair word boxes.

Special needs children can create a storyboard with the support of a paraprofessional, their teacher or a resource specialist. They can also narrate the story of how they all found the words, using a tape recorder.

Word Study Museum Within the Classroom

This strategy has been presented in detail so it can be used by the teachers within their own classrooms. In addition, the way the activity is described and the mention at the end of the description of how the activity can address family literacy, ELL, and special needs children's talents, provides an example of other audiences a teacher should consider in curriculum design. Almost every general education teacher and reading specialist will have to differentiate instruction to address the needs of special education and ELL learners. Family or shared literacy is a major component of all literacy instruction.

Children can create either single or multiple exhibits, museum style, within their classrooms celebrating their word study. They can build actual representations of the type of study they have done, including word trees (made out of cardboard or foam board), elaborate word boxes and games, word history timelines or murals, and word study maps. They can develop online animations, Kids Spiration graphic organizers, quick movies, digital photo essays, and PowerPoint presentations to share the word they have identified. The classroom or the gym or cafeteria can be transformed into a gallery space. Children can author brochure descriptions for their individual, team or class exhibits. Some children can volunteer to be tour guides or docents for the experience. Other children can work to create a banner for the museum. The children can name the museum themselves and send out invitations to its opening to parents, community, staff members and peer or younger classes.

Depending on their age and grade level, children can also develop interactive games and quizzes focused on particular exhibits. An artist or a team of class artists can design a poster for the exhibit, while other children choose to build the exhibits. Another small group can work on signage and a catalogue or register of objects within the exhibit. Greeters who will welcome parents and peers to the exhibit can be trained and can develop their own scripts.

If the children are in Grades 4-6, they can also develop their own visitor feedback forms and design word-themed souvenirs. The whole museum within the school or classroom can be captured digitally or with a regular camera. The record of this event can be hung near the word walls. Of course, the children can use many of their newly recognized and owned words to describe the event.

The Word Study Museum activity can be used with either a phonics-based or a balanced literacy approach. It promotes additional writing, researching, discussing, and reading about words.

It is also an excellent family literacy strategy in that families can develop their own Word Exhibits at home. This activity can also support and celebrate learners with disabilities. It can be presented in dual languages by children who are ELL learners and fluent in more than a single language..

Relationship Between Word Analysis Skills and Reading Comprehension

The explicit teaching of word analysis requires that the teacher pre-select words from a given text for vocabulary learning. These words should be chosen based on the storyline and main ideas of the text. The educator may even want to create a story map for a narrative text or develop a graphic organizer for an expository text. Once the story mapping and/or graphic organizing have been done, the educator can compile a list of words which relate to the storyline and/or main ideas.

The number of words that require explicit teaching should only be two or three. If the number is higher than that, the children need guided reading and the text needs to be broken down into smaller sections for teaching. When broken down into smaller sections, each text section should only have two to three words which need explicit teaching.

Some researchers, including Tierney and Cunningham, believe that a few words should be taught as a means of improving comprehension.

It is up to the educator whether the vocabulary selected for teaching needs review before reading, during reading, or after reading.

Introduce vocabulary BEFORE READING if...

- Children are having difficulty constructing meaning on their own. Children themselves have previewed the text and indicated words they want to know.
- The teacher has seen that there are words within the text which are definitely necessary for reading comprehension
- The text itself, in the judgment of the teacher, contains difficult concepts for students to grasp.

Introduce vocabulary DURING READING if...

- Children are already doing guided reading.
- The text contains words which are crucial to its comprehension and students will have trouble comprehending it, if they are not helped with the text.

Introduce vocabulary AFTER READING if...

- The children themselves have shared words which they found difficult or interesting
- The children need to expand their vocabulary
- The text itself is one that is particularly suited for vocabulary building.

Strategies to support word analysis and enhance reading comprehension include:

- Use of a graphic organizer such as a word map
- Semantic mapping
- Semantic feature analysis
- Hierarchical and linear arrays
- Preview in context
- Contextual redefinition
- Vocabulary self-collection

Identification of Common Morphemes, Prefixes, and Suffixes

This aspect of vocabulary development is to help children look for structural elements within words which they can use independently to help them determine meaning.

Some teachers choose to directly teach structural analysis. In particular, those who teach by following the phonics-centered approach for reading do this. Other teachers who follow the balanced literacy approach introduce the structural components as part of mini lessons that are focused on the students' reading and writing.

Structural analysis of words as defined by J. David Cooper (2004) involves the study of significant word parts. This analysis can help the child with pronunciation and constructing meaning.

The term list below is generally recognized as key structural analysis components.

Root Words
This is a word from which another word is developed. The second word can be said to have its "root" in the first, such as *vis, to see,* in visor or vision. This structural component can be illustrated by a tree with roots to display the meaning for children. Children may also want to literally construct root words using cardboard trees to create word family models.

ELL learners can construct these models for their native language root word families, as well for the English language words they are learning. ELL learners in the fifth and sixth grade may even appreciate analyzing the different root structures for contrasts and similarities between their native language and English.

Learners with special needs can focus in small groups or individually with a paraprofessional on building root word models.

Base Words
These are stand-alone linguistic units which cannot be deconstructed or broken down into smaller words. For example, in the word *re-tell*, the base word is "tell."

Contractions
These are shortened forms of two words in which a letter or letters have been deleted. These deleted letters have been replaced by an apostrophe.

Prefixes
These are beginning units of meaning which can be added (the vocabulary word for this type of structural adding is "affixed") to a base word or root word. They cannot stand alone. They are also sometimes known as "bound morphemes," meaning that they cannot stand alone as a base word. Examples are *re-, un-,* and *mis-*.

Suffixes
These are ending units of meaning which can be "affixed" or added on to the ends of root or base words. Suffixes transform the original meanings of base and root words. Like prefixes, they are also known as "bound morphemes," because they cannot stand alone as words. Examples are *-less, -ful,* and *-tion*.

Compound Words
These occur when two or more base words are connected to form a new word. The meaning of the new word is in some way connected with that of the base word. Examples are *firefighter, newspaper,* and *pigtail*.

Inflectional Endings
These are types of suffixes that impart a new meaning to the base or root word. These endings in particular change the gender, number, tense, or form of the base or root words. Just like other suffixes, these are also termed "bound morphemes." Examples are *–s* or *-ed*.

Comments
Definitions are included because the structural analysis components are explicitly taught in schools which advocate the phonics-centered approach and are also incorporated into the word work component of the schools which advocate the balanced literacy approach for instruction.

Definition questions—that is, multiple choice questions which have only a single right answer—test whether the teacher candidate has memorized the appropriate terminology. They constitute no less than 15% of the multiple choice question on the test. Therefore, by taking the time to memorize these easy definitions, scores are likely to improve.

Some of these activities are presented in detail to help answer the constructed response questions of the test.

Knowledge of Greek and Latin Roots That Form English Words

Knowledge of Greek and Latin roots which comprise English words can measurably enhance children's reading skills and can also enrich their writing.

Word Webs

Sharon Taberski (2000) does not advocate teaching Greek and Latin derivatives in the abstract to young children. However, when she comes across (as is common and natural) specific Greek and Latin roots while reading to children, she uses that opportunity to introduce children to these rich resources.

For example, during readings on rodents (a favorite of first and second graders), Taberski draws her class's attention to the fact that beavers gnaw at things with their teeth. She then connects the "dent" root or derivative to the children's lives, other words they are familiar with or experiences. The children then volunteer "*dentist,*" "*dental,*" "*denture.*" Taberski begins to place these in a graphic organizer, or word web.

When she has tapped the extent of the children's prior knowledge of "dent" words, she shares with them the fact that *dens/dentis* is the Latin word for teeth. Then she introduces the word "indent," which she has already previewed with them as part of their conventions of print study. She helps them to see that the "indenting" of the first line of a paragraph can even be related to the "teeth" Latin root in that it looks like a "print" bite was taken out of the paragraph.

Taberski displays the word web in the Word Wall Chart section of her room. The class is encouraged throughout, say, a week's time to look for other words to add to the web. Taberski stresses that for her, as an elementary teacher of reading and writing, the key element of the Greek and Latin word root web activity is the children's coming to understand that if they know what a Greek or Latin word root means, they can use that knowledge to figure out what other words mean.

She feels the key concept is to model and demonstrate for children how fun and fascinating Greek and Latin root study can be.

Greek and Latin Roots Word Webs With an Assist from the World Wide Web

Older children in Grades 3-6 can build on this initial print activity by searching online for additional words with a particular Greek or Latin root which has been introduced in class.

They can easily do this in a way that authentically ties in with their own interests and experiences by reading reviews for a book which has been a read-aloud online or by just reading the summaries of the day's news and printing out those words which appear in the stories online that share the root discussed.

The children can be encouraged to circle these instances of their Latin or Greek root and also to document the exact date and URL for the citation. These can be posted as part of their own online web in the word wall section study area. If the school or class has a website or webpage, the children can post this data there as a special Greek and Latin root word page.

Expanding the concept of the Greek and Latin word web from the printed page to the World Wide Web nicely inculcates in the child habits of lifelong reading and researching online. This beginning expository research will serve children well in intermediate level content area work and beyond.

Use of Syllabification as a Word Identification Strategy

Strategy: *Clap Hands, Count Those Syllables as They Come!!* (Taberski, 2000)

The objective of this activity is for children to understand that every syllable in a polysyllabic word can be studied for its spelling patterns in the same way that monosyllabic words are studied for their spelling patterns.

The easiest way for the K-3 teacher to introduce this activity to the children is to share a familiar poem from the poetry chart (or to write out a familiar poem on a large experiential chart).

First the teacher reads the poem with the children. As they are reading it aloud, the children clap the beats of the poem and the teacher uses a colored marker to place a tic (/) above each syllable.

Next, the teacher takes letter cards and selects one of the polysyllabic words from the poem which the children have already "clapped" out.

The children use letter cards to spell that word on the sentence strip holder or it can be placed on a felt board or up against a window on display. Together the children and teacher divide the letters into syllables and place blank letter cards between the syllables. The children identify spelling patterns they know.

Finally, as part of continued small group syllabification study, the children identify other polysyllabic words they clapped out from the poem. They make up the letter combinations of these words. Then they separate them into syllables with blank letter cards between the syllables.

Children who require special support in syllabification can be encouraged to use many letter cards to create a large butcher paper syllabic (in letter cards with spaces) representation of the poem or at least a few lines of the poem. They can be told that this is for use as a teaching tool for others. In this way, they authenticate their study of syllabification with a real product that can actually be referenced by peers.

Techniques for Identifying Compound Words
The teaching of compound words should utilize structural analysis techniques. (See above section on structural analysis.)
Here are some other strategies for helping students to identify and read compound words.
- Use songs and actions to help children understand the concept that compound words are two smaller words joined together to make one bigger word
- Use games like concentration, memory and Go Fish for students to practice reading compound words
- Use word sorts to have students distinguish between compound words and nonexamples of compound words

Identification of Homographs
Homographs are words that are spelled the same but have different meanings. A subgroup within this area includes words that are spelled the same, have different meanings, and are pronounced differently. Some examples of homographs include:
- Lie
- Tear
- Bow
- Fair
- Bass

Teaching homographs can be interesting and fun for the students. Incorporating them into passages where the students can use the context clues to decipher the different meanings of the homographs. Games are also a good strategy for using to help students understand multiple meaning words. Jokes and riddles are usually based on homographs, and students love to make collections or books of these.

Semantic Feature Analysis
This technique for enhancing vocabulary skills by using semantic cues is based on the research of Johnson and Pearson (1984) and Anders and Bos (1986). It involves young children in setting up a feature analysis grid of various subject content words, which is an outgrowth of their discussion about these words.

For instance, Cooper (2004) includes a sample of a Semantic Features Analysis Grid for Vegetables. .

Vegetables	Green	Have Peels	Eat Raw	Seeds
Carrots	-	+	+	-
Cabbage	+	-	+	-

Note that the use of the + for yes, - for no, and possible use for + and - if a vegetable like squash could be both green and yellow.

Teachers of children in grade one and beyond can design their own semantic analysis grids to meet their students' needs and to align with the topics the kids are learning. Select a category or class of words (could be planets, rodent family members, winter words, weather words).

Use the left side of the grid to list at least three if not more items that fit this category. The number of actual items listed will depend on the age and grade level of the children with three or four items fine for K-1 and up to 10-15 for Grades 5 and 6. Brainstorm with the children or if better suited to the class, the teacher may list on his or her own features that the items have in common. As can be noted from the example excerpted from *Cooper's Literacy: Helping Children Construct Meaning (*2004), these common features such as vegetables' green color, peels, and seeds are usually fairly easy to identify.

Show the children how to insert the notations +, -, and even ? (If they are not certain) on the grid. The teacher might also explore with the children the possibility that an item could get both a + and a -. For example, a vegetable like broccoli might be eaten cooked or raw depending on taste and squash can be green or yellow.

Whatever the length of the grid when first presented to the children (perhaps as a semantic cue lesson in and of itself tied in to a text being read in class), make certain that the grid as presented and filled out is not the end of the activity.

Children can use it as a model for developing their own semantic feature grids and share them with the whole class. Child-developed grids can become part of a Word Work center in the classroom or even be published in a Word Study Games book by the class as a whole. Such a publication can be shared with parents during open school week and evening visits and with peer classes.

Contextual Redefinition

This strategy encourages children to use the context more effectively by presenting them with sufficient context BEFORE they begin reading. It models for the children the use of contextual clues to make informed guesses about word meanings.

To apply this strategy, the teacher should first select unfamiliar words for teaching. No more than two or three words should be selected for direct teaching. The teacher should then write a sentence in which there are sufficient clues supplied for the child to successfully figure out the meaning. Among the types of context clues the teacher can use are compare/contrast, synonyms, and direct definition.

Then the teacher should present the words only on the experiential chart or as letter cards. Have the children pronounce the words. As they pronounce them, challenge them to come up with a definition for each word. After more than one definition is offered, encourage the children to decide as a whole group what the definition is. Write down their agreed upon definition with no comment as to its accurate meaning.

Then share with the children the contexts (sentences the teacher wrote with the words and explicit context clues). Ask the children to read the sentences aloud and come up with a definition for each word. Make certain that as they present their definitions, the teacher does not comment. Ask that they justify their definitions by making specific references to the context clues in the sentences. As the discussion continues, direct the children's attention to their previously agreed upon definition of the word. Facilitate their discussing the differences between their guesses about the word when they saw only the word itself and their guesses about the word when they read it in context. Finally, have the children check their use of context skills to correctly define the word by using a dictionary.

Development of Word Analysis Skills by Individual Students

This type of direct teaching of word definitions is useful when children have dictionary skills and the teacher is aware of the fact that there are insufficient clues about the words in the context to help the students define it. In addition, struggling readers and students from ELL backgrounds may benefit tremendously from being walked through this process that highly proficient and successful readers apply automatically.

By using this strategy, the teacher can also "kid watch" and note the students' prior knowledge as they guess the word in isolation. The teacher can also actually witness and hear how various students use context skills.

Through their involvement in this strategy, struggling readers gain a feeling of community as they experience the ways in which their struggles and guesses resonate with other peers' responses to the text.

ELL learners can share their accounts in their native language first and then translate (with the help of the teacher) these accounts into English with both the native language and the English language versions of the word exploration posted.

Skill 1.8 **Demonstrate knowledge of phonemic awareness (e.g. rhyming, segmenting, blending sounds) and the alphabetic principle in reading acquisition**

Phonological Awareness

Phonological awareness means the ability of the reader to recognize the sounds or phonemes of spoken language. This recognition includes how these sounds can be blended together, segmented (divided up), and manipulated (switched around). This awareness eventually leads to phonics, a method for decoding language by unlocking letter-sound or grapheme-phoneme relationships.

Development of phonological skills for most children begins during the pre-K years. Indeed, by the age of 5, a child who has been exposed to fingerplays and poetry can recognize a rhyme. Such a child can demonstrate phonological awareness by filling in the missing rhyming word in a familiar rhyme or rhymed picture book. The procedure of filling in a missing word is called the cloze procedure. It can be used in oral or print literacy activities.

One teaches children phonological awareness by directly pointing out the sounds made by letters singly (as in /b/) or in combination (as in /bl/), and to recognize individual sounds in words.

Phonological awareness skills include but are not limited to the following:

1. Rhyming and syllabification
2. Blending sounds into words—such as pic-tur-bo-k
3. Identifying beginning or initial phonemes and ending or final phonemes in short, one-syllable words
4. Breaking words down into sounds, which is also called "segmenting" words
5. Removing initial sounds and substituting others. An example is /bat/ minus the /b/ with an /m/ substituted becomes /mat/.

The Role of Phonological Awareness in Reading Development

Instructional methods to teach phonological awareness may include any or all of the following:

1. Auditory games during which children recognize and manipulate the sounds of words, separate or segment the sounds of words, take out sounds, blend sounds, add in new sounds, or take apart sounds to recombine them in new formations.

2. Snap game in which the teacher says two words. The children snap their fingers if the two words share a sound, which might be at the beginning or end of the word. Children hear initial phonemes most easily, followed by final ones. Medial or middle sounds are most difficult for young children to discriminate. One sees this in their oral responses as well as in their invented spelling. Silence occurs if the words share no sounds. Children love this simple game and it also helps with classroom management.

3. Language games model for children identification of rhyming words. These games help inspire children to create their own rhymes.

4. Read books that rhyme such as *Sheep in a Jeep* by Nancy Shaw or *The Fox on a Box* by Barbara Gregorich.

5. Share books with children that use alliteration (words that begin with the same sound) such as *Avalanche, A to Z*.

Assessment of Phonological Awareness

These skills can be assessed by having the child listen to the teacher say two words. Then ask the child to decide if these two words are the same word repeated twice or two different words.

When making this assessment, if using two different words, make certain that they only differ by only one phoneme, such as /d/ and /g/.

Children can be assessed using make-believe words as long as they're familiar to them.

The Role of Phonological Processing in the Development of Individual Students

Children who are raised in homes where English is not the first language or where standard English is not spoken, may have difficulty with hearing the difference between similar sounding words like "send" and "sent." Any child who is not in a home, day care, or preschool environment in which English phonology operates may have difficulty perceiving and demonstrating the differences between English language phonemes. If children cannot hear the difference between words that "sound the same" like "grow" and "glow," they will be confused when these words appear in a print context. Sadly, this confusion will naturally impact their comprehension.

Considerations for teaching phonological processing to ELL children include recognition by the teacher that what works for the English-Language-speaking child from an English-Language-speaking family, does not necessarily work in other languages.

Research recommends that ELL children learn to read initially in their first language. It is critical for ELL children to learn to speak English before being taught to read English. Research supports that oral language development lays the foundation for phonological awareness.

All phonological instruction programs must be tailored to the children's learning backgrounds. Rhymes and alliteration introduced to ELL children should be read or shared with them in their first language, if at all possible.

Struggling Readers

"Students who cannot read by age 9 are unlikely to become fluent readers and have a greater tendency to drop out."
Beth Antunez

Among the causes of reading difficulties for some children (and adults) are auditory trauma or ear infections that affect their ability to hear speech. Such children need one-on-one support with articulation and perception of different sounds. When a child says a word such as "parrot" incorrectly, repeat it back as a question with the correct pronunciation. If the child gets the sound correctly after your question, all is well. Extra support was needed. If the child still has difficulty with pronunciation after repeated instances, then consult with a speech therapist or audiologist. Early identification of medical conditions that affect hearing is crucial to reading development.

Points to Ponder
Phonological awareness is auditory.
It does not involve print.
It begins before children have learned letter-sound relationships.
It is the basis for the successful teaching of phonics and spelling.
It can and must be taught and nurtured.
It precedes and must be in place before the alphabetic principle can be taught.

Phonemic Awareness

"The two best predictors of early reading success are alphabetic recognition and phonemic awareness."
Marilyn Jager Adams

"In order to benefit from formal reading instruction, children must have a certain level of phonemic awareness. . . . Phonemic awareness is both a prerequisite for and a consequence of learning to read."
Hallie Kay Yopp

Phonemic awareness is a specific skill within the broader category of phonological awareness. Probably developing fairly late, it is the knowledge that words are comprised of individual phonemes that can be blended. Theorist Marilyn Jager Adams who researches early reading has outlined five basic types of phonemic awareness tasks.

Task 1- Ability to hear rhymes and alliteration.
For example, the children would listen to a poem, rhyming picture book or song and identify the rhyming words heard which the teacher might then record or list on chart.

Task 2- Ability to do oddity tasks (recognize the member of a set that is different [odd] among the group. For example, children might look at pictures of grass, a garden and a rose, answering, Which one starts with a different sound?

Task 3 –The ability to orally blend words and split syllables.
For example, the children can say the first sound of a word and then the rest of the word and put it together as a single word.

Task 4 –The ability to orally segment words.
For example, the ability to count sounds. The child would be asked to count or clap the sounds in "hamburger."

Task 5- The ability to do phonics manipulation tasks.
For example, replace the "r" sound in rose with a "p" sound.

The Role of Phonemic Awareness in Reading Development

Children who have problems with phonics generally have not acquired or been exposed to phonemic awareness activities at home or in preschool-2. This includes extensive songs, rhymes and read–alouds.

Instructional Methods

Since the ability to distinguish between individual sounds, or phonemes, within words is a prerequisite to association of sounds with letters and manipulating sounds to blend words—a fancy way of saying "reading"—the teaching of phonemic awareness is crucial to emergent literacy (early childhood K-2 reading instruction). Children need a strong background in phonemic awareness in order for phonics instruction (sound-spelling relationship-printed materials) to be effective.

Instructional methods that may be effective for teaching phonemic awareness can include:

- Clapping syllables in words
- Distinguishing between a word and a sound
- Using visual cues and movements to help children understand when the speaker goes from one sound to another
- Incorporating oral segmentation activities which focus on easily distinguished syllables rather than sounds
- Singing familiar songs (e.g. Happy Birthday, This Old Man) and replacing key words with those of a different ending
- Dealing children a deck of picture cards and having them sound out the words for the pictures on their cards or calling for a picture by asking for its first and last sound.

Consideration for ELL Students

Given the demographics of our country with its influx of New Americans, the likelihood is great that you will be teaching at least some children who are from a non-native-English-speaking background. Therefore, as a conscientious educator, it is important that you understand the special factors involved in supporting children's second language literacy development.

Not all English phonemes are present in various ELL native languages; for example, the sound of /th/ does not appear in Spanish. Some native language phonemes may and do conflict with English phonemes.

It is recommended that all teachers of reading and particularly those who are working with ELL students use meaningful, student-centered, and culturally customized activities. These activities may include language games, word walls, and poems. Some of these activities might, if possible, be initiated in the child's first language and then reiterated in English.

Reading and the ELL Learner

Research has shown that there is a positive and strong correlation between a child's literacy in his or her native language and his or her learning of English. The degree of native language proficiency and literacy is a strong predictor of English language development. Children who are literate and engaged readers in their native language can easily transfer their skills to a second language (i.e. English).

What this means is that educators should not approach the needs of ELL learners in reading the same as they do native speakers. Those children whose families are not from a focused oral literacy and reading culture in the native language will need additional oral language rhymes, read-alouds, and singing as supports for reading skills development in both their native and the English language.

Assessment of Phonemic Awareness

Teachers can maintain ongoing logs and rubrics for assessment throughout the year of phonemic awareness for individual children. Such assessments would identify particular stated reading behaviors or performance standards, the date of observation of the child's behavior (in this context-phonemic activity or exercise), and comments.

The rubric or legend for assessing these behaviors might include the following descriptors:
- demonstrates or exhibits reading behavior consistently,
- makes progress/strides toward this reading behavior, and
- has not yet demonstrated or exhibited this behavior.

Depending on the particular phonemic task the teacher models, the performance task might include:

- Saying rhyming words in response to an oral prompt
- Segmenting a word spoken by the teacher into its beginning, middle and ending sounds
- Counting correctly the number of syllables in a spoken word

Phonological awareness involves the recognition that spoken words are composed of a set of smaller units such as onsets and rimes, syllables, and sounds.

Phonemic awareness is a specific type of phonological awareness which focuses on the ability to distinguish, manipulate and blend specific sounds or phonemes within an individual word.

Think of phonological awareness as an umbrella and phonemic awareness as a specific spoke under this umbrella.

Phonics deals with printed words and the learning of sound-spelling correlations, while phonemic awareness activities are oral.

In reviewing reading research and theory, new distinctions and definitions appear often. The body of reading knowledge changes over time. The information and definitions in this guide are those accepted in the year of its publication and the time of its authoring and updating. As changes occur in accepted theories, they will be made in the guides and in the certification exams.

"If you believe that you learn to read by reading, you must learn to want to read. Reading to children, therefore models both the 'how' and 'why' of reading."
Helen Depree and Sandra Iversen, *Early Literacy in the Classroom*

"The long talk that parents have put off about the ways of the world might need to be an introduction to the facts about the English alphabet."
Terrence Moore, Ashbrook Center Fellow and Principal of Ridgeview Classical Schools in Fort Collins, Colorado

The Alphabetic principle is sometimes called graphophonemic awareness. This term means that written words are composed of letter (graphemes) which represent the sounds (phonemes) of written words.

Development of the Understanding that Print Carries Meaning

This understanding is demonstrated every day in the elementary classroom as the teacher holds up a selected book to read aloud to the class. The teacher explicitly and deliberately talks aloud about how to hold the book, focuses the class on looking at its cover, points to where to start reading, and sweeps her hands in the direction to begin, left to right.

When writing the morning message on the board, the teacher reminds the children that the message begins in the upper left hand corner at the top of the board to be followed by additional activities and a schedule for the rest of the day.

When the teacher invites children to make posters of a single letter such as *b* and list items in the classroom, their home, or outside which start with that letter, the children are concretely demonstrating that print carries meaning.

Strategies for Promoting Awareness of the Relationship between Spoken and Written Language

- Writing down what the children say on a language chart.
- Highlighting the uses of print products found in the classroom such as labels, yellow sticky pad notes, labels on shelves and lockers, calendars, signs, and directions.
- Reading together big-print and oversized books to teach print conventions such as directionality.
- Practicing how to handle a book: How to turn pages, to find the top and bottom of pages, and how to tell the difference between the front and back covers.
- Discussing and comparing with children the length, appearance and boundaries of specific words. For example, children can see that the names Dan and Dora share certain letters and a similar shape.
- Having children match oral words to printed words by forming an echo chorus as the teacher reads poetry or rhymes aloud and they echo the reading.
- Having the children combine, manipulate, switch and move letters to change words.
- Working with letter cards to create messages and respond to the messages that they create.

The Role of Environmental Print in Developing Print Awareness

Children can create an environmental print book, which contains collaged symbols of their favorite lunch or breakfast foods. The children cut and clip symbols from food packages and then place them in alphabetical order in their class-made book. Magazines and catalogues are another source of environmental print that is accessible with ads for child centered products. Supermarket circulars and coupons from the newspaper are also excellent for engaging children in using environmental print as reading, especially when combined with dramatic play centers or prop boxes.

What is particularly effective in using environmental print is that it immediately invites the child from ELL background into print awareness, through the familiarity of commercial logos and packaging symbols used.

Development of Book Handling Skills

Understanding the value and importance of the concepts of print for beginning readers developed out of the work of Marie Clay in New Zealand. Assessment of these skills typically occurs in kindergarten and into first grade as necessary.

The following skills are part of the assessment process:

- Print carries a message – The students can demonstrate this skill even if unable to read the text by pretending to read. This may be demonstrated even if the child does not demonstrate any of the other concepts.
- Book organization – Students demonstrate an understanding of the organization of books by being able to identify the title, cover, author, left to right progression, top to bottom order, and one to one correspondence. Students may learn these skills individually as they become more familiar with books.
- Print Consistencies- This is the understanding that text is made up of letters which form words and which are then combined to form sentences. As the beginning reader makes these connections, they will next develop the concept of capital letters at the beginning and basic punctuation marks.
- Letter Identification- The final stage of the concepts of print assessment involves the identification of both upper- and lower-case letters. More advanced students may begin to recognize some of the most common spelling patterns in beginning texts.

Have the children identify the front cover, back cover, and title page of a specific book.

Model storytelling with the book held so that the audience can see the illustrations shown to them. Then have children demonstrate the skills for their peers.

Have children search through the class libraries for special features on the fronts or backs of books as they help return the books to their bins. Have the children display and talk about the special symbols they have found.

Review with the children, in an age- and grade-appropriate format, additional parts of the book as appropriate during mini-lessons and read-alouds. These additional parts of the book can include title pages, dedication page, table of contents, copyright date and glossary.

Strategies for Promoting an Understanding of the Directionality of Print

In order to become proficient readers, young students need to develop a complete understanding that all print is read from left to right and top to bottom. Modeling is one of the most important strategies a teacher can use to develop this understanding in children. The use of Big Books, poems and charts are strategies teachers can use in both large and small group instruction. Simple questions can engage the students to pay closer attention to these skills (i.e. "We are going to read this passage, where should I put my pointer to start reading?").

Directionality of print should also be taught during the writing process. In language experience stories, interactive writing, and Kidwriting©, the teacher can incorporate explicit modeling and instruction in these skills. Sometimes it may be necessary to provide children with a dot at the top left corner of the paper in order to provide a visual reminder of where to begin.

Techniques for Promoting the Ability to Track Print in Connected Texts

Model directionality and one-to-one word matching by pointing to words, while using a Big Book, pocket chart, or poem written out on a chart. As you repeatedly lead the children in this reading, they can follow along and eventually track the print and make one-to-one matches on the connected text independently. They can also practice by using a pointer (all children love to use the pointer because then pleasure becomes associated with the reading) or their fingers to follow the words. Children happily volunteer to be the point person. Even before Vanna White, the joy of "signifying letters" had tremendous appeal for children.

Copy down a brief, familiar rhyme (perhaps from a favorite book or song) and post it in the room at child's eye level, so the children can independently walk around and read it.

Copy down a brief or familiar rhyme or poem on individual word cards. Then challenge the children in small groups or independently to reassemble and display the cards on a pocket chart. As children "play" with constructing and reconstructing this pocket chart, they will develop an awareness of directionality, one-on-one matching of print to spoken words, spacing, and punctuation.

Model interactive emergent writing with the class. While the teacher is noting down the weather, deliberately ask and have the children suggest where the first word in that report should go. Top or bottom of the board? Will the first letter be upper case or lower case? What goes at the end of the sentence?

Create with the children sing-song repetitions/rules for using capitals, periods, commas, etc. Encourage the children to begin reciting these sing-songs as soon as they identify specific concepts of print in connected texts.

Model for children how, when pointing at words, they can start at the top and move from left to right. Tell the children that if there are more words to the sentence they are reading under the first line of print, they must go back to the left and under the previous line. Young children enjoy practicing this kinesthetic "return sweep." You might want to teach them to identify the need to do this by saying "Don't fall asleep at the page" or "Time to get to the 'return sweep' stage!" Post this saying and encourage them to singsong as they joyously take ownership of their reading.

Have even beginning readers "read" through the text to find letters they recognize in the story and then share some of the text that includes these specific letters to whet their appetite for reading.

Strategies for Promoting Letter Knowledge and Letter Formation

Engage the children in a Tale Trail game. Use a story they have already heard or read. Ask the children to circle certain letters and then reread the story, sharing the letters they have circled.

Give the children lots of opportunities to do letter sorts. Pass out word cards which have the targeted letter on them. Ask the children to come up and display their answers to questions like these about a given letter, say, *R*.

R as the first letter--rose, rise, ran,
R as the last letter--car, star, far,
R with "a" t after it--start, heart, part, smart
R, two r's in the middle of a word-- carry, sorry, starry

Play "What's in a Name?" Select a student's name. For example, write the name "William" on a sentence strip. Have the children count the number of letters in the name and how many of them appear twice. Allow them to talk about which letter is upper case and which letters are lower case. Have the students chant the name. Then rewrite the name on another sentence strip. Have the strip cut into separate letters and see if someone from the class can reassemble it correctly.

As you read a book with or to children, ask that they show you specific letters or lower case or upper case letters. Read the text first and encourage as many children to come up and identify the letters as possible. Use a Big Book and have felt and sandpaper letters available for display as well. If grade, age and developmentally appropriate, have children then write the letter they identified themselves, or it might be even more fun to have them construct it using pipe cleaners, Playdough or coded colored markers (different colors for upper and lower case letters).

Play "letter leap" with the children and have them look carefully at the room to identify labeled items that begin with a specific letter by "leaping" over to them and placing a large lettered placard next to them. Children who are advanced in letter formation can then be challenged to "leap" through the classroom when called upon to literally "letter" unlabeled objects.

Recognition that Phonemes are Represented by Letters and Letter Pairs

As young children begin to learn to read, connections are made between the printed letters on the page and the sounds they have heard in language. Phonemic awareness activities are crucial for building this bridge. Students have engaged in many auditory activities. At this time, it is important the teacher use explicit and systematic methods to demonstrate to the students how these auditory sounds are represented on a page by letters or sometimes letter pairs. As this occurs, students can begin to decode text and move toward becoming proficient readers.

Use of Reading and Writing Strategies for Teaching Letter-sound Correspondence

Provide children with a sample of a single letter book (or create one from environmental sources, newspapers, coupons, circulars, magazines or your own text ideas). Make sure that your already published or created sample includes a printed version of the letter in both upper and lower case forms. Make certain that each page contains a picture of something that starts with that specific letter and also has the word for the picture. The book you select or create should be a predictable one in that when the picture is identified, the word can be read.

Once the children have been provided with your sample and have listened to it being read, challenge them to each make a one letter book. Often it is best to focus on familiar consonants for the single letter book or the first letter of the child's first name. By using the first letter of the child's first name, he or she is invited to develop a book which tells about him or her and the words that he or she finds. This is an excellent way to have the reading and writing workshop enhance the teaching of the alphabetic principle. Encourage children to be active writers and readers by finding words for their book on the classroom word wall, in alphabet books in the special alphabet book bin and in grade and age appropriate pictionaries, (dictionaries for younger children which are filled with pictures).

Of course, the richest resource within the reading and writing workshop classroom for teaching and fostering the alphabetic principle lies in the use of alphabet books as anchor books for inspiring students' writing. While young children in grades K-1 will do better with the one-letter-book authoring activity, children in Grades 2 and beyond can truly be inspired and motivated by alphabet books to enhance their own reading, writing and alphabetic skills. Furthermore, use of these books which have and are being produced in a variety of formats to enhance social studies, science and mathematical themes, provide an opportunity for even young children to create a meaningful product that authenticates their content study as it enhances alphabetic skills and, of course, print awareness

An annotated bibliography of selected alphabet books has been provided in the bibliography section of this guide. It was limited by space considerations, but the teacher can with no expense and with much pleasure catch up on the latest titles and identify those most appropriate for the grade taught, by visiting a bookstore. Hold the print book in hand and then consider selecting an alphabet book that has a particularly inviting concept, art style, or adaptable format within the children's capacity to use as a model.

For instance, Tina Hoban uses actual color photographs of letters in her *26 Letters and 99 Cents*. Children may want to make clay letters or create letter sculptures to develop their own alphabet book similar to Hoban's. If nutrition is the science topic, children might want to examine Ehlert's very accessible *Eating the Alphabet: Fruits and Vegetables from A to Z*. This, combined with an examination of the fruits and vegetables in a local store (perhaps a pleasant walk from the school and a quick break from the routine), can yield a wonderful alphabet book on fruits and vegetables which can also include those fruits and vegetables eaten in various cultures (e.g., mangos, plantains, pomegranates, etc.).

The alphabet book can also offer the class a chance to work collaboratively using a template page created by the teacher. Completion of this collaborative work can be shared with peers in another class and parents and be kept in the classroom library as a model for the following year's class with recognition and acceptance of the authors!

Assessment Throughout the Year of Graphophonemic Awareness

The teacher will want to maintain individual records of children's reading behaviors demonstrating alphabetic principle/graphophonemic awareness.

The following performance standards should be part of a record template form for each child in Grades K-1 and beyond as needed (depending on ELL or special needs):
- Match all consonant and short vowel sounds.
- Read one's own name.
- Read one syllable words and high frequency words.
- Demonstrate ability to read and understand that as letters in words change, so do the sounds.
- Generate the sounds from all letters including consonant blends and long vowel patterns. Blend those different sounds into recognizable words.
- Read common sight words.
- Read common word families.

Recognize and use knowledge of spelling patterns when reading: run/running, hop/hopping.

The following template can be used by teachers to record student progress for each child in Grades K-1 and beyond as needed (depending on ELL or special needs):

Reading Progress

Skill Area	Mastered	Making Progress	Not Yet	Comments
Matches all consonant and short vowel sounds				
Reads one's own name				
Reads one syllable words and high frequency words				
Demonstrates ability to read and understand that as letters in words change, so do the sounds				
Generates the sounds from all letters including consonant blends and long vowel patterns. Blend those different sounds into recognizable words				
Reads common sight words				
Reads common word families				
Recognizes and uses knowledge of spelling patterns when reading: run/running, hop/hopping				

Any record kept of an individual child's progress should include each date of observation and some legend or rubric detailing the level of performance, standard acquisition, or mastery.

Development of Alphabetic Knowledge in Individual Students

Researchers Laura M. Justice and Helen K. Ezell (2002) evaluated alphabetic knowledge and print awareness in pre-school children from low-income households. In their post-tests, children who had participated in shared reading sessions that emphasized a print focus outperformed their control group peers (other Head Start children) on three measures of print awareness: words in print, print recognition, and alphabetic knowledge.

Other researchers, including Chaney (1994), have demonstrated a statistically significant and inverse relationship between household income and children's performance on measures of print awareness and the alphabetic principle.

Lonigan (1999) found that substantial group differences existed on a variety of pre-literacy tasks administered to 85 preschool children from lower- and middle-income households. The researchers looked at environmental print, print and book reading conventions, and alphabet knowledge. Results showed that preschool children from middle-income households showed significantly higher levels of skill across all print awareness tasks in comparison with preschoolers from low-income households.

Obviously, this data highlights the importance of extensive alphabetic knowledge activities and print awareness opportunities for some children from low-income households in Grades K-1 and even beyond, if necessary.

Two other studies undertaken by Ezell and Justice (in the year 2000) suggested that structuring adult-child shared book reading interactions to include an explicit print awareness and alphabetic principle focus resulted in a substantial increase in children's verbal interactions with print.

This work highlights the importance of not only classroom and preschool emphasis on print awareness and alphabetic principle routines, but also the need for teachers to reach out to parents and to model for them these shared reading experiences so that family life can parallel the classroom experiences. Many schools currently have parent volunteers and reading buddy programs. Training of these volunteers, particularly in high need, low-economic-status communities are certainly warranted.

David J. Chard and Jean Osborn (1999) have reflected on the guidelines necessary for teachers to use in selecting supplemental phonics and word-recognition materials for addressing students with learning disabilities.
They note that an important way to help children with reading disabilities figure out the system underlying the printed word is leading them to understand the alphabetic principle. Children with learning disabilities (LD) in particular benefit from organized instruction that centers on letters, sounds, and the relations between sounds and letters. They also benefit from instruction that offers practice with word-recognition patterns and word families that share similar letter patterns.

Children who are LD also benefit from opportunities to apply what they are learning to the reading and re-reading of stories and other texts. Such texts contain a high portion of words which reflect the letters, sounds, and spelling patterns the children are learning.

For special needs children, a beginning reading program should include the following elements of alphabetic knowledge instruction:

- A variety of alphabetic knowledge activities in which the children learn to identify and name both upper and lower case letters.
- Games, songs, and other activities that help children to learn to name the letters quickly.
- Writing activities that encourage children to practice the letters which they are writing.
- A sensible sequence of letter introduction that can be adjusted to the needs of the children.

Skill 1.9   Demonstrate an understanding of genre patterns, and the influences of purpose, context and genre in constructing meaning

Authors use various ways to tell a story while employing various literary techniques. If teachers want students to understand the technique, they need to teach them the characteristics of each narrative genre. It may be necessary to draw the students' attention to the elements and structure of narratives as well the strategies they can use for reading each of the genres. Before students actually read a selection, the teacher can address the literary techniques, forms and vocabulary in mini-lessons to provide them with knowledge about what they will be reading. This helps students to become more engaged with the text and to have an idea of what they should think about as they are reading.

Narrative Genres

Prose fiction is literature about imaginary people, places and events. This narrative genre can be used to stimulate students' imaginations while considering the author's view of the world. This genre includes novels, short stories and plays, each of which has its own distinctive characteristics. To varying degrees, they all have a setting, conflict, plot, climax and resolution.

Short story is a narrative with usually only one focus and a more limited world view. Students should determine whether the person telling the story is a narrator or is a character within the story. They should take note of the central conflict and determine why the characters act as they do. As a response to the story, they can decide how they feel about the characters and their actions and ask questions about the message that the author is trying to convey in the story..

A **novel** is a longer work of fiction, often with sub-plots. During the reading the students should identify subplots and understand their relationship to the main plot of the novel. They must be aware of the motives of the various characters and of their own reactions to characters' actions.

Prose non-fiction is literature that is about real events, times and places. It includes essays, journals, articles, letters, biographies and autobiographies. Much of contemporary nonfiction reads like fiction with suspense, expression and ingenuity of style. Because it is vivid and personal, it can provide the students with a model for their own writing. When students are reading for information, they need to keep this purpose in mind and may need time and instruction to help them summarize or restate the main ideas.

Poetry communicates ideas and feelings through an arrangement of words and sounds. Poetry can be used to capture a mood, tell a story or explore different ideas. There are various literary techniques authors use in writing poetry, which the teacher can discuss with the class through mini-lessons.

Plays can be read for the purpose of performance or for literary effect. Students should pay attention to the literary devices that the author uses. When reading a play, students can work on putting expression into their reading so that they can bring the characters to life.

There are six different types of texts that are often used in a school setting. Each type has a specific use within the classroom depending on the purpose for reading set forth by the teacher. The types vary from the genres of reading and should not be confused.

Wordless Books are generally used to increase discussion and develop vocabulary. These books are good for generating ideas for writing or discussions among students. They provide pictures filled with details to serve as a springboard to oral language development or to increase the quality of description in writing.

Predictable Texts allow the beginning reader to feel successful with the process of reading in a rapid manner. Words or phrases are repeated over and over so that students can participate in the act of reading. They are also generally very much enjoyed by students due to the natural rhythm that develops via the repetitions. However, teachers should quickly move on from this type of text so that children can begin to attend to the words and not rely on their auditory memory alone.

Controlled Vocabulary Texts are usually used to increase the high frequency vocabulary of students. Sight word reading vocabulary is critical to later success with more advanced reading tasks. This type of book generally has a very slim plot or story line and is more beneficial for word recall than building comprehension.

Decodable Texts emphasize specific phonics skills. They are often found in sets that span many different phonics skills. The stories are usually progressive as the skills learned in earlier books are reinforced in later books. As with controlled vocabulary texts, these books rarely have well developed story lines and are not well suited to comprehension development. However, they do have a significant place in helping students unlock the code to reading.

Authentic Literature is the type of reading that most people are familiar with, and is the goal of all reading. All children should experience the reading of authentic literature or real stories. These can be fiction or nonfiction but should provide numerous details and allow for the development of comprehension skills. They range in difficulty and length, but are the core of reading.

Created, Easy to Read Texts encompass teacher-created reading passages or books to fill a specific purpose within the curriculum or for a group of students.

Students should be aware of the purpose for reading so that they know what thinking is expected of them. When reading any text, students need to employ certain strategies. Teachers should engage the students in the reading process and model the appropriate strategies of:

- connecting
- making meaning
- questioning
- predicting
- inferring
- reflecting
- evaluating

Major Nonfiction Genres

Essay

An essay is a short work of nonfiction that gives the author's opinion on a specific topic. While nonfiction essays are expository, they also tend to be subjective and can include narrative. Essays can also be literary criticism, political manifestos, arguments, observations, or even personal reflections. One basic form is the five paragraph essay, which consists of an introductory paragraph, three paragraphs about the topic and a concluding paragraph. Other forms of essay include:

- Descriptive – provides a vivid picture of a location, person, object, event or debate.

- Narrative – tells a story as a way of presenting a point of view or opinion on a topic

- Compare and contrast - develops the relationship between two or more objects

- Persuasive – attempts to persuade the reader to accept or agree with an idea or a point of view

Argumentative – argues one side of an issue giving supporting evidence

Biography

A biography is a written account of a person's life. It usually highlights specific aspects of personality, gives insight into events in someone's life and often includes intimate details that are not widely known. A biography is written about a subject and so is in third person point of view.

Autobiography

An autobiography is an account of a person's life written by that person. When one is telling about one's life the opinions expressed may be exaggerated or events may be omitted. It is written in the first person point of view.

Memoir

A memoir is a type of autobiography, but usually deals with only one or two aspects of the author's life. It is not as structured as an autobiography as it is usually only about one section of the author's life rather than the entire life. Like the autobiography, a memoir is usually written in the first person point of view.

Editorial

An editorial is a statement or a news article written by a news organization. It expresses the opinion of the editor or writer on topics that may be of interest to the readers. Such writing is usually short and always labeled as being an editorial or opinion piece.

Textbook

A textbook presents information on a subject area and includes many different topics. The book is divided into chapters, each one focusing on a topic. There are many features in a textbook, such as a table of contents, index and glossary along with photos, charts, maps, and diagrams.

News Article

A news article presents information on recent events of interest. These writings answer the 5W's and How and may be accompanied by photos or illustrations.

Textual Features

In order for students to make the most of their reading experiences they should know the various features of texts that can help them understand the material. These include:

- **Paragraphs** – ideas are arranged into paragraphs with each one centered around one main ides. There is a beginning sentence, three or four middle sentences and a concluding sentence. The **topic sentence** may be anywhere in the paragraph. All the other sentences are designed to provide more information about the topic sentence. The **concluding sentence** brings closure to the.
- **Glossary** – this section of a text provides definitions for words in the text. Throughout the text, words that are included in the glossary are written in bold so that they are easily identifiable.
- **Graphic Features** – some of the graphic features included in texts are maps, charts, diagrams and illustrations designed to elaborate on information presented in the text.

Illustrations can be key supports for emergent and early readers. Teachers should not only use wordless stories (books which tell their narratives through pictures alone), but can also make targeted use of Big Books for read-alouds, so that young children become habituated in the use of illustrations as an important component for constructing meaning. The teacher should model for the child how to refer to an illustration for help in identifying a word in the text the child does not recognize. Children can also go on a "picture walk" with the teacher as part of a mini-lesson or guided reading, and anticipate the story (narrative) using the pictures alone to construct meaning.

Skill 1.10   Recognize and demonstrate understanding of the factors that influence early literacy and language acquisition and the different stages at which literacy occurs

There are several different factors that influence early literacy and language acquisition. They include:

- The intellectual, social and emotional development of the child
- The culture of the family
- Socio- economic circumstances
- The support the child receives in reading development in the home – presence of print, books and the reading level of the parents
- Prior experience with printed materials
- Parental attitudes toward reading
- Attendance in a pre-school setting

Children learn more readily at an early age. This is why teaching the basic skills of reading at an early age are so important in reading development. Many children enter school with a deficiency in prior knowledge because they haven't been read to at home. In Kindergarten, teachers should surround the children with print, read to them at every opportunity and balance the reading with instruction about letters and sounds.

Teachers need to comprehend the stages of literacy development in order to provide the right instruction for each child in their classrooms. These stages and their characteristics are:

0 to 4 years
- enjoys having an adult read to them
- likes to pretend to read books
- reads pictures of familiar books
- recognizes some of the letters of the alphabet
- practices printing their own name
- starts to sound out letters

Beginning Literacy – 5 – 7 years
- Starts to develop phonemic awareness
- Can associate letters with sounds
- Starts to sound out words
- Can recognize some sight words
- Uses picture clues
- Starts to use context clues when reading
- Uses invented spelling when writing

Beginning Fluency – 7 to 8 years
- Has a repertoire of sight vocabulary
- Can read familiar stories fluently
- Practices reading with a partner
- Can retell stories with comprehension
- Has greater speed and accuracy when reading
- Finds it easy to write and spell familiar words

Literacy 9 – 12 years
- Reads fluently
- Comprehends what is read
- Has an expanded vocabulary
- Writes for various purposes
- Can use a dictionary for help with spelling
- Can express personal tastes in reading

The variation in literacy backgrounds that children bring to reading can make teaching more difficult. Often a teacher has to choose between focusing on the learning needs of a few students at the expense of the group, or focusing on the group at the risk of leaving some students behind academically. This situation is particularly critical for children with gaps in their literacy knowledge who may be at risk in subsequent grades for becoming "diverse learners."

Areas of Emerging Evidence

- **Experiences with print (through reading and writing) help preschool children develop an understanding of the conventions, purpose, and functions of print.** Children learn about print from a variety of sources and in the process come to realize that print carries the story. They also learn how text is structured visually (i.e., text begins at the top of the page, moves from left to right, and carries over to the next page when it is turned). While knowledge about the conventions of print enables children to understand the physical structure of language, the conceptual knowledge that printed words convey a message also helps children bridge the gap between oral and written language.
- **Phonological awareness and letter recognition contribute to initial reading acquisition by helping children develop efficient word recognition strategies (e.g., detecting pronunciations and storing associations in memory.)** Phonological awareness and knowledge of print-speech relations play an important role in facilitating reading acquisition. Therefore, phonological awareness instruction should be an integral component of early reading programs. Within the emergent literacy research, viewpoints diverged on whether acquisition of phonological awareness and letter recognition are preconditions of literacy acquisition or whether they develop interdependently with literacy activities such as story reading and writing.

- **Storybook reading affects children's knowledge about, strategies for, and attitudes towards reading.** Of all the strategies intended to promote growth in literacy acquisition, none is as commonly practiced, nor as strongly supported across the emergent literacy literature as storybook reading. Children in different social and cultural groups have differing degrees of access to storybook reading. For example, it is not unusual for a teacher to have students who have experienced thousands of hours of story reading time, along with other students who have had little or no such exposure.

Design Principles in Emergent Literacy

- **Conspicuous Strategies.** As an instructional priority, conspicuous strategies are a sequence of teaching events and teacher actions used to help students learn new literacy information and relate it to their existing knowledge. Conspicuous strategies can be incorporated in beginning reading instruction to ensure that all learners have basic literacy concepts. For example, during storybook reading teachers can show students how to recognize the fronts and backs of books, locate titles, or look at pictures and predict the story, rather than assume children will learn this through incidental exposure. Similarly, teachers can teach students a strategy for holding a pencil appropriately or checking the form of their letters against an alphabet sheet on their desks or the classroom wall.

- **Mediated Scaffolding.** Mediated scaffolding can be accomplished in a number of ways to meet the needs of students with diverse literacy experiences. To link oral and written language, for example, teachers may use texts that simulate speech by incorporating oral language patterns or children's writing. Or teachers can use daily storybook reading to discuss book-handling skills and directionality-concepts that are particularly important for children who are unfamiliar with printed texts. Teachers can also use repeated readings to give students multiple exposures to unfamiliar words or extended opportunities to look at books with predictable patterns, as well as provide support by modeling the behaviors associated with reading. Teachers can act as *scaffolds* during these storybook reading activities by adjusting their demands (e.g., asking increasingly complex questions or encouraging children to take on portions of the reading) or by reading more complex text as students gain knowledge of beginning literacy components.

- **Strategic Integration.** Many children with diverse literacy experiences have difficulty making connections between old and new information. Strategic integration can be applied to help link old and new learning. For example, in the classroom, strategic integration can be accomplished by providing access to literacy materials in classroom writing centers and libraries. Students should also have opportunities to integrate and extend their literacy knowledge by reading aloud, listening to other students read aloud, and listening to tape recordings and videotapes in reading corners.

- **Primed Background Knowledge.** All children bring some level of background knowledge (e.g., how to hold a book, awareness of directionality of print) to beginning reading. Teachers can utilize children's background knowledge to help children link their personal literacy experiences to beginning reading instruction, while also closing the gap between students with rich and students with impoverished literacy experiences. Activities that draw upon background knowledge include incorporating oral language activities (which discriminate between printed letters and words) into daily read-alouds, as well as frequent opportunities to retell stories, look at books with predictable patterns, write messages with invented spellings, and respond to literature through drawing.

Emergent literacy research examines early literacy knowledge and the contexts and conditions that foster that knowledge. Despite differing viewpoints on the relation between emerging literacy skills and reading acquisition, strong support was found in the literature for the important contribution that early childhood exposure to oral and written language makes to the facility with which children learn to read

Skill 1.11 Demonstrate an understanding of ways adults support and facilitate language acquisition

Although it is clear that everyone is born with an innate sense for language, this does not develop without help from adults. Children need to be read to and talked to using the correct pronunciation of words. Prior to coming to school, children should be familiar with books and the stories they can read from pictures. Not all parents, however, are aware of the need to read to their children before they reach school age. For many children the first experiences they have with reading is when they enter Kindergarten.

Along with reading to children and providing instruction in phonemic awareness, teachers also have to help parents teach their children. One method of doing this is to have a meeting with parents at the beginning of the year outlining your expectations for reading at home. Children should be expected to take books home each night for home reading. Regular communication with the parents is also necessary to keep the cycle of reading running smoothly.

The classroom is also a place where other adults from the community can read to the children. Inviting the principal, mayor or other person into the class to read to the children helps them understand that reading is important and is something that everyone does.

COMPETENCY 2.0   **APPLICATION OF THEORETICAL AND KNOWLEDGE BASES OF READING IN INSTRUCTION**

Skill 2.1   Demonstrate an understanding of the relationship between reading and writing instruction and of how writing and reading support each other at different developmental levels.

Reading Emphasis in Middle School

Reading for comprehension of factual material - content area textbooks, reference books, and newspapers - is closely related to study strategies in the middle/junior high. Organized study models, such as the SQ3R method, a technique that makes it possible and feasible to learn the content of even large amounts of text (Survey, Question, Read, Recite, and Review Studying), teach students to locate main ideas and supporting details, to recognize sequential order, to distinguish fact from opinion, and to determine cause and effect relationships.

Strategies

Teacher-guided activities that require students to organize and to summarize information based on the author's explicit intent are pertinent strategies in middle grades. Evaluation techniques include oral and written responses to standardized or teacher-made worksheets.

Reading of fiction introduces and reinforces skills in inferring meaning from narration and description. Teaching-guided activities in the process of reading for meaning should be followed by cooperative planning of the skills to be studied and of the selection of reading resources. Many printed reading for comprehension instruments as well as individualized computer software programs exist to monitor the progress of acquiring comprehension skills.

Older middle school students should be given opportunities for more student-centered activities - individual and collaborative selection of reading choices based on student interest, small group discussions of selected works, and greater written expression. Evaluation techniques include teacher monitoring and observation of discussions and written work samples.

Certain students may begin some fundamental critical interpretation - recognizing fallacious reasoning in news media, examining the accuracy of news reports and advertising, explaining their reasons for preferring one author's writing to another's. Development of these skills may require a more learning-centered approach in which the teacher identifies a number of objectives and suggested resources from which the student may choose his course of study. Self-evaluation through a reading diary should be stressed. Teacher and peer evaluation of creative projects resulting from such study is encouraged.

Reading aloud before the entire class as a formal means of teacher evaluation should be phased out in favor of one-to-one tutoring or peer-assisted reading. Occasional sharing of favored selections by both teacher and willing students is a good oral interpretation basic.

Reading Emphasis in High School

Students in high school literature classes should focus on interpretive and critical reading. Teachers should guide the study of the elements of inferential (interpretive) reading - drawing conclusions, predicting outcomes, and recognizing examples of specific genre characteristics, for example - and critical reading to judge the quality of the writer's work against recognized standards. At this level students should understand the skills of language and reading that they are expected to master and be able to evaluate their own progress.

Strategies

The teacher becomes more facilitator than instructor - helping the student to make a diagnosis of his own strengths and weaknesses, keeping a record of progress, and interacting with other students and the teacher in practicing skills.

Despite the requisites and prerequisites of most literature courses, students should be encouraged to pursue independent study and enrichment reading.

Ample opportunities should be provided for oral interpretation of literature, special projects in creative dramatics, writing for publication in school literary magazines or newspapers, and speech/debate activities. A student portfolio provides for teacher and peer evaluation.

When preparing to read a book, the analyst should become acquainted with the elements of the story such as setting, characterization, style (language, both technically with regard to dialect but also structurally with regard to use of description, length of sentences, phrases, etc.), plot (particularly conflicts and pattern), tone (what is the *attitude* of the writer toward characters, theme, etc.) and particularly theme (the message or point the story conveys). It's not essential to know the writer's biography, but it is often helpful, especially in responding from the analyst's point of view.

Literature is written to evoke a personal response in readers. Once the analyst has a grip on the story—a thorough understanding of the story—then an analysis of one's own response to it is in order.

The following questions are useful:

- Do you respond emotionally to one of the characters? Why? Is a character similar to someone you know or have known?
- Is the setting evocative for you because of a place, situation, or milieu that you have experienced and that had meaning for you? Why?
- Did the vocabulary, descriptions, or short or long sentences have impact on you? Why? For example, short, simple sentence after short, simple sentence may be used deliberately, but do you find it annoying?
- Do you agree with the author's attitude toward the characters, setting, story, etc.? For example, has a character been written unsympathetically that you felt deserved more consideration? Does the author demonstrate a distaste for the setting he has chosen, and do you feel he is being unjust? Or do you experience the same distaste?

Reading is personal. Responding to it personally adds important dimensions to an analysis for others.

Skill 2.2 **Demonstrate knowledge of how to construct instructional plans in which assessment, goals, instruction and reassessment are connected and continuous**

Writing a lesson plan is not simply writing down a list of items that a teacher will cover in one class period. In order to write an effective instructional plan, the teacher has to ask himself/herself three vital questions:

>What do you want the students to learn?
>How are you going to teach them?
>How will you know when they have achieved the objective?

Goal

Start with the mandated goal for the lesson. This helps to determine what you and the students should be doing throughout the lesson. It gives you the purpose and the rationale. Look at the broad aims for the unit and then determine your goal for the lesson. Ask yourself what you expect the students to be able to do at the end of the lesson.

Objectives

These are the specific outcomes that you will teach in the lesson. The way you design the lesson will depend on your answers to these questions:

- What will the students do during this lesson?
- What will they have to do to accomplish the objective?
- What are the standards that you will use to determine whether or not students have achieved the objective?
- What assessment will you use to determine whether the objectives have been achieved?

You have to look at the background knowledge that students must possess in order to accomplish the objectives. Do you need to re-teach any concepts?

Materials

List the materials that the students will need to work with during the lesson. What preparations do you need to make before you start to teach the lesson?

Description of the Lesson

This is a description of how you intend to teach the specific lesson. Use Bloom's Taxonomy to deconstruct the objectives into what you expect the students to be able to do.

Procedure

These are the nuts and bolts of your lesson. Procedure consists of the following components:

- Introduction – how will you introduce the lesson
- Main Activity – the focus of the lesson
- Closure – how will you clue up the lesson
- Activities – what will the students do to demonstrate that learning has taken place

Assessment

Have the students learned what you intended them to learn? This is where you determine whether or not students have achieved the intended outcome or whether you need to reteach the lesson in a different manner.

The rule of thumb for planning instructional lessons is to begin with the end in mind. Then determine how you are going to get there and how you will know if the students have arrived.

Skill 2.3 **Demonstrate knowledge of explicit instructional strategies to teach students how to monitor their own word identification strategies, comprehension, and comprehension strategies**

There are five key strategies for child reading of informational/expository texts.

Inferencing is a process that involves the reader making a reasonable judgment based on the information given and engages children to literally construct meaning. In order to develop and enhance this key skill in children, they might have a mini lesson where the teacher demonstrates this by reading an expository book aloud (i.e. one on skyscrapers for young children) and then demonstrates for them the following reading habits: looking for clues, reflecting on what the reader already knows about the topic, and using the clues to figure out what the author means/intends.

Identifying main ideas in an expository text can be improved when the children have an explicit strategy for identifying important information. They can make this strategy part of their everyday reading style, "walking" through the following exercises during guided reading sessions. The child should read the passage so that the topic is readily identifiable to him or her. It will be what most of the information is about.

Next the child should be asked to be on the lookout for a sentence within the expository passage that summarizes the key information in the paragraph. Then the child should read the rest of the passage or excerpt in light of this information and also note which information in the paragraph is less important. The important information the child has identified in the paragraph can be used to formulate the author's main idea. The child reader may even want to use some of the author's own language in stating that idea.

Monitoring means self-clarifying: As one reads, the reader often realizes that what he or she is reading is not making sense. The reader then has to have a plan for making sensible meaning out of the excerpt. Cooper and other balanced literacy advocates have a stop and think strategy which they use with children. The child reflects, "Does this make sense to me?" When the child concludes that it does not, the child then either re-reads, reads ahead in the text, looks up unknown words or asks for help from the teacher.

What is important about monitoring is that some readers ask these questions and try these approaches without ever being explicitly taught them in school by a teacher. However, these strategies need to be explicitly modeled and practiced under the guidance of the teacher by most, if not all child readers.

Summarizing engages the reader in pulling together into a cohesive whole the essential bits of information within a longer passage or excerpt of text. Children can be taught to summarize informational or expository text by following these guidelines. First they should look at the topic sentence of the paragraph or the text and ignore the trivia. Then they should search for information which has been mentioned more than once and make sure it is included only once in their summary. Find related ideas or items and group them under a unifying heading. Search for and identify a main idea sentence. Finally, put the summary together using all these guidelines.

Generating questions can motivate and enhance children's comprehension of reading in that they are actively involved. The following guidelines will help children generate meaningful questions that will trigger constructive reading of expository texts. First children should preview the text by reading the titles and subheadings. Then they should also look at the illustrations and the pictures. Finally they should read the first paragraph. These first previews should yield an impressive batch of specific questions.

Next, children should get into a Dr. Seuss mode and ask themselves a "THINK" question. Make certain that the children write down the question. Then have them read to find important information to answer their "think" question. Ask that they write down the answer they found and copy the sentence or sentences where they found the answer. Also have them consider whether, in light of their further reading through the text, their original question was a good one or not.

Ask them to be prepared to explain why their original question was a good one or not. Once the children have answered their original "think" question, have them generate additional ones and then find their answers and judge whether these questions were "good" ones in light of the text.

Strategies for Identifying Point of View, Distinguishing Facts from Opinions and Detecting Faulty Reasoning in Informational/Expository Texts

Expository texts are full of information which may or may not be factual and which may reflect the bias of the editor or author. Children need to learn that expository texts are organized around main ideas. Expository content is commonly found in newspapers, magazines, content textbooks, and informational reference books (i.e. atlas, almanac, yearbook of an encyclopedia).

The five types of expository texts (also called "text structures") to which the children should be introduced through modeled reading and a teacher facilitated walk through are:

Description text: This usually gives the characteristics or qualities of a particular topic. It can be depended upon to be factual. Within this type of text, the child reader has to use all of his or her basic reading strategies, because these types of expository texts do not have explicit clue words.

Causation or Cause-Effect text: This text is one where faulty reasoning may come into play and the child reader has to use inferential and self-questioning skills to assess whether the stated cause-effect relationship is a valid one. Clue words to look for are: "therefore", "the reasons for", "as a result of", "because", "in consequence of", and "since." The reader must then decide whether the relationship is valid. For example, does the ventricle pump blood into the heart?

Comparison text: This is an expository text which gives contrasts and similarities between two or more objects and ideas. Many social studies, art, and science text books in class and non-fiction books include this contrast. Key words to look out for are: like, unlike, resemble, different, different from, similar to, in contrast with, in comparison to, and in a different vein. It is important that as children examine texts which are talking about illustrated or photographed entities can review the graphic representations for clues to support or contradict the text.

Collection text: This text presents ideas in a group. The writer presents a set of related points or ideas. This text structure is also called a listing or a sequence. The author frequently uses clue words such as first, second, third, finally, and next to alert the reader to the sequence. Based on how well the writer structures the sequence of points or ideas, the reader should be able to make connections. It is important the writer make clear in the expository text how the items are related and why they follow in that given sequence. Simple collection texts that can be literally modeled for young children include recipe making. A class of first graders, beginning readers and writers, were literally spellbound by a teacher's presentation of a widely known copyrighted collection text. The children were thrilled as the author followed the sequences of the recipe, and the children finally took turns stirring the food until it was creamy and smooth. The children enjoyed eating their Cream of Farina from a commercial cereal box which had cooking directions on it.

The children had constructed meaning from this five-minute class demonstration and would now pay close attention to collection texts on other food and product instruction boxes because this text had become an authentic part of their lives.

Response structure expository texts present a question or response followed by an answer or a solution. Of course, entire mathematics text books and some science and social studies text books are filled with these types of structures. Again it is important to walk the child reader through the excerpt and to sensitize the child to the clue words which signal this type of structure. These words include, but are not limited to, such phrases as "the problem is," "the question is," "you need to solve for," "one probable solution would be," "an intervention could be," "the concern is," and "another way to solve this would be."

Newspapers provide wonderful features which can be used by the teacher as read-alouds to introduce children Grades 3-6 to point of view distinctions, specifically, editorials, editorial cartoons and key sports editorial cartoons. Children can also come to understand the distinction between fact and fiction when they examine a newspaper advertisement or a supermarket circular for a product they commonly use, eat, drink or wear which includes exaggerated claims about what the product can actually do for the individual in question.

Finally, the fact versus opinion distinction can be nicely explored if a teacher takes the children online to look at some celebrity websites and walks them through some exaggerated claims made about their particular movie star favorites. It is very important at some point, if the children have access to the internet, that the teacher show them how to examine websites, look at who developed a particular website and consider how credible the developers of the site are.

Use of Reading Strategies for Different Texts

As children progress to the older grades (3-6), it is important for the teacher to model for them that in research on a social studies or science exploration, it may not be necessary to read every single word of a given expository information text. For instance, if the child is trying to find out about hieroglyphics, he or she might only read through those sections of a book on Egyptian or Sumerian civilization which dealt with picture writing. The teacher, assisted by a child, should model how to go through the table of contents and the index of a book to identify only those pages which deal with picture writing. In addition, other children should come to the front of the room or to the center of the area where the reading group is meeting. With the support of the teacher, they should skim the book for illustrations or diagrams of picture writing which is the focus of their need.

Children can practice the skills of skimming texts and scanning for particular topics that connect with their social studies, science and mathematics content-area interests for their grade level.

Use of Comprehension Skills Before, After, and During Reading

Cooper (2004) advocates that the child ask himself or herself what a text is about before he or she reads it and even during reading of the text. The child should be continually questioning himself or herself as to whether the text confirmed his or her predictions. Of course, after completing the text, the child can then review the predictions and verify whether they were correct.

Using another strategy, the child reader looks over the expository text subheadings, illustrations, captions and indices to get an idea about the book. Then the child, still before reading the text, decides whether he or she can find the answer to his or her question.

Use of Oral Language Activities to Promote Comprehension

Taberski advocates using the "Stopping to Think About" strategy with expository texts as well as fictional ones. This strategy is centered on the reader using three steps as he or she goes through the expository text. These steps may be expressed as questions.

> What do I, the reader, think is going to happen?
> What clues in the text or illustrations or graphics lead me to think that this is going to happen?
> How can I prove that I am right by going back to the text to demonstrate that this does happen or is suggested by actual clues in the text?

Taberski (2000) deliberately uses expository texts that relate to her grade's social studies and science lessons to model for children how to "stop and think" about the way an expository text is organized. She sometimes deliberately reads aloud a section of a text or a chapter of a non-fiction book so that the children can consider what they have learned about the topic and how it is organized. Then together as a whole class or as a guided reading group, they make predictions about what is coming next.

Development of Reading Comprehension Skills and Strategies for Individual Students

While all child readers can benefit from explicit expository reading strategies, the English Language Learner can truly get a gateway for understanding second language materials by working with a native English-language-speaking buddy on the question-generating strategy. Both the buddy (a peer) and the teacher should alert the English Language Learner to how much of a resource illustrations and pictures can be for constructing meaning. If the teacher has time to work individually with the English Language Learner, the daily newspaper, which is replete with graphics, photos and text, is a wonderful tool for honing expository reading skills using these strategies.

The five strategies for enhancing expository reading skills are not beyond use with learners with special needs. However, rather than be offered in an array, these strategies would have to be presented one at a time, probably one-on-one, with explicit teacher modeling and then done as shared reading and shared writing with the specific child.

Highly proficient readers might enjoy sharing their skills with other peers and could serve as the newspaper reading buddies for special needs students. They might not only support special needs grade level or younger peers in reading through a designated newspaper section every day, but might also collaborate or oversee their peers or younger peers in designing a word search or crossword puzzle based on that particular section of the newspaper.

Use of editorial sports page cartoons is a good way to introduce special needs learners to opportunities for identifying point of view. They can also create their own takes on the topics of the editorial cartoons using an accessible, non-threatening storyboard format for their commentary.

The Role of Oral Language Fluency in Facilitating the Comprehension of Informational/Expository Texts

Children at the middle and secondary levels of education who are studying social studies content have been exposed to what social studies educators call re-enactments. This is a Reader's Theater-version of history and cultural study based completely on fact and established historical texts and documents.

Even young children will enjoy and gain tremendous additional expository comprehension facility when they are asked to dramatize a well-known historical document or song. They may act out the preamble to the Constitution or read aloud as a chorus the Declaration of Independence or dramatize the Battle Hymn of the Republic. This gives children an opportunity to examine in deep form the vocabulary, syntactic, and semantic clues of these texts. They then have to use their oral instruments (voices) to express the appropriate expression for the texts. If the children are in Grades 4 and above, they can also be asked to explain in writing how they used the word, syntactic and semantic clues to interpret their oral language recitation. Recitation and writing can be a powerful experience for children Grades 4 and up as they build their expository reading and writing skills.

Use of Writing Activities to Promote Comprehension

K-W-L Strategy

This is a graphic organizer strategy which activates children's prior knowledge and also helps them to target their reading of expository texts. This focus is achieved through having the children reflect on three key questions.

Before the child read the expository passage:
"What do I *K*now?" and "What do I or we *W*ant to find out?"

After the child has read the expository passage:
"What have I or we *L*earned from the passage?"

What is excellent about this strategy, which is broadly used and easily implemented in almost any classroom, is that it is almost totally student-centered and powerfully focuses the child's attention on the actual reading of expository passages. The K-W-L strategy also helps the child prepare for a potential writing task.

When the teacher first introduces the K-W-L strategy, the children should be allowed sufficient time to brainstorm what all of them in the class or small group actually know about the topic. The children should have a three-columned K-W-L worksheet template for their journals and there should be a chart up front to record the responses from class or group discussion. The children can write under each column in their own journal, and should also help the teacher with notations on the chart. This strategy involves the children actually gaining experience in note-taking and having a concrete record of new data and information they have gleaned from the passage about the topic.

Depending on the grade level of the participating children, the teacher may also want to focus them toward considering categories of information they hope to find out from the expository passage. For instance, they may be reading a book on animals to find out more about an animal's habitats during the winter or about its mating habits.

When children are working on the middle-section (*W*ant) strategy sheet, the teacher may give them a chance to share what they would like to learn further about the topic and help them to express it in question format.

K-W-L is useful and can even be introduced as early as Grade 2 with extensive teacher support. It not only serves to support the child's comprehension of a particular expository text, but also models for children a format for note-taking. Beyond note-taking, when the teacher wants to introduce report writing, the K-W-L format provides excellent outlines and question introductions for at least three paragraphs of a report.

Cooper (2004) recommends this strategy for use with thematic units and with reading chapters in required science, social studies, or health textbooks.
In addition to its usefulness with thematic unit study, K-W-L is wonderful for providing the teacher with a concrete format to assess how well children have absorbed pertinent new knowledge within the passage (by looking at the third *L*earn section). Ultimately, it is hoped that students will learn to use this strategy, not only under explicit teacher direction with templates of K-W-L sheets, but also on their own by informally writing questions they want to find out about in their journals and then going back to their own questions and answering them after reading.

Use of Text Features (e.g. Index, Glossary), Graphic Features (e.g. Charts, Maps) and Reference Materials

Traditionally, the aspects of expository text reading comprehension have been taught in a dry format using reference books from the school or public library, particularly, the Atlas, Almanac, and large geography books. Although these worthy library and perhaps classroom library books can still be used, it is much easier to take a simple newspaper to introduce and provide children with daily ongoing, authentic experiences in learning these necessary skills as they also keep up with real world events that affect their daily lives.

They can go on a chronological hunt through the daily newspaper and discover the many formats of schedules contained therein. For instance, some newspapers include a calendar of the week with literary, sports, social, movie and other public events. Children can also go on scavenger hunts through various sections of the newspaper and on certain days find full blown timelines detailing famous individual's careers, business histories, and milestones in the political history of a nation or even key movies made by a famous movie director up for an Oscar.

The nature of the newspaper reportage and the public's need to know the why and wherefore behind the story of natural disasters, company takeovers, political downfalls and uprisings leads newspapers to represent events graphically and to use cause /effect diagramming and comparison/contrast wording. If the teacher specifically wants to make certain that the students come away with this material, he or she can pre-clip "teaching" stories from the news for the child and introduce them in a special News Center.

After children have been walked through these comparison/contrast news writings and cause/effect diagramming as it appears in the newspaper, they can be challenged to find additional examples of these text structures in the news or challenged to reframe or rewrite familiar stories using these text structures. They can even use desktop publishing to re-author the stories using the same text structures.

If a class participates in a local Newspaper in Education program, in which the children receive a free newspaper two to three times a week in the classroom, the teacher can teach index skills using the index of the newspaper by having children compete or cooperate in small groups to find various features.

Map and chart skills take on much more relevance and excitement when the children work on these skills using sport charts detailing the batting averages and pass completions of their favorite players or perhaps the box scores of their older siblings' football and baseball games. Maps dealing with holiday weather become meaningful to children as they anticipate a vacation.

Ability to Apply Reading Skills for Various Purposes

What is really intriguing about the use of newspapers as a model and an authentic platform for introducing children to recognizing and using expository text structures, features and references, is that the children can demonstrate their mastery of these structures by putting out their own newspapers detailing their school universe. They can also create their own timelines for projects or research papers using newspaper models.

Application of Comprehension Strategies for Electronic Texts

If the class gets newspapers in the classroom as part of an ongoing Newspapers in Education program, it is natural and easy for the teacher to take the time to show children how the same news is covered online. All of the newspapers have e-news. Children can first do a K-W-L on what they know or think they know about e-news and then actually review their specific daily newspaper's site. With the support of the teacher or an older peer, they can examine the resource and perhaps note the following differences in electronic text:

- Use of moving pictures and video to document events
- Use of sound clips in addition to written text
- Use of music/sound effects not in printed text
- Links to other web resources and to other archived articles

Naturally, this can lead to much rich discussion and to further detailed web versus print news resource analysis. For children in Grades 5 and 6, this might even include a research investigation of a particular news story or event including broadcast media coverage.

Development of Reading Comprehension Skills and Strategies for Individual Students

Both English Language Learners and struggling readers can benefit from the structure and format of the K-W-L approach. It allows them to share their prior experiences and knowledge of the topics covered in the expository text through natural conversation. It provides them with a natural device for the teacher or tutor to customize and to scaffold instruction to meet their linguistic and experiential backgrounds. Through the discussion and sharing of other children's comments, struggling readers and children from ELL backgrounds have an opportunity to learn how to use questions to "walk through" and take notes on expository writing.

Highly proficient readers can do a comparative expository news event study between print accounts, e-news reportage, and broadcast media coverage. They can prepare charts and their own news mock-up to show the similarities and contrasts between which aspects of the event get covered in which media format. They may also want to write to actual reporters and editors from the different media to share their insights and see if these professionals are willing to respond.

"If we want children to become strategic readers, then we create classrooms that reinforce the strategies we've demonstrated and allow children to practice on books that match their needs."
Sharon Taberski

Skill 2.4   Demonstrate knowledge of instructional approaches to foster higher-order, critical, reflective thinking about texts

Developing critical thinking skills in students is not as simple as developing other skills. Effective teachers realize that critical thinking skills must be taught within the contexts of specific subject matter. For example, Language Arts teachers can teach critical thinking skills through novels; Social Studies teachers can teach critical thinking skills through primary source documents or current events; Science teachers can teach critical thinking skills by having students develop hypotheses prior to conducting experiments.

There are three general types of critical thinking skills:

Analysis is the systematic exploration of a concept, event, term, piece of writing, element of media, or any other complex item. It is the exploration of the parts that make up a whole. For example, when analyzing a piece of literature, one might focus on a particular character to determine how that character adds significance to the whole novel. In biology, one could analyze the findings of an experiment to see if the results might indicate significance for something even larger than the experiment itself. A social studies teacher could ask students to analyze the events leading up to World War II: doing so would require that students look at the various components (e.g., smaller world events prior to World War II) and determine how those components, when added up together, caused the war.

Synthesis is the opposite of analysis. In analysis, we take a whole and examine its parts. With synthesis, we take different aspects and make them one whole. For example, a Language Arts teacher could ask students to synthesize two works of distinct literature. Let's say that we take *The Scarlet Letter* and *The Crucible*, two works both featuring life in Puritan America, written about one century apart. A student could synthesize the two works and come to conclusions about Puritanical life. An Art teacher could ask students to synthesize two paintings from the Impressionist era and come to conclusions about the features that distinguish that style of art.

Evaluation involves making judgments. Whereas analysis and synthesis seek answers and hypotheses based on investigations, evaluation seeks opinions. For example, a social studies teacher could ask students to evaluate the quality of Richard Nixon's resignation speech. To do so, they would assess its value. In contrast, analysis would keep judgment out of the assignment: it would have students focus possibly on the structure of the speech (i.e., Does an argument move from emotion to logic?). When evaluating a speech, a piece of literature, a movie, or a work of art, we seek to determine its value. Teaching good evaluation skills requires not just that students learn how to determine whether something is good or not—it requires that they learn how to support their evaluations. So if a student claims that Nixon's speech was effective in what the President intended the speech to do, the student would need to explain how this is so. Notice that evaluation will probably utilize the skills of analysis and/or synthesis, but that the purpose is ultimately different.

In general, critical thinking skills should be taught through assignments, activities, lessons, and discussions that cause students to think on their own. While teachers can and should provide students with the tools to think critically, they will ultimately become critical thinkers if they have to use those tools themselves. Teachers must provide students the tools to evaluate, analyze, and synthesize. Let's take political speeches as an example. Students will be better analyzers, synthesizers, and evaluators if they understand some of the basics of political speeches. Therefore, a teacher might introduce concepts such as rhetoric, style, persona, audience, diction, imagery, and tone. The best way to introduce these concepts would be to provide students with multiple, good examples of these things. Once they are familiar with these critical tools, students will be in a better place to apply them individually to political speeches—and then be able to analyze, synthesize, and evaluate political speeches on their own.

Skill 2.5 Demonstrate an understanding of different decoding strategies and of instructional approaches to teach students how to use them

The Relationship Between Oral and Written Vocabulary Development and Reading Comprehension

Biemiller's (2003) research documents that those children entering fourth grade with significant vocabulary deficits demonstrate increasing reading comprehension problems. Evidence shows that these children do not catch up, but rather continue to fall behind.

Strategy One: Word Map Strategy

This strategy is useful for children Grades 3-6 and beyond. The target group of children for this strategy includes those who need to improve their independent vocabulary acquisition abilities. The strategy is essentially teacher-directed learning in which children are "walked through" the process. They are helped by the teacher to identify the type of information that makes a definition. They are also assisted in using context clues and background understanding to construct meaning.

The word-map graphic organizer is the tool teachers use to complete this strategy with children. Word map templates are available online from the Houghton Mifflin website and from READWRITETHINK, the website of the NCTE (see webliography section). The word map helps the children to visually represent the elements of a given concept.

The children's literal articulation of the concept can be prompted by three key questions: What is it? What is it like? What are some examples?

For instance, the word "oatmeal" might yield the word map provided below.

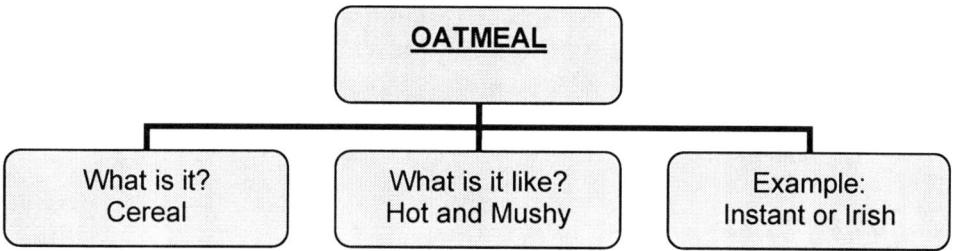

The procedure to be used in sharing this strategy with children is to select three concepts the children are familiar with. Then show them the template of a word map. Tell them that the three questions asked on the map and the boxes below helps readers and writers to see what they need to know about a word. Next, help the children to complete at least two word maps for two of the three concepts that were pre-selected. Then have the children select a concept of their own to map either independently or in a small group. As the final task for this first part of the strategy, have the children, in teams or individually, write a definition for at least one of the concepts using the key things about it listed on the map. Have the children share these definitions aloud and talk about how they used the word maps to help them with the definitions.

For the next part of this strategy, the teacher should pick up an expository text or a textbook the children are already using to study mathematics, science or social studies. Then either locate a short excerpt in which a particular concept is defined or use the content to write model passages of definition on his or her own.

After the passages are selected or authored, the teacher should duplicate them. Then they should be distributed to the children along with blank word map templates. The children should be asked to read each passage and then to complete the word map for the concept in each passage. Finally, have the children share the word maps they have developed for each passage. Give them a chance to explain how they used the word in the passage to help them fill out their word map. End by telling them that the three components of the concept—class, description, example—are just three of the many components for any given concept.

This strategy has assessment potential because the teacher can literally see how the students understand specific concepts by looking at their maps and hearing their explanations. The maps the students develop on their own demonstrate whether they have really understood the concepts in the passages. This strategy serves to ready students for inferring word meanings on their own. By using the word map strategy, children develop concepts of what they need to know to begin to figure out an unknown word on their own. It assists the children in Grades 3 and beyond to connect prior knowledge with new knowledge.

This word map strategy can be adapted by the teacher to suit the specific needs and goals of instruction. Illustrations of the concept and comparisons to other concepts can be included in the word mapping for children Grades 5 and beyond. This particular strategy is also one that can be used with a research theme in other content areas.

Strategy Two: Preview in Context

This is a direct teaching strategy which allows the teacher to guide the students as they examine words in context prior to reading a passage. Before beginning the strategy, the teacher selects only two or three key concept words and then reads carefully to identify passages within the text that evidence strong context clues for the word.

Then the teacher presents the word and the context to the children. As the teacher reads aloud, the children follow along. Once the teacher has finished the read aloud, the children re-read the material silently. After the silent re-reading, the children will be coached by the teacher to a definition of one of the key words selected for study. This is done through a child-centered discussion. As part of the discussion, the teacher asks questions which get the children to activate their prior knowledge and to use the contextual clues to figure out the correct meaning of the selected key words. Make certain that the definition of the key concept word is ultimately made by the children.

Next, help the children begin to expand the word's meaning. Do this by having them consider the following for the given key concept word: synonyms, antonyms, and other contexts or other kinds of stories/texts where the word might appear. This is the time to have the children check their responses to the challenge of identifying word synonyms and antonyms by having them go to the thesaurus or the dictionary to confirm their responses. In addition, have the children place the synonyms or antonyms they find in their word boxes or word journals. The recording of their findings will guarantee them ownership of the words and deepen their capacity to use contextual clues.

The main point to remember in using this strategy is that it should only be used when the context is strong. It will not work with struggling readers who have less prior knowledge. Through listening to the children's responses as the teacher helps them to define the word and its potential synonyms and antonyms, the teacher can assess their ability to successfully use context clues. The key to this simple strategy is that it allows the teacher to draw the child out and to grasp his or her thinking process via his or her responses. The more talk from the child, the better.

The Role of Systematic, Noncontextual Vocabulary Strategies

Strategy One: Hierarchical and Linear Arrays

The very complexity of the vocabulary used in this strategy description may be unnerving for the teacher. Yet this strategy included in the Cooper (2004) literacy instruction is really very simple once it is outlined directly for children.

By using the term "hierarchical and linear arrays", Cooper really is talking about how some words are grouped based on associative meanings. The words may have a "hierarchical" relationship to one another. For instance, an undergraduate or a first grader is lower in the school hierarchy than the graduate student and second grader. Within an elementary school, the fifth grader is at the top of the hierarchy and the pre-K or kindergartener is at the bottom of the hierarchy. By the way, the term for this strategy obviously need not be explained in detail to K-3 children, but might be shared with some grade- and age-appropriate modifications with children in Grades 3 and beyond. It will enrich their vocabulary development and ownership of arrays they create.

Words can have a linear relationship to one another in that they run a spectrum from bad to good. We might, for example, from K-3 experiences, use a spectrum of "pleased-happy-overjoyed." These relationships can be displayed in horizontal boxes connected with dashes. Below is another way to display hierarchical relationships.

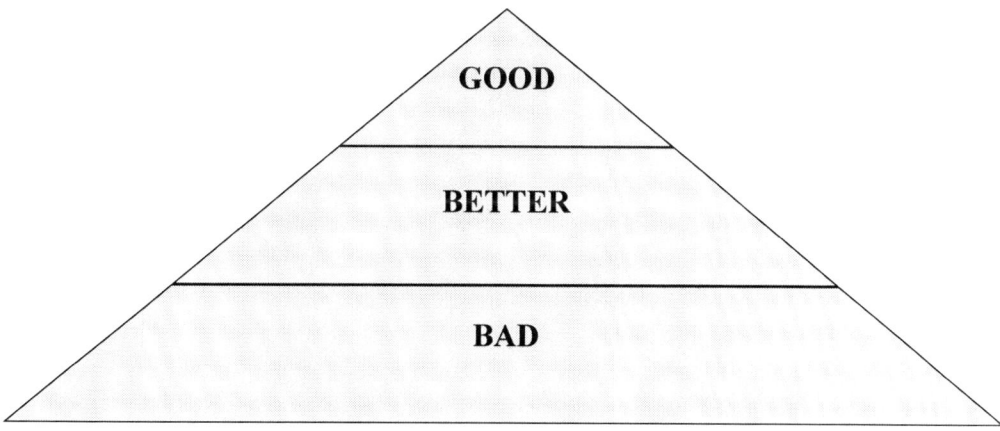

Once you get past the seemingly daunting vocabulary words, the arrays turn out to be another neat, graphic organizer tool which can help children see how words relate to one another.

To use this graphic organizer, the teacher should pre-select a group of words from a read-aloud or from children's writing. Show the children how the array will look using arrows for the linear array and straight lines for the hierarchy. In fact, invite some children up to draw the straight hierarchy lines as the tools are presented, so they have a role in developing even the first hierarchical model. Do one hierarchy array and one linear array with the pre-selected word with the children. Talk them through filling out (or helping the teacher to fill out) the array. After the children have had their own successful experience with arrays, they can select the words from their independent texts or familiar, previously read favorites to study. They will also need to decide which type of array, hierarchical or linear, is appropriate. For fifth and sixth graders, this choice can and should be voiced using the now "owned" vocabulary words "hierarchical array" and "linear array."

This strategy is best used after reading, since it will help the children to expand their word banks.

Contextual Vocabulary Strategies

Vocabulary Self-Collection. This strategy is one in which children, even on the emergent level from Grade 2 and up, take responsibility for their learning. It is also by definition a student centered strategy, which demonstrates student ownership of their chosen vocabulary.

This strategy is one that can be introduced by the teacher early in the year, perhaps even the first day or week. The format for self-collection can then be started by the children. It may take the form of a journal with photocopied template pages and can be continued throughout the year.

To start, ask the children to read a required text or story. Invite them to select one word for the class to study from this text or story. The children can work individually, in teams or in small groups. The teacher can also do the self-collecting so that this becomes the joint effort of the class community of literate readers. Tell the children that they should select words which particularly interest them or which are unique in some way.

After the children have had time to make their selections and to reflect on them, make certain that they have time to share them with their peers as a whole class. When each child shares the word which he or she has selected, have them provide a definition for the word. Each word that is given should be listed on a large experiential chart or even in a Big Book format, if that is age and grade appropriate. The teacher should also share the word he or she selected and provide a definition. The teacher's definition and sharing should come somewhere in the middle of the children's recitations.

The dictionary should be used to verify the definitions. When all the definitions have been checked, a final list of child-selected (and single teacher-selected) words should be made.

Once this final list has been compiled, the children can record it in their word journals or they may opt to record only those words they find interesting in their individual journals. It is up to the teacher at the onset of the vocabulary self-collection activity to decide whether the children have to record all the words on the final list or can eliminate some. The decision made at the beginning by the teacher must be adhered to throughout the year.

To further enhance this strategy, children, particularly those in Grades 3 and beyond, can be encouraged to use their collected words as part of their writings or to record and clip the appearance of these words in newspaper stories or online. This type of additional recording demonstrates that the child has truly incorporated the word into his or her reading and writing. It also habituates children to be lifelong readers, writers, and researchers.

One of the nice things about this simple but versatile strategy is that it works equally well with either expository or narrative texts. It also provides children with an opportunity to use the dictionary.

Assessment is built into the strategy. As the children select the word for the list, they share how they used contextual clues and through their response to definitions offered by peers, prior knowledge can be assessed.

What is most useful about this strategy is that it documents that children can learn to read and write by reading and writing. The children take ownership of the words in the self-collection journals and that can also be the beginning of writer observation journals as they include their own writings. They also use the word lists as a start for writers' commonplace books. These books are filled with newspaper, magazine, and functional document clippings using the journal words.

This activity is a good one for demonstrating the balanced literacy belief that vocabulary study works best when the words studied are chosen by the child.

The Relationship between Oral Vocabulary and the Process of Identifying and Understanding Written Words

One way to explore the relationship between oral vocabulary and the comprehension of written words is through the use of Oral Records (which are discussed at length in the Appendix).

In *On Solid Ground: Strategies for Teaching Reading K-3*, Sharon Taberski (2000) discusses how oral reading records can be used by the K-3 teacher to assess how well children are using cueing systems. She notes that the running record format can also show visual depictions for the teacher of how the child thinks as he or she reads. The notation of miscues in particular shows how a child "walks through" the reading process. They indicate if and in what ways the child may require guided support in understanding the words he or she reads aloud. Taberski notes that when children read they need to think about several things at once. First, they must consider whether what they are reading makes sense (semantic or meaning cues). Next, they must know whether their reading "sounds right" in terms of Standard English (syntactic and structural cues). Third, they have to weigh whether their oral language actually and accurately matches the letters the words represent (visual or graphophonic cues).

In taking the running record and having the opportunity firsthand to listen to the children talk about the text, the teacher can analyze the relationship between the child's oral language and word comprehension. Information from the running record provides the teacher with a road map for differentiated cueing system instruction.

For example, when a running record is taken, a child often makes a mistake but then self-corrects by selecting from various cueing systems. These include "M" for meaning, "S" for syntax, and "V" for visual. The use of a visual cue means that the child is drawing on his or her knowledge of spelling patterns. Of course, Taberski cautions that any relationship between oral language and comprehension that the teacher draws from an examination of the oral-reading records must be drawn using a series of three or more of the child's oral reading records, taken over time.

A teacher can review children's records over time to note their pattern of miscues and which cues they have the greatest tendency to use in their self-corrections. Whichever cueing system the children use to the greatest extent, it is necessary for the teacher to offer support in also using the other cueing systems to construct correct meaning. Taberski suggests that while assessing running records to determine the relationship between oral language and meaning the children read from "just right" books.

Skill 2.6 Demonstrate an understanding of the instruction of comprehension strategies, including modeling when and how to orchestrate multiple comprehension strategies and their scaffolding

See Skills 1.10 and 2.3

Skill 2.7 **Demonstrate knowledge of explicit instruction and scaffolding for learning study skills and strategies (e.g., note-taking and test-taking)**

Tests are essential instructional tools. They can greatly influence students' learning and should not be taken lightly nor given without due regard for the importance of preparation. Several studies indicate conclusively that students perform better when they understand beforehand what type of test they are going to take and why they are taking it. If students perceive a test to be important or to have relative significance, they will perform better. In a recent study, students who were informed by their teachers as to how their test scores were to be used, and who were also urged by their teachers to put forth their best effort, scored higher on the Differential Aptitudes Test than students who did not receive this coaching.

Motivation to perform well on tests begins with how well the student wants to do on an exam. This intrinsic motivation is an internal drive by the student who aspires to do his or her best in school.

Extrinsic motivation may be as simple as a student wanting to learn a basic mathematical skill to complete a remedial math class or as complex as a student needing to pass a Pre-Calculus class to take an AP (Advanced Placement) Calculus class during senior year to gain college credit and enter Stanford or Harvard University as an early college admissions applicant.

Students will also attain higher test scores if they are familiar with the format of the test. It is important for the student to know whether he or she will be taking a multiple-choice test or an essay test. Teachers can help students boost their test performance by providing them with explicit information in regard to the content of the test.

If the focus is on improving student performance on tests, then students must become familiar with the diversity of test-taking formats. Students must understand that there are basic study skills and preparations that maximize student performance and learning outcomes. In researching the effects of sleep deprivation on student learning and test-taking, Carlyle Smith, a professor of psychology at Trent University in Ontario determined that students who were taught a complex logic game of memorization and then deprived of sleep, their performance in the game was diminished by 30% over a group of students who had received full rest. For students, the best performance for test-taking begins with a good night's sleep.

Effective test-taking includes an ability to size up testing formats and quickly eliminate incorrect answers from a list of possible choices. A student has a 25% chance of guessing the correct answer from a choice of four answers and a 50% chance once the decoys and incomplete answers have been eliminated from the remaining two answers. Knowing how the test is constructed will get a student those better odds.

Objective Tests

Most objective tests will include multiple-choice questions, and matching and true/false questions that include a selection of answer choices. The correct answer can be found using a simple process of elimination of decoy or incomplete answers. Helping students review material needed for the tests and providing them sample practice questions will increase student-testing performance. Listed below are basic strategies for taking multiple-choice tests such as the SAT, ACT, state tests and class assessment:

- Read the questions and the answers thoroughly
- Look for decoy or partial answers and eliminate them
- Make an educated guess from the answers that remain
- For true/false answers, if any part of the answer given is false, then the entire answer is false, so you have a 50-50 chance of getting a correct response from true/false
- Answer the easy questions first and spend more time on the harder questions.
- Listen to your gut instinct on tests; usually your first instinct is correct, but don't be afraid to second guess your gut if you know for a fact that part of the answer that you've chosen has a false component embedded in it.

Subjective Tests

Subjective tests put the student in the driver's seat. These types of assessments usually consist of short answer, longer essays or problem solving that involves critical thinking skills requiring definitive proof from the short reading passages to support the answer. Sometimes teachers provide rubrics that include assessment criteria for high scoring answers and projects. The bottom line is that studying and preparing for any type of test will result in better student performance and achievement on tests.

Skill 2.8 **Demonstrate knowledge of how to evaluate the level of text difficulty and appropriateness of reading materials and programs for a variety of instructional purposes and learning situations**

Awareness of Text Leveling

The classroom library in the context of the balanced literacy approach to reading instruction is focused on leveled books. These are books which have been leveled with the support of Fountas and Pinnell's *Guided Reading: Good First Teaching for All Children* and *Matching Books to Readers: Using Leveled Reading in Guided Reading, K-3*.

The books which are leveled according to the designations need to be stored in bins or crates with front covers facing out. This makes them much easier for the children to identify. In that way the children can go through the appropriate levels and find those books that they are particularly interested and which are also at the right level for them to read. These are books which the children can read with the right degree of reading accuracy. When young children can see the cover of a book, they are more likely to flip through it until they can independently identify its appeal. Then they will read a little bit of the book to see if it's "just right."

"Just right" leveled books that children can read on their own need to be available for them during independent reading. The goal is for the more fluent readers to select books on their own. Ultimately, the use of leveled books helps the children, in addition to the teacher, decide which books are "good" or "just right" for them.

Levels are indicated by means of blue, yellow, red, and green dot stickers on the books' right upper corners which parallel emergent, early, transitional, and fluent reading stages. They are then kept in containers with other "blue," "yellow," "red," and "green" books.

Lists and resources other than Fountas and Pinnell which can be used to match children with "just right" books include the Reading Recovery level list. Ultimately, the teacher has to individualize whatever leveling is used in the library to address individual learners' needs.

Awareness of the Challenges and Supports in a Text

Illustrations can be key supports for emergent and early readers. Teachers should not only use wordless stories (books which tell their narratives through pictures alone), but can also make targeted use of Big Books for read-alouds, so that young children become habituated to the use of illustrations as an important component for constructing meaning. The teacher should model for the child how to reference an illustration for help in identifying a word in the text the child does not recognize. Of course, children can also go on a picture walk with the teacher as part of a mini-lesson or guided reading and anticipate the story (narrative) using the pictures alone to construct meaning.

Decodability: Use literature which contains examples of letter-sound correspondences you wish to teach. First, read the literature with the children or read it aloud to them. Then take a specific example from the text and have the children reread it as the teacher points out the letter-sound correspondence. Then ask the children to go through the now familiar literature to find other letter-sound correspondences. Once the children have correctly made the letter-sound correspondences, have them share similar correspondences they find in other works of literature.

Cooper (2004) suggests that children can become word detectives so that they can independently and fluently decode on their own. The child should learn the following word detective routines so that he or she can function as an independent fluent reader who can decode words on his or her own. First, the child should read to the end of a sentence. Then the child should search for word parts which he or she knows and also try to decode the word from the letter sounds. As a last resort, the child should ask someone for help or look up the word in the dictionary.

Techniques for Determining Students' Independent, Instructional and Frustration Reading Levels

Instructional reading is generally judged to be at the 95 percent accuracy level, although Taberski places it at between 92 and 97 percent. Taberski tries to enhance the independent reading levels by making sure that readers on the instructional reading levels read a variety of genres and have a range of available and interesting books within a particular genre.

Taberski's availability for reading conferences helps her to both assess firsthand her children's frustration levels and to model ongoing teacher/reader book conversations by scheduling child-initiated reading conferences when she personally replenishes their book bags.

In order to allay children's frustration levels in their reading and to foster their independent reading, it is important to some children that the teacher personally take time out to hear them read aloud and to check for fluency and expression. Children's frustration level can be immeasurably lessened if they are explicitly told by the teacher after they have read aloud that they need to read without pointing and that they should try chunking words into phrases which mimic their natural speech.

Assessment of the Reading Development of Individual Students

For young readers who are from ELL backgrounds, even if they have been born in the United States, the use of pictures validates their story-authoring and story-telling skills and provides them with access and equity to the literary discussion and book talk of their native-English-speaking peers. These children can also demonstrate their storytelling abilities by drawing sequels or prequels to the story detailed in the illustrations alone. They might even be given the opportunity to share the story aloud in their native language or to comment on the illustrations in their native language.

Since many stories today are recorded in two or even three languages at once, discussing story events or analyzing pictures in a different native language is a beneficial practice that can be accomplished in the twenty-first century marketplace.

Use of pictures and illustrations can also help the K-3 educator assess the capabilities of children who are struggling readers if the children's learning strength is spatial. Through targeted questions about how the pictures would change if different plot twists occurred or how the child might transform the story through changing the illustrations, the teacher can begin to assess struggling reader's deficits and strengths.

Children from ELL backgrounds can benefit from listening to a recorded version of a particular story which they can read along with the tape. This gives them another opportunity to hear the story correctly pronounced and presented and to begin to internalize its language structures. In the absence of taped versions of some key stories or texts, the teacher may want to make sound recordings herself or himself.

Highly proficient readers can also be involved in creating these literature recordings for use with ELL peers or younger peers. This of course develops oral language proficiency and also introduces these skilled readers to the intricacies of supporting ELL reading instruction. When they actually see their tapes being used by children, they will be tremendously gratified.

Skill 2.9 **Demonstrate an understanding of how literacy needs differ across the content areas (e.g. science, math, art)**

See Skills 2.5 and 2.4

Skill 2.10 **Demonstrate an understanding of how to appropriately use texts (e.g. nonprint materials, media, trade books, textbooks, and electronic texts) within diverse genres for multiple purposes and lifelong learning**

Reading is an inherent component of every subject area taught in schools today. Content area reading (science, social studies, etc.) can sometimes be much more difficult for students. Typically, the information is nonfiction and contained in smaller amounts of text. Deciphering content area reading requires a unique set of strategies in order to best acquire the necessary information.

Text Format. Teaching children that nonfiction texts are laid out differently than fictional texts is important. Often times the format of the text provides an automatic organizational tool to help chunk information. Key words or section headings can help provide students with catch phrases with which they can remember the information. They can also help students to scan a large amount of information to find the individual components required to answer comprehension questions. Index and table of content skills can provide additional support.

Summarizing. As stated before, content subjects generally attempt to convey a great deal of information in a smaller amount of text. This is where the idea of summarizing can be so valuable and productive. Teaching the students to be able to take larger amounts of information and break it down into four or five sentences allows them to manage more details and learning. It also helps them to make connections and compartmentalize the information.

Graphic Organizers are pictorial methods of organizing information to help the student remember it more efficiently. Graphic organizers can be complex or simple, provided to the student or drawn from memory. The key is that the method or organizing tool used will help the students classify the information to be learned into smaller pieces with common characteristics. They also help the students to begin to see relationships between the concepts. Graphic organizers work well as study aids to help students acquire more information. Some graphic organizers can use pictures or other visual cues to help the students remember the items to be learned.

Semantic Mapping. In this strategy of organizing information the students use a visual representation to show how words or concepts are interrelated. This is a form of graphic organizer. In semantic mapping, the new knowledge is directly linked to the prior information. Sometimes called concept mapping, semantic maps allow the learner to see relationships between words or concepts and tie them to their own background knowledge in a meaningful manner.

Use of Reading Strategies for Different Texts

As children progress to the older grades (3-6), it is important for the teacher to model for them that in research on a social studies or science exploration, it may not be necessary to read every single word of a given expository information text. For instance, if the child is trying to find out about hieroglyphics, he or she might only read through those sections of a book on Egyptian or Sumerian civilization that deal with picture writing. The teacher, assisted by a child, should model how to go through the table of contents and the index of the book to identify those pages that deal with picture writing.

Children need to understand and to be comfortable with the fact that not every single expository text is meant to be read thoroughly and completely.

With the advent of the Internet, the art of research and study skills in texts is becoming lost. It is, however, a skill that needs to be emphasized and explained to students. Understanding reference materials will provide the students with the necessary foundational skills to better prepare them for future learning.

Students should be able to locate the information they need for projects or to further their learning. In order to be able to find the information they need, students will need knowledge of using indexes, table of contents and other time saving helpers.

Furthermore, students need to be taught how to read and interpret graphs, charts and maps that are found within reference materials and content specific materials. Being able to correctly interpret these types of information will better allow the student to draw the appropriate conclusions. It will enhance the knowledge the student gains from reading and provide further clarification.

Once children understand how to access and interpret the information contained in content specific materials or reference materials they can then begin to analyze it to clarify their thinking process and make the connections to their own life or information from other texts. Sometimes, the students will find conflicting pieces of information that they will be able to examine more deeply.

Processing information in this way takes reading to an even higher, more involved level. It also requires students to find their own method for integrating it into their personal schema for later recall.

Teaching students specific study skills like note-taking, summarizing, using graphic organizers, semantic mapping, and time management will allow for effective use of the reference materials available to them.

See Also Skill 2.3

Skill 2.11 Demonstrate knowledge of a variety of children's/adolescent literature, including multicultural literature, and how to mediate it to enhance instruction

The major literary genres include allegory, ballad, drama, epic, epistle, essay, fable, novel, poem, romance, and the short story.

Allegory: A story in verse or prose with characters representing virtues and vices. There are two meanings, symbolic and literal. John Bunyan's *The Pilgrim's Progress* is a well-known example of this genre.

Ballad: A story told or sung, usually in verse and accompanied by music. Literary devices found in ballads include the refrain, or repeated section, and incremental repetition, or anaphora, for effect. Earliest forms were anonymous folk ballads. Later forms include Coleridge's Romantic masterpiece, "The Rime of the Ancient Mariner."

Drama: Plays – comedy, modern, or tragedy - typically in five acts. Traditionalists and neoclassicists adhere to Aristotle's unities of time, place and action. Plot development is advanced via dialogue. Literary devices include asides, soliloquies and the chorus representing public opinion. Greatest of all dramatists/playwrights is William Shakespeare. Other dramaturges include Ibsen, Williams, Miller, Shaw, Stoppard, Racine, Moliére, Sophocles, Aeschylus, Euripides, and Aristophanes.

Epic: Long poem usually of book length reflecting values inherent in the generative society. Epic devices include an invocation to a muse for inspiration, purpose for writing, universal setting, protagonist and antagonist who possess supernatural strength and acumen, and interventions of a God or the gods. Understandably, there are very few epics: Homer's *Iliad* and *Odyssey*, Virgil's *Aeneid*, Milton's *Paradise Lost*, Spenser's *The Fairie Queene*, Barrett Browning's "Aurora Leigh," and Pope's mock-epic, *The Rape of the Lock*.

Epistle: A letter or other work in the form of a letter.

Essay: Typically a prose work of limited length focusing on a topic and propounding a definite point of view in an authoritative tone. Great essayists include Carlyle, Lamb, DeQuincy, Emerson and Montaigne, who is credited with defining this genre.

Fable: Terse tale offering up a moral or exemplum. Chaucer's "The Nun's Priest's Tale" is a fine example of a *bete fabliau* or beast fable in which animals speak and act in characteristically human ways, illustrating human foibles. Aesop's fables have been adapted and repeated for centuries.

Legend: A traditional narrative or collection of related narratives, popularly regarded as historically factual but usually a mixture of fact and fiction.

Myth: Stories that are more or less universally shared within a culture to explain its history and traditions.

Novel: A long form of fictional prose containing a variety of characterizations, settings, local color and regionalism. Most have complex plots, expanded description, and attention to detail. Some of the great novelists include Austen, the Brontes, Twain, Tolstoy, Hugo, Hardy, Dickens, Hawthorne, Forster, and Flaubert.

Poem: Rhythmic, often figurative works. Sub-genres include fixed types of literature such as the sonnet, elegy, ode, pastoral, and villanelle. Unfixed types of poetry include blank verse and dramatic monologue.

Romance: A highly imaginative tale set in a fantastical realm dealing with the conflicts between heroes, villains and/or monsters. "The Knight's Tale" from Chaucer's *Canterbury Tales*, *Sir Gawain and the Green Knight* and Keats' "The Eve of St. Agnes" are prime representatives.

Short Story: Typically a terse narrative, with less development of characters. May include description, author's point of view, and tone. Poe emphasized that a successful short story should create one focused impact. Considered to be great short story writers are Hemingway, Faulkner, Twain, Joyce, Shirley Jackson, Flannery O'Connor, de Maupassant, Saki, Edgar Allen Poe, and Pushkin.

Children's Literature is a genre of its own and emerged as a distinct and independent form in the second half of the eighteenth century. *The Visible World in Pictures* by John Amos Comenius, a Czech educator, was one of the first printed works and the first picture book. For the first time, educators acknowledged that children are different from adults in many respects. Modern educators acknowledge that introducing elementary students to a wide range of reading experiences plays an important role in their mental, social and psychological development. The following are some of the most common forms of literature specifically for children:

Traditional Literature: Traditional literature opens up a world where right wins out over wrong, where hard work and perseverance are rewarded, and where helpless victims find vindication—all worthwhile values that children identify with even as early as kindergarten. In traditional literature, children will be introduced to fanciful beings, humans with exaggerated powers, talking animals, and heroes that will inspire them. For younger elementary children, these stories in Big Book format are ideal for providing predictable and repetitive elements that can be grasped by these children.

Folktales/Fairy Tales: Some examples: The Three Bears, Little Red Riding Hood, Snow White, Sleeping Beauty, Puss-in-Boots, Rapunzel and Rumpelstiltskin. Adventures of animals or humans and the supernatural characterize these stories. The hero is usually on a quest and is aided by other-worldly helpers. More often than not, the story focuses on good and evil and reward and punishment.

Fables: Animals that act like humans are featured in these stories and usually reveal human foibles or sometimes teach a lesson. A good example is Aesop's Fables.

Myths: These stories about events from the earliest times, such as the origin of the world, are considered true in the cultures from which they are derived.

Legends: These are similar to myths except that they tend to deal with events that happened more recently. Example: Arthurian legends.

Tall Tales: Examples include Paul Bunyan, John Henry, and Pecos Bill. These are purposely exaggerated accounts of individuals with superhuman strength.

Modern Fantasy: Many of the themes found in these stories are similar to those in traditional literature. The stories start out based in reality, which makes it easier for the reader to suspend disbelief and enter worlds of unreality. Little people live in the walls in *The Borrowers* and time travel is possible in *The Trolley to Yesterday*. Including some fantasy tales in the curriculum helps elementary-grade children develop their senses of imagination. These often appeal to ideals of justice and issues having to do with good and evil; because children tend to identify with the characters, the message is more likely to be retained.

Science Fiction: Robots, spacecraft, mystery, and civilizations from other ages often appear in these stories. Most presume advances in science on other planets or in a future time. Most children like these stories because of their interest in space and the "what if" aspect of the stories. Examples: *Outer Space and All That Junk* and *A Wrinkle in Time*.

Modern Realistic Fiction: These stories are about real problems that real children face. By finding that their hopes and fears are shared by others, young children can find insight into their own problems. Young readers also tend to experience a broadening of interests as the result of this kind of reading. It's good for them to know that a child can be brave and intelligent and can solve difficult problems.

Historical Fiction: *Rifles for Watie* is an example of this kind of story. Presented in a historically accurate setting, it's about a 16-year-old boy who serves in the Union army. He experiences great hardship but discovers that his enemy is an admirable human being. It provides a good opportunity to introduce younger children to history in a beneficial way.

Biography: Reading about inventors, explorers, scientists, political and religious leaders, social reformers, artists, sports figures, doctors, teachers, writers, and war heroes help children to see that one person can make a difference. They also open new vistas for children to think about when they choose an occupation to fantasize about.

Informational Books: These are ways to learn more about specific topics. A book like *Polar Wildlife* by Kamini Khanduri shows pictures and facts that will capture the imaginations of young children.

Skill 2.12   Demonstrate an understanding of how technology can be used to enhance instruction

With a wide selection of educational software on the market, it is important for an educator to be able to evaluate a program before purchasing it. Software can vary greatly in content, presentation, skill level, and objectives and it is not always possible to believe everything that is advertised on the package. If a teacher is in the position of having to purchase a computer program for use in the classroom without any prior knowledge of the program itself, it is useful to have some guidelines to follow. Once a program has been purchased and the shrink-wrap has been removed, many vendors are reluctant to allow its return because of a possible violation of copyright laws or damage to the software medium. For this reason it is important to preview the software personally before buying it. If a vendor is reluctant to allow the teacher to preview a program prior to its purchase, it is sometimes possible to get a preview copy from the publisher.

Many school districts have addressed this problem by publishing a list of approved software titles for each grade level in much the same way that they publish lists of approved text books and other classroom materials. In addition, most districts have developed a software evaluation form to be used by any instructor involved in the purchase of software that is not already on the approved list. Use of a software evaluation form can eliminate a lot of the risk involved when shopping for appropriate titles for the classroom. In many districts, all software is evaluated by the actual instructors who will use it and the completed evaluation forms are made available for the perusal of other prospective buyers.

The first thing that must be considered before purchasing software is its compatibility with the computer on which it is to be used. If the program will not run efficiently on the computer in the classroom because of hardware limitations, there is no need to continue the evaluation process. Some of the restrictions to consider are the operating system (Windows or Mac) for which the particular software package was developed, the recommended memory size, the required hard drive space, the medium type (floppy disk or CD-ROM), the type of monitor, and the need for any special input devices such as a mouse, joystick, or speech card. If a network is used in the classroom or school for which the program is to be purchased, it is also important to know if the program is networkable. Often, programs with a lot of graphics encounter difficulties when accessed from a network.

There are three general steps to follow when evaluating a software program. First, one must read the instructions thoroughly to familiarize oneself with the program, its hardware requirements, and its installation.

Once the program is installed and ready to run, the evaluator should first run the program as it would be run by a student, without deliberate errors but making use of all the possibilities available to the student. Thirdly, the program should be run making deliberate mistakes to test the handling of errors. One should try to make as many different kinds of mistakes as possible, including those for incorrect keyboard usage and the validity of user directions.

Most software evaluation forms include the same types of information. There is usually a section for a general description of the program consisting of the intended grade level, additional support materials available, the type of program (game, simulation, drill, etc), stated goals and objectives, and the clarity of instructions. Other sections will provide checklists for educational content, presentation, and type and quality of user interaction with the program. Once a software package has been thoroughly tested, the teacher will be able to make an intelligent decision regarding its purchase.

When dealing with large class sizes and at the same time trying to offer opportunities for students to use computers, it is often necessary to use a lot of ingenuity. If the number of computers available for student use is limited, the teacher must take a tip from elementary school teachers who are skilled at managing centers. Students can be rotated singly or in small groups to the computer centers as long as they are well oriented in advance to the task to be accomplished and to the necessary rules. Rules for using the computer should be emphasized in advance with the whole class prior to individual computer usage and then prominently posted.

If a computer lab is available for use by the curriculum teacher, the problem of how to give each student the opportunity to use the computer as an educational tool might be alleviated, but a whole new set of problems must be dealt with. Again, the rules to be observed in the computer lab should be discussed before the class enters the lab and students should have a thorough understanding of the assignment. When a large group of students is visiting a computer lab, it is very easy for expensive hardware to suffer from accidental or deliberate harm if the teacher is not aware of what is going on at all times. Students need to be aware of the consequences for violating the rules because it is tempting to experiment and show off to their peers.

Unfortunately, students who have access to computers outside of school often feel like they know everything already and are reluctant to listen to instruction on lab etiquette or program usage. The teacher must be constantly on guard to prevent physical damage to the machines from foreign objects finding their way into disk drives, key caps from disappearing from keyboards (or being rearranged), or stray pencil or pen marks from appearing on computer systems. Experienced students might also try to save games on hard drives, move files into new directories or eliminate them altogether, create passwords to prevent others from using machines, etc.

At the same time, other students need a lot of assistance to prevent accidents caused by inexperience. It is possible to pair inexperienced students with more capable ones to alleviate some of the problem. Teachers must constantly rotate around the room and students must be prepared before their arrival in the lab so that they know exactly what to do when they get there.

To a novice, computers might appear to be very complicated machines, but in reality it is not very difficult to operate one of today's "user-friendly" computers. Basically, all that is required is to attach the computer to the power source and turn it on. Most machines are configured to boot up into a menu of programs from which the user has merely to point and click at the desired choice.

For the computer to boot up from the hard drive to follow the instructions for which it has been configured, it is necessary to remove any diskettes from the floppy disk drive before turning on the power. Otherwise, the computer will not boot up into its menu from the hard drive, but rather will try to find the necessary boot up instructions on the floppy disk.

When preparing to shut down the computer, it is important to close all programs that are currently in use. This includes saving anything that needs to be kept for future sessions on the computer. When a program is not properly exited, important data might be lost and the computer might not boot up to the proper menu next time it is turned on. It is just a matter of good housekeeping to put away everything in its proper place before leaving. If the program was accessed from a DOS prompt or menu, the computer should be returned to the same starting place before turning off the machine. Programs accessed from Windows should be exited, all windows should be closed, and Windows itself should be exited by selecting File Exit before the power is turned off. MacIntosh computers are much like Windows in that all programs should be exited and all windows closed before choosing SYSTEM and SHUT DOWN. Once everything is properly closed, the computer will give the user a message ["It is safe to turn off your computer"] and the computer can be turned off.

Internet usage agreements define a number of terms of technology use that students must agree to in order to have access to school computers. Students must exercise responsibility and accountability in adhering to technology usage during the school day. Students who violate any parts of the computer usage agreement may have future access to school computers or other educational technology denied or blocked.

District and school policies are developed to provide a consistent language of expectation for students using school technology. Districts are liable for the actions of students and teachers in school communities who use publicly funded and legislatively funded technology. The standards of usage for school computers are created to maximize student use for educational purposes and to minimize student surfing to non-educational sites that minimize learning during class times. Time allowance for computer usage is often limited for students.

Federal and state funding to districts also carry technology expectations as conditions of funding, so the chain of expectation starts from top management to school communities. Given the predatory nature of some users of the Internet, the policies and procedures for school usage are necessary to keep students safe when they are using computers for educational purposes.

Beyond computer usage in schools, other electronics like iPods, Walkmans, and cell phones are prohibited in classrooms. The distractions these devices provide impede educational access for students struggling to maintain focus on the lesson objectives. An effective teacher underscores in the classroom that the focus on learning will be exclusive of electronic distractions and inappropriate computer use.

Students who have their computer privileges revoked due to abuse of the Internet agreements may find that academic progress may be jeopardized, especially if the students do not own computers or do not have Internet access beyond the classrooms.

Teachers should monitor the activities of students who are using computers and actively respond to students who misuse public technology intended to enhance the learning process and access for all students.

The Internet and other research resources provide a wealth of information on thousands of interesting topics for students preparing presentations or projects. Using search engines like Google, Microsoft and Infotrac, students can search multiple Internet resources with one subject search. Students should have an outline of the purpose of a project or research presentation that includes:

- Purpose - identify the reason for the research information
- Objective - having a clear thesis for a project will allow the students opportunities to be specific on Internet searches
- Preparation - when using resources or collecting data, students should create folders for sorting through the information. Providing labels for the folders will create a system of organization that will make construction of the final project or presentation easier and less time-consuming
- Procedure - organized folders and a procedural list of what the project or presentation needs to include will create A+ work for students and A+ grading for teachers
- Visuals or artifacts - choose data or visuals that are specific to the subject content or presentation. Make sure that poster boards or Power Point presentations can be visually seen from all areas of the classroom. Teachers can provide laptop computers for Power Point presentations.

When a teacher models and instructs students in the proper use of search techniques, the teacher can minimize wasted time in preparing projects and wasted paper from students who print every search. In some school districts, students are allowed a minimum number of printed pages per week. Since students have Internet accounts for computer usage, the school's librarian and teachers in classrooms can easily monitor printing.

READING

Having the school's librarian or technology expert as a guest speaker in classrooms provides another method of sharing and modeling proper presentation preparation using technology. Teachers can also appoint technology experts from the students in a classroom to work with others on projects and presentations. In high schools, technology classes provide students with upper-class teacher assistants who fill the role of technology assistants.

The wealth of resources for teachers and students seeking to incorporate technology and structured planning for student presentations and projects is as diverse as the presentations.

Skill 2.13 Demonstrate an understanding of how to teach students to recursively apply strategies for planning, drafting, revising, and editing texts to different genres for a variety of purposes and audiences

In the past teachers have assigned reports, paragraphs and essays that focused on the teacher as the audience with the purpose of explaining information. However, for students to be meaningfully engaged in their writing, they must write for a variety of reasons. Writing for different audiences and aims allows students to be more involved in their writing. If they write for the same audience and purpose, they will continue to see writing as just another assignment. Listed below are suggestions that give students an opportunity to write in more creative and critical ways.

- Write letters to the editor, to a college, to a friend, to another student aimed at the intended audience.
- Write stories to be read aloud to a group (the class, another group of students, to a group of elementary school students) or published in a literary magazine or class anthology.
- Write plays to be performed.
- Have students discuss the parallels between the different speech styles we use and writing styles for different readers or audiences.
- Allow students to write a particular piece for different audiences.
- Expose students to writing that is on the same topic with a different audience and have them identify the variations in sentence structure and style
- Make sure students consider the following when analyzing the needs of their audience.

    Why is the audience reading my writing? Do they expect to be informed, amused or persuaded?
    What does my audience already know about my topic?
    What does the audience want or need to know? What will interest them?
    What type of language suits my readers?

Remind your students that it is not necessary to identify all the specifics of the audience in the initial stage of the writing process but that at some point they must make some determinations about audience.

- **Values**- What is important to this group of people? What is their background and how will that affect their perception of your speech?
- **Needs**- Find out in advance what the audience's needs are. Why are they listening to you? Find a way to satisfy their needs.
- **Constraints**- What might hold the audience back from being fully engaged in what you are saying, or agreeing with your point of view, or processing what you are trying to say? These could be political reasons, which make them wary of your presentation's ideology from the start, or knowledge reasons, in which the audience lacks the appropriate background information to grasp your ideas. Avoid this last constraint by staying away from technical terminology, slang, or abbreviations that may be unclear to your audience.
- **Demographic Information**- Take the audience's size into account, as well as the location of the presentation.

Listening to students sitting on the steps that lead into the building that houses their classrooms, teachers will hear dialogue that may not even be intelligible to them. The student who is writing to his peers will need to know and understand the peculiarities of that discourse in order to be very effective with them. This is a good example for students of what it means to tailor language for a particular audience and for a particular person.

This is a good time to teach the concept of jargon. Writing to be read by a lawyer is different from writing to be read by a medical doctor. Writing to be read by parents is different from writing to be read by the administrator of the school. Not only are the vocabularies different, but the formality/informality of the discourse will need to be adjusted. Things to be aware of in determining what the language should be for a particular audience hinges on two things: vocabulary and formality/informality. The most formal language does not use contractions or slang. The most informal language will certainly use contractions and the slang that is appropriate for the particular audience. Formal language will use longer sentences and will not sound like a conversation. The most informal language will use shorter sentences—not necessarily simple sentences—but shorter constructions and will sound like a conversation.

Novels use formal language only when a particular character would speak that way, such as a lawyer or a school superintendent. It's jarring to read a novel that has a construction worker using formal language. Using examples of various characters and dialogue from fiction is useful in helping students understand this crucial aspect of writing.

Journalistic Writing

News reporters generally become excellent writers because they get a lot of practice, which is a principle most writing teachers try to employ with their students. Also, news writing is instructive in skills for writing clearly and coherently.

Reporters generally write in two modes: straight reporting and feature writing. In both modes, the writer must be concerned with accuracy and objectivity. The reporter does not write his opinions. He or she does not write persuasive discourse. The topic is typically assigned, although some experienced reporters have the opportunity to seek out and develop their own stories.

Feature writing is more like an informative essay although it may also follow the inverted pyramid model. This form of reporting focuses on a topic designed to be interesting to at least one segment of the readership—sports enthusiasts, travelers, vacationers, families, women, food lovers, etc. The article will focus on one aspect of the area of interest, such as a particular experience for the vacationing family. The first sentence might read something like this: "Lake Lure offers a close-to-home relaxing weekend getaway for families in East Tennessee." The development can be an ever-widening pyramid of details focused particularly on what the family can experience at Lake Lure but also include directions for how to get there.

Other Forms of Expository Writing

Although much business-letter writing has been relegated to email communications, letters are still a valuable form of communication. A carefully written letter can be powerful. It can alienate, convince, persuade, entice, motivate, or create goodwill.

As with any other communication, it is worthwhile to learn as much as possible about the receiver. This may be complicated if there will be more than one receiver of the message. It may be better to send more than one form of the letter to the various receivers in some cases.

Purpose is the most powerful factor in writing a business letter. What is the letter expected to accomplish? Is it intended to get the receiver to act or to act in a specific manner? Are you hoping to see some action take place as the result of the letter? If so, you should clearly define for yourself what the purpose is before you craft the letter.

Reasons for choosing the letter as the channel of communication include:

It's easy to keep a record of the transaction.
The message can be edited and perfected before it is transmitted.
It facilitates the handling of details.
It's ideal for communicating complex information.
It's a good way to disseminate mass messages at a relatively low cost.

Business letters typically use formal language. They should be straightforward and courteous. The writing should be concise and special care should be taken to leave no important information out. Clarity is very important; otherwise, it may take more than one exchange of letters or phone calls to get the message across.

A complaint is a different kind of business letter. It can come under the classification of a "bad news" business letter, and there are some guidelines that are helpful when writing this kind of letter. A positive writing style can overcome much of the inherent negativity of a letter of complaint. No matter how much in the right you may be, maintaining self-control and courtesy and avoiding demeaning or blaming language is more likely to be effective. Abruptness, condescension, or harshness of tone will not help achieve your purpose, particularly if you are requesting a positive response such as reimbursement for a bad product or some help in righting a wrong that may have been done to you. It's important to remember that you want to solve the specific problem and to retain the goodwill of the receiver, if possible.

Induction is better than deduction for this type of communication. Beginning with the details and building to the statement of the problem generally has the effect of softening the bad news. It's also useful to begin with an opening that will serve as a buffer. The same is true for the closing. It's good to leave the reader with a favorable impression by writing a closing paragraph that will generate goodwill rather than bad.

Email has revolutionized business communications. It has most of the advantages of business letters and the added ones of immediacy, lower cost, and convenience. Even very long reports can be attached to an email. On the other hand, a two-line message can be sent and a response received immediately, bringing together the features of a postal system and the telephone. Instant messaging goes even one step further. It can do all of the above—send messages, attach reports, etc.—and still have many of the advantages of a telephone conversation.

Skill 2.14 **Demonstrate an understanding of the purpose of publication of student writing in literacy acquisition**

See Competency 2.0

Skill 2.15 **Demonstrate an understanding of deliberate vocabulary instruction across grades and content areas**

See Skill 2.5

Skill 2.16 **Demonstrate knowledge of how to plan and implement instruction that addresses the strengths and needs of all students**

See previous Skills

Skill 2.17 **Demonstrate an understanding of instructional decisions to accommodate learners with social, cultural, linguistic and cognitive differences**

See Skill 2.8

Skill 2.18 **Demonstrate knowledge of various instructional grouping strategies to motivate and engage all students (e.g. flexible, whole class, small group, individual, ability/achievement) and the issues associated with each**

Teachers should look at flexible grouping within the classroom setting. Although students may be grouped for ability at different times, this should not be the standard. Some of the various instructional grouping strategies that teachers can use in the classroom are:

- Whole class instruction – used to introduce new materials and strategies to the whole class
- Small group instruction – used for small groups of students who need more instruction on an objective
- Students working alone in teacher-directed activities – this enables the teacher to give one-on-one instruction or to assess how students are progressing
- Collaborative groups – students working together on a project
- Circle sharing – student discussion, such as author's chair
- Partner groups – paired reading, think par share, etc.

Skill 2.19   Demonstrate an understanding of how to create safe and respectful environment for all students

Since students come to school from such varied backgrounds and teachers often don't know the circumstances of the home, it is important to make the school a place where they can feel safe and cared for. There must be a positive school environment where there is a spirit of trust, collaboration and high expectations for all students. When students feel safe at school, they are more likely to attend regularly, cooperate in class and achieve to the best of their ability. Effective schools are inviting not only to students, but to parents as well. Teachers should make sure they provide students with opportunities to build self-esteem.

The features of a safe and caring school are:

- A healthy, safe and organized environment
- High morale
- Positive school attitude
- A clear mission designed to promote student achievement
- Quality instruction in the classroom
- Respectful interactions between students and teachers
- Communication with parents on a regular basis
- Acknowledgement that making mistakes is a part of learning

Skill 2.20   Demonstrate an understanding of how to organize programmatic activities to encourage reading (e.g. book clubs, read-a-thons) with an understanding of differences between extrinsic and intrinsic motivation

There are many ways teachers can encourage reading for pleasure in their classrooms. One of the best ways is to read aloud from a novel each day, even with grades as young as Grade 2. For Kindergarten and Grade 1, choosing picture books by one author at a time will help students realize that different authors write on different topics and in different ways. Author studies in all grades will encourage students to seek out books by that author and read them on their own.

Even within the content areas, there is a wealth of fiction that relates to the theme at hand and provides the students with background information that will help them with their studies. For example, when studying Colonial America in Social Studies, there are many picture books that teachers can use as introductions for lessons. Devoting a portion of the class to read aloud from a novel about that period in history will help students to develop an interest in reading about the themes and help them understand how much enjoyment that reading can bring.

Monthly book clubs are also an excellent way of getting age-appropriate reading material into students' hands. Since these book clubs offer books at fairly inexpensive prices, parents realize that they can get more value for their money when they order each month. Book fairs at school provide students with the chance to win books for themselves and their classrooms.

Read-a-thons encourage reading because students realize that by reading they are helping a cause. Some of these offers which include prizes for the students or the teacher or school could initiate this kind of motivation.

COMPETENCY 3.0 READING MATERIALS AND INSTRUCTION AND READING ENVIRONMENT

Skill 3.1 Identify and use texts, trade books, and other print and non-print materials to foster appreciation of reading for students who are at various levels and from various cultures

Not every student in your class will be at the same level of reading. By using guided reading to teach strategies at different levels in the same classroom, teachers can also choose books related to topics of study in other subjects and at the students' levels of interest. There is a wealth of resources available about all the cultures of the world and this could be a starting point for a discussion about how all these cultures are similar and different.

By choosing books at an individual student's reading level, the student will then realize the value of reading for information and at the same time experience success with reading the text.

To get started in choosing appropriate books, teachers first look at the range of differences in culture and reading levels in the class. Conducting an interest survey with students will also prove valuable in choosing books that they will want to read. Genre studies, author studies and guided reading are just three ways that this can be incorporated into any class.

A search of the library resources in the school is one way to get started with choosing books for the classroom. The amount of money you may have to spend on a classroom library will depend on the budget of the school or the school district. Teachers should search online for a list of books that are appropriate for the students at a particular grade level, keeping in mind that they should align with the state-mandated standards for the curriculum.

The monthly book club order will also have a good selection of books for teachers to choose from. When a class has a large order, this gives the teacher much needed funds to buy more books and the teacher also gets free books for the classroom. There are also catalogs from all the major publishers with lists of books on just about every subject imaginable.

Skill 3.2 Identify strategies appropriate for a variety of printed materials and identify texts that are appropriate for a specific reading purpose

See Skill 2.11

Skill 3.3 Identify strategies for recognizing and evaluating students' attitudes and needs, and suggest books/materials in a variety of genres at appropriate difficulty levels to meet those needs

See Skill 2.11

Skill 3.4 **Identify techniques for providing opportunities for creative and personal responses to reading**

Responding to literature is one of the most important parts of reading. From the responses that students give to what they have read, teachers can determine the level of comprehension. It takes practice for students to be able to respond critically to a text because they have the idea that all published authors are perfect and they should not criticize what they write.

Some of the strategies that teachers can use to provide opportunities for students to give creative and personal responses to their reading include:

- Reading conferences – ask a student to read a section of the text and then tell why he or she chose that section. Teachers can also ask students why they are reading a certain book or ask about their favorite author.
- Reading Surveys – teachers can devise a list of questions to find out what students are reading, how they decide what books to read, and how students feel about the topics or language used in the book.
- Daily reading time – this could be a set time when everyone in the class is reading, including the teacher, or it could be a center activity for a small group of children.
- Literature Circles – using the role sheets developed by Harvey Daniels in *Voice and Choice in a Student-Centered Classroom*, students take on different roles each day. They discuss the chapter or book, find new vocabulary words, illustrate a scene or pose questions for the group.
- Reader's Theatre – students adapt part of the book or story and make it into a choral reading with expression that shows how they felt about what they have read.

Responding to literature does not always take the form of written responses. In a Reader's Workshop, students can choose to respond to what they read through art, painting, song, dance or any number of ways to show an interpretation of the reading. Interviewing the author or asking students to change a scene so that the result is different are other examples of ways to invoke personal responses to reading.

Students who have a hard time coming up with a response would benefit from a sheet listing ideas for ways they can respond. These usually take the form of open-ended sentences such as:
- The character I liked the best was
- The character that is most like me is
- If I were _____, I would have

Skill 3.5 **Demonstrate an understanding of a variety of approaches to teaching reading and of methods to organize instruction effectively**

See Competency 2.0

Skill 3.6 **Identify strategies for exposing students to a variety of genres and help them understand the characteristics of each genre**

See Competency 2.0

Skill 3.7 **Identify various purposes for reading**

Whenever you are reading, there is a purpose behind the activity. For some it is simply a love of reading. Students must also understand the various purposes for reading different types of texts. These include:

- To understand the main idea of the text or the author's purpose
- To find the mood of the text
- To appreciate the author's use of language
- To learn about different topics
- To get ideas for writing and research
- To understand the author's argument

Skill 3.8 **Demonstrate an understanding of how to use a variety of non-print sources, how to use study aids and how to interpret graphics**

See Competency 2.0

Skill 3.9 **Identify strategies to purposefully integrate the language arts into all content areas, including the use of technology**

Some of the activities that teachers can use to integrate language arts into the content areas of the curriculum include:

- Use thematic units that incorporate reading, writing, math, social studies and science with activities that are interrelated
- Have a quick-write at the end of content area instruction in which students record what they learned in this class. This is often referred to as using a Learning Log.
- Use shared reading with students paired for reading the text
- Introduce content area topics by reading from a picture book about the topic
- Use process writing for all writing activities across the curriculum
- Use interactive writing
- Oral reports
- Use of cartoons in writing assignments
- Written retellings of the text material
- Math journals (Science journals, Social Studies journals)
- Write informational texts
- Jot notes for research

Media's impact is immense and ever increasing. As children, we watch programs on television that are amazingly fast-paced and visually rich. Parents' roles as verbal and moral teachers are diminishing in response to the more stimulating guidance of the television set. Modern media's effect on education in particular provides special challenges and opportunities for teachers and students.

Thanks to satellite technology, urban classrooms and rural villages can receive instructional radio and television programs. CD-ROMs can allow students to learn information through a virtual reality experience. The Internet allows instant access to unlimited data and connects people across all cultures through shared interests. Educational media, when used in a productive way, enriches instruction and makes it more individualized, accessible, and economical.

Skill 3.10 **Identify components of a balanced literacy program, (word study, reading aloud, shared reading, guided reading, independent reading, writing, speaking, viewing and listening) and sensitivity to a developmental continuum**

A teacher that employs a balanced literacy curriculum in his or her classroom makes choices on a daily basis in planning lessons that will benefit the students. This approach to teaching reading integrates all components of language arts and uses multiple strategies to help students develop as fluent readers. The main purpose is to integrate reading, writing, listening, speaking and viewing so that each is not a separate part of learning to read.

Reading aloud to students is a main part of balanced literacy. However, the focus is on modeling the skills and strategies and then allowing students time to practice on their own. The components of a balanced literacy curriculum are the following:

- Shared reading
- Guided reading
- Independent reading
- Shared writing
- Guided writing
- Independent writing

Reading and writing in a shared setting models the correct methods for students. In small group settings, guided reading and writing teaches them the strategies they need to develop as independent readers and writers. Word Study is one such example of small group work that can take place. This involves the teacher taking time to meet with children from Grades 3-6 in a small group of no more than six children for a word study session. The children selected for this group are those who need to focus more on the relationship between spelling patterns and their consonant sounds.

It is important that this not be a formalized traditional reading group that meets at a set time each week or biweekly. Rather, the group should be spontaneously formed by the teacher based on a quick inventory of the selected children's needs at the start of the week. Taberski has templates in her book of *Guided Reading Planning Sheets*. These sheets are essentially targeted word and other skills sheets with her written dated observations of children who are in need of support to develop a given skill ("kid watching"--see Dictionary).

READING

The teacher should try to meet with this group for at least two consecutive 20-minute periods each day. Over those two meetings, the teacher can model a Making Words Activity. Once the teacher has modeled making words the first day, the children would then make their own words. On the second day, the children would "sort" their words.

Other topics for a word study group within the framework of the Balanced Literacy Approach that Taberski advocates are inflectional endings, prefixes and suffixes, and/or common spelling patterns. It should be noted that theorists would classify this as a structural analysis activity because the structural components (i.e. prefixes, suffixes, and spelling patterns) of the words are being studied.

Discussion Circles or Literature Circles are another way of having students involved in reading and writing in a balanced literacy framework. Cooper believes that children should not be "taught" vocabulary and structural analysis skills. Flesch and E.D. Hirsch, who are key theorists of the Phonics approach and advocates of Cultural Literacy (a term coined by and associated with E. D. Hirsch), believe that specific vocabulary words at various grade and age levels need to be mastered and MUST be explicitly taught in schools. As far as J. David Cooper is concerned, all the necessary and meaningful vocabulary (for the child and ultimately adult reader) can't possibly be taught in the classroom. For Cooper, it is far more important that children be made aware of and become interested in learning words by themselves. Cooper feels that by reading and writing, children develop a love for and a sense of ownership of words. All of Cooper's suggested Structural Analysis word strategies are therefore designed to foster children's love of words and a desire to "own" more of them through reading and writing.

Discussion Circles are activities that fit nicely into the Balanced Literacy Lesson Format as part of a SHARE (see Dictionary of Terms). After the children conclude a particular text, Cooper suggests that they get together in discussion circles to respond to the book. This activity works well from Grades 3-6 and beyond. The teacher-coach might suggest that the children focus on words of interest they encountered in the text. These can also be words that they heard if the text was read aloud. Children can be asked to share something funny or upsetting or unusual about the words. Through this focus on children's response to words as the center of the discussion circle, peers become more interested in word study.

Skill 3.11   Identify ways to use flexible grouping to accommodate students' needs

See Skill 2.18

Skill 3.12 Identify the influences of family and peers as well as ethnic, socioeconomic, regional, and cultural factors as they relate to reading development

The goal of teaching children to read can be best accomplished when schools solicit the help of parents, members of the community and other professionals. One of the easiest ways to initiate this is to invite these groups into the classroom to read to the children and to observe what is happening within the confines of the classroom. Through regular communication with parents and a Curriculum Night at school, teachers can teach parents to help their children at home. A parents' night can be arranged with a videotape of the class in which individual questions and concerns can be addressed.

Parents and community members come from diverse backgrounds and experiences. Many of them may feel that the job of teaching reading falls solely on the shoulders of the teacher. Teachers can help these parents realize that reading to and with the children at home is one of the best ways of promoting reading. Simple activities such as having children read and write shopping lists can be a reading experience.

When children are experiencing reading difficulties, intervention from other professionals may be necessary. This includes support from a Language Assistance Teacher, testing professionals and the reading specialist.

Skill 3.13 Identify ways to include parents as partners in the literacy development of their children

Classrooms should be places where the students are surrounded by print. There should be a classroom library where the students can select books for home reading. The books can be arranged by reading level so that students know how to choose books with which they will experience success. They can also be arranged by theme or author so that students with a particular interest can choose a specific book. Newspapers are a source of reading and there are many newspaper publishers that provide this resource free to schools. Setting up a newspaper center in which students have to read sections of the paper and answer questions or create projects is another way of getting them to read and gain information at the same time.

Children who come from family backgrounds where English is not spoken may lack a solid understanding of its syntactic and visual structure. Therefore, as they are being recorded for progress using the oral running record, they may need additional support from their teacher and from an English Language teacher in examining the structure and meaning of English. A child from a non-native English-Language-speaking background may often pronounce words that make no sense to him or her and just go on reading. They have to learn to stop to construct meaning. This child may have to be prompted to self-correct. Children from non-native English-Language-speaking backgrounds can benefit from independent reading opportunities and from listening to a familiar story on tape while reading along. This also gives them practice in listening to standard English oral reading. Often these children can begin to internalize the language structures by listening to the book on tape several times.

Skill 3.14 Identify techniques for creating a literate environment in which students can connect purposes of reading to their personal lives

The Role of Literature in Developing Literacy

The balanced literacy approach advocates the use of "real literature"—recognized works of the best of children's fiction and non-fiction trade books and winners of such awards as the Newberry and Caldecott medals—for helping children develop literacy.

Balanced literacy advocates argue that:

- Real literature engages young readers and assures that they will become lifelong readers.

- Real literature also offers readers a language base that can help them expand their expressiveness as readers and as writers.

- Real literature is easier to read and understand than grade-leveled texts

In some districts in the United States, the phonics-only approach is heavily embedded. However, the majority of school districts would describe their approach to reading as the balanced literacy approach, which includes phonics work as well as the use of real literature texts. To contrast the phonics and balanced literacy approaches as opposite is inaccurate, since a balanced approach includes both.

It is important to go online and to visit the key resources of the National Council of Teachers of English and the International Reading Association to keep abreast of the latest research in the field.

TEACHER CERTIFICATION STUDY GUIDE

Strategies for Planning, Organizing, Managing, and Differentiating Reading Instruction to Support the Reading Development of All Students

The physical setup of your classroom is exceedingly important to support the effective development of all children.

The homey look of the classroom belies its deliberate design as a space where children can experience, practice, share and learn. Some teachers have done away with the large desk and use smaller tables instead. Sharon Taberski advocates for young children K-3 adjusting the height of the table legs so the children can use the tables as writing spaces and sit on the floor. Taberski gives each of her children a personal 12"x 9"x 2" tray on which they place their home possessions, books, homework, folder, etc. This is kept in a small storage unit near the coat closet during the day.

Children put their completed homework in a wire basket and notes from parents or the office in a second wire basket. Supplies such as pencils, markers, crayons, scissors, and erasers are not brought from home, but rather available for all in the class from "community" containers at the center of each of the children's tables.

All the children's reading, writing, and individual math folders are stored together in plastic bins in the meeting area. Every child has an individual book bag which is kept in one of two large wicker baskets set in different areas of the room.

This storing of materials away from children decreases their fiddling with their belongings during class, makes the room look much neater, and frees the children to focus on their learning experiences rather than where their belongings are at any given time of day.

As you can see on the accompanying diagram, the 10'x10' meeting area is the center of classroom learning. This is where the whole class is gathered at the beginning of the reading and the writing workshop and for sharing sessions. It is also the demonstration and modeling center for both the teacher and for children.

Generally, the presenter sits on the adult chair (in some balanced literacy classrooms, this is a rocking chair) near the easel with the chart. Generally, this chair and the easel are strategically positioned so that the teacher can see the door and any visitors or urgent messages from the office. Rearranging furniture during the day takes away from instruction time and is disruptive. Have a designated comfortable section of the room that can be a gathering place for a literacy community and then organize the rest of the classroom activities around that center.

The conference table which is at the back of the room (see diagram) is another key piece of classroom space furniture. It is the place where four or five children and the teacher can confer, wait and do their work. Having children come to a set conference table rather than the teacher's going to them (although some teachers do advocate going to the children) saves time, as far as Taberski is concerned. It serves to keep her and the children on task.

READING 102

Taberski keeps two separate trays of supplies: a small magnetic board, letters, chalkboard, chalk, sentence strips, index cards, and blank books for demonstrations during her conferences. She believes that teachers should store materials close to where they are used so they don't have to take time from the children to get up and get the materials.

The Classroom Library

On tables, Taberski generally keeps book crates with books that are not leveled. Children choose from these books during the first independent reading session of the day, which is from 8:40-9:00. During the second reading session (9:30-10:20) children select books from the leveled reading bins which are stored on the bookcase shelves.

In addition to leveled books, which have already been discussed, Taberski also maintains a non-leveled, nonfiction library which includes dictionaries, atlases, almanacs and informational books related to the themes, projects and investigations that the children will undertake throughout the year.

Taberski and other balanced literacy advocates also generally include at least 10-15 Big Books which they routinely use to engage children with the text.

Since Guided Reading with groups of six children is a major part of the balanced literacy approach, Taberski and other disciplined and dedicated teacher-educators "bundle" six copies of selected books so that they can distribute them to their guided reading groups whenever they choose. Taberski models the concept of a home library collection for the children by keeping books which she particularly likes in a bookcase behind her chair. She sometimes places "her" books on the easel so that they can be shared by the children and returned to her.

Wall Works

Much of creating a family atmosphere lies in the use of classroom walls to document the children's learning experiences, skills work, and readings.

Generally at least one wall in a reading classroom is the Chart Wall. Charts with various spelling patterns discussed in class can be posted. If a child later has issues or concerns with that particular pattern, he or she should be directed to look at and review the chart.

One of the centerpieces of the K-2 classroom is the High Frequency Word Chart. This is a growing list of commonly used words which the teacher tapes under the appropriate beginning letter according to the children's directions. At the end of each month, the newest high frequency words go into the children's folders and become part of their spelling words. In this way, reading, writing, and spelling are all intricately connected.

Another thing teachers can do to inspire students to become readers is to assign a book that you have never read before and read along with them, chapter by chapter. Run a contest in which the winner gets to pick a book that you and they will read chapter by chapter. If you are excited about it and are experiencing satisfaction from the reading, that excitement will be contagious. Be sure that the discussion sessions allow for students to relate what they are thinking and feeling about what they are reading. Lively discussions and the opportunity to express feelings will lead to more spontaneous reading.

You can also hand out a reading list of your favorite books and spend some time telling the students what you liked about each. Make sure the list is diverse. It's good to include nonfiction along with fiction. Don't forget that a good biography or autobiography may encourage students to read beyond thrillers and detective stories.

When the class is discussing the latest movie, whether formally as a part of the curriculum or informally and incidentally, if the movie is based on a book, this is a good opportunity to demonstrate how much more can be derived from the reading than from the watching. Or how the two combined make the experience more satisfying and worthwhile.

Share with your students the excitement you have for reading. Successful writers are usually good readers. The two go hand-in-hand.

Supplies for children K-3 and beyond may include:

A red plastic double pocket reading folder
A blue plastic double pocket reading folder
A four-section pressed board spelling/poetry folder
A 4" x 6" assessment notebook for reading
A 4" x 6" assessment notebook for writing
A reading response notebook (loose-leaf 60 pages)
A handwriting notebook

The Reading Folder contains the assessment notebooks, the reading response notebooks, a Weekly Reading Log, and the strategy sheets the child may be using that particular week.

The Assessment Notebook is a key evaluative tool and a recording document for the conscientious balanced literacy specialist. The teacher uses the notebook to record a child's record, the retellings of stories shared by the child, and summaries of talks about leveled books read. Within the assessment books, the teacher also has notes about the child's progress, the strategies the child has learned to use well, the books he or she has read and those strategies the child still needs to practice. These assessment notebooks must be kept accessible so that the teacher can use them to confer with the child, parents, and administrator as needed.

The reading response notebook becomes a compilation of reading strategy sheets and children's writings and art in response to literature. The Weekly Reading Log allows the child to maintain for himself or herself the titles of books read and to write a bit about the narrative, style, and genre of each given book.

Book Bags: These are 10" x 12" heavy duty plastic bags which keep 3-10 books a child is working on during his or her free time. The teacher generally matches the children to the books and changes these books as needed.

Writing Folders

Children keep several pieces of writing in their folders at a time. Within the writing folder is also a handwriting notebook and a beginning word book as well. The Spelling/Poetry Folder is one which helps children focus on the sequence of letters in words and learn more about how words work. Advocates of the balanced literacy approach have a definite schedule for the teaching of reading and writing workshop from which they generally do not deviate. A sample follows.

8:40-9:00- FIRST INDEPENDENT READING/WORD STUDY GROUP

9:00-9:30- MEETING-WHOLE GROUP SESSION in the meeting area
Read Aloud, Shared Reading, or Shared Writing

9:30-10:30- READING WORKSHOP
Reading Conferences or Guided Reading
Second Independent Reading
Reading Share 10:20-10:30

10:30-10:40- Writing Mini Lesson or Writing Share

10:40-11:20- Writing Workshop, Writing Conferences, Guided Writing, Modeled Writing, Independent Writing

(11:10-11:20)- Writing Share

Adjustment of Reading Instruction Based on Ongoing Assessment

Keeping cumulative records helps the teacher learn about the cueing systems that children use. It is important for the teacher to adjust reading instruction based on the pattern of miscues gathered from several successive reading records. When the teacher carefully reviews a given student's substitutions and self-corrections, certain patterns begin to surface. A child may use visual cues as he or she reads and adds meaning to self-correct. To the alert teacher, the reliance on visual miscues indicates that the reader doesn't make sense of what she is reading. This means that the teacher needs to check to see what cueing system the child uses when he or she is reading "just right" books. Children who use meaning and structure but not visual/graphophonic cues need to be reminded and facilitated to understand the importance of getting and reconstructing the author's message. They have to be able to share the author's story, not their own.

Not only can and should the teacher use the material in the children's ongoing assessment notebook to adjust the child's current instruction but the material also serves to document for the child his or her growth as a successful reader over time. In addition, if the same concerns surface over the use of a particular cueing system or high frequency word, the teacher can adjust the class wall chart and even devote a whole class lesson to the particular element.

Skill 3.15   Identify ways to increase learners' motivation to read independently for information and pleasure

Instructional Reading Strategies for Promoting the Development of Particular Reading Skills

Phonemic awareness can be developed through using leveled books that deal with rhyming words and segmenting phonemes into words. Children can also work with word or letter strips to continue the poems from the books and create their own "sequels" to the phoneme-filled story. They can also create an in-style rhyming story using some of the same phonemes from the leveled story they have heard.

Word Identification- Selective Cue Stage. Sometimes children have not yet experienced an awareness of the conventions of print and labeling in their own home environments. The teacher or an aide may have to go on a label adventure and support children in recognizing or affixing labels to parts of the classroom, halls and school building. A neighborhood walk with a digital or hand-held camera may be required to help children identify uses and functions of print in society. A classroom photo essay or bulletin board could be the outgrowth of such an activity.

Sight Vocabulary- Beginning readers may enjoy outdoing Dolch (1936), who compiled the best-known sight vocabulary word list. They can create their own class version of this list with illustrations and even some comments about why they have nominated certain words for the list.

Uses of Large Group, Small Group, and Individualized Reading Instruction

The framework for organizing the balanced literacy classroom is referred to as the one book-whole class mode. What this means is that everyone in the class has experiences with the same book. Everyone in the class discusses the literature. The teacher starts by activating prior knowledge and developing the context or background for the piece of literature. Some of the children may have less prior knowledge or context with which to frame the book. The teacher will need to provide a preview of the book or develop key concepts to provide a stronger base for what the class will read together.

Some children will have to work with a paraprofessional or with a reading tutor before the class studies the book. Different modes of reading, such as read-alouds, shared reading or guided reading, are accommodated within the class. Student reader choices can also include cooperative reading, reading with a partner, or independent reading.

Following the reading, the children respond in literature circles and/or in the whole class or in writing.

Strategies for Selecting and Using Meaningful Reading Materials at Appropriate Levels of Difficulty

Matching young children with "just right" books fosters their reading independently no matter how young they are. The teacher needs to have an extensive classroom library of books. Books that emergent readers and early readers can be matched with should have fairly large print, appropriate spacing so that the reader can easily see where word begins and ends, and few words on each page so that the young reader can focus on all important concerns of top-to-bottom, left-to-right, directionality, and the one-to-one match of word to print.

Illustrations for young children should support the meaning of the text and language patterns and predictable text structures should make these texts appealing to young readers. Most important, the content of the story should relate to the children's interests and experiences as the teacher knows them.

Only after all these considerations have been addressed can the teacher select "just right" books from an already leveled bin or list. In a similar fashion, when the teacher is selecting books for transitional and fluent readers, the following ideas need to be taken into account:

The book should take at least two sittings to read, so children can get used to reading longer books. The fluent and transitional reader needs to deal with more complex characters and more intricate plotting. Look for books that set the stage for plot development with a compelling beginning. Age appropriateness of the concepts, plot and themes is important so that the child will sustain interest in the book. Look for book features such as a list of chapters to help children navigate through the book.

Series books are wonderful to introduce at this point in the children's development.

Creation of an Environment that Promotes Love of Reading

The aforementioned creation of the meeting area and the reading chair (sometimes a rocking chair) with throw pillows around it promotes a love of reading. Beyond that, some classrooms have adopted an author's hat decorated with pictures of famous authors and book characters which children wear when they read from their own works.

Many classrooms also have children's storyboards, artwork, story maps, pop-up books, and "in the style of" writing inspired by specific authors. Some teachers buy calendars for the daily schedule which celebrate children's authors or types of literature. Children are also encouraged to bring in public library books and special books from their home libraries. The teacher can model this habit of sharing beautiful books and inviting stories from his or her home library.

In addition, news stories about children's authors, series books, television versions of books, theatrical film versions of books, stuffed toy book character decorations and other memorabilia related to books can be used to decorate the room.

Various chain bookstores including Barnes & Noble and Borders give out free bookmarks and promotional display materials related to children's books which can be available in the room for children to use as they read independently or in their guided groups. They might even use these artistic models to inspire their own book-themed artifacts.

Strategies for Promoting Independent Reading in the Classroom and at Home

Pre-select books for children that are "just right" for them. Provide children with a quiet, relaxing space within the classroom where they can go to read these books. Don't get upset if they seem to take a break or wander around the room after fifteen minutes. Adults take breaks as well.

Make certain that the children who are reading independently fill in their weekly logs. Beyond telling what books they were reading and how many pages they have read, have the children respond to the following prompts:

This week I was successful at . . .

Next week I plan to . . .

A response can also be an illustration or a sentence or two about the book.

Deliberately assign a child or a pair of children to read Big Books. These are a guaranteed success for the children because they have already been shared in class. Some children enjoy reading these independently using big rulers to point at words. This provides them with a sense of mastery over the words and ownership of their independent reading.

Some children enjoy working on their own strategy sheet, such as a story map, character map, or storyboard panel, to demonstrate how they can apply a strategy to their own independent learning.

Uses of Instructional Technology to Promote Reading Development

One of the most interesting ways in which the web complements the Reading and Writing Workshop involves the proliferation of author specific websites. If used judiciously, these web resources allow authors to be "present" in the classroom and allow children to write, question, discuss and share their literacy experiences with the authors themselves. Children can also readily become part of a distanced community of peers who are also reading works by a given author.

For instance, children who have been introduced to the work of Faith Ringgold, the author of *Tar Beach*, can easily visit her online site, www.faithringgold.com. Here they will not only find extensive biographic data on Ringgold, but they will also be able to learn a song inspired by her main character, Cassie. They will be able to help illustrate a new story Ringgold has put up on the website and also see if any of the questions they may have generated in their shared or independent reading of her books has already been answered in the "frequently asked questions" section of her web resource. A few of the author websites respond online to individual children's questions.
There are even some reader response web resources such as the Spaghetti Review website where young readers can post their response to different books they are reading. **http://www.book-club-review.com/view.php?cid=1**

Awareness of Strategies and Resources for Supporting Individual Students

See Skill 3.13

Highly proficient readers can sometimes support early readers through a partner relationship. Some children, particularly the emergent and beginning early readers, benefit from reading books with partners. The partners sit side-by-side and each one takes turns reading the entire text.

Use of talking book and author web resources provides special needs learners with visual- or auditory-handicapping conditions immediate contact with authors. This can lead to direct sharing in the joy of oral language storytelling. In addition to the accessibility of the keyboard, children's responses to literature can be shared with a broad network of other readers, including close and distance peers. Technology literally invites special needs learners into the circle of connected readers and writers.

Skill 3.16 **Identify ways to use the connection between reading and writing to foster and enhance communication skills in all students**

See Skills 3.10 and 3.15

COMPETENCY 4.0 READING COMPREHENSION

Skill 4.1 Demonstrate an understanding of instructional techniques such as modeling, scaffolding, and appropriate questioning strategies to enhance students' understanding of text

In order to discover multiple layers of meaning in a literary work, the first step is a thorough analysis, examining such things as setting, characters and characterization, plot (focusing particularly on conflicts and pattern of action), theme, tone, figures of speech, and symbolism. It is useful, in looking for underlying themes, to consider the author's biography, particularly with regard to setting and theme, and the date and time of the writing, paying particular attention to literary undercurrents at the time the work was written as well as the political and social milieu.

Once the analysis is complete and data accumulated on the historical background, determine the overt meaning. What does the story say about the characters and their conflicts, where does the climax occur, and is there a denouement? Once the forthright, overt meaning is determined, then begin to look for undercurrents and sub-themes that are related to the author's life and to what is going on in the literary, political, and social background at the time of writing.

In organizing of the presentation, it is usually best to begin with an explication of the overt level of meaning and then follow up with the other messages that emerge from the text.

To *interpret* means essentially to read with understanding and appreciation. It is not as daunting as it is made out to be. Simple techniques for interpreting literature are as follows:

- **Context:** This includes the author's feelings, beliefs, past experiences, goals, needs, and physical environment. Incorporate an understanding of how these elements may have affected the writing to enrich an interpretation of it.
- **Symbols:** Also referred to as a sign, a symbol designates something that stands for something else. In most cases, it stands for something that has a deeper meaning than its literal denotation. Symbols can have personal, cultural, or universal associations. Use an understanding of symbols to unearth a meaning the author might have intended but not expressed, or even something the author never intended at all.
- **Questions:** Asking questions, such as "How would I react in this situation?" may shed further light on how readers feel about the work.

Essential terminology and literary devices germane to literary analysis include alliteration, allusion, antithesis, aphorism, apostrophe, assonance, blank verse, caesura, conceit, connotation, consonance, couplet, denotation, diction, epiphany, exposition, figurative language, free verse, hyperbole, iambic pentameter, inversion, irony, kenning, metaphor, metaphysical poetry, metonymy, motif, onomatopoeia, octava rima, oxymoron, paradox, parallelism personification, quatrain, scansion, simile, soliloquy, Spenserian stanza, synecdoche, terza rima, tone, and wit.

Skill 4.2 Demonstrate an understanding of appropriate and effective uses of oral and silent reading

In oral reading, the student that is reading aloud provides a link between the author and those students listening to the spoken words. Oral reading not only helps the reader develop fluency but allows the teacher to further develop listening skills in the students. If they have to listen to find the answer to a particular question, then they will listen more intently. Therefore, teachers should give students a reason for listening other than knowing when their turn to read comes or where the reader left off.

Oral reading, whether it is to a group or just one-on-one with the teacher, helps students develop expression in reading. Students can read aloud and tape the reading or read in pairs. However, they should always be provided with time to practice before they are expected to read aloud in class.

Teachers should inform the students of the purposes of oral reading. These purposes can include:

- Enjoyment of a story
- Responding to student writing
- To gain information about a subject
- To build confidence and develop fluency
- To practice reading with expression

Silent reading involves students reading to themselves. Some teachers regularly have a silent reading period in the class, such as Drop Everything And Read (DEAR). Silent reading allows students to read books and stories that interest them at their own pace. They do not have to practice the reading beforehand and they should be allowed to exchange books that they find too hard. The five finger rule is one that teachers can instruct the students in so that they can recognize right away whether or not the book will be one they will have success with. The idea behind silent reading is to encourage the students to read for pleasure. When using this rule, students put up one finger for each mistake they make or for each word they don't know when reading one page. If they raise all five fingers in the course of reading one page, they should put the book back and make another choice.

Teachers need to model silent reading for students. During the time allotted for this activity, teachers should also be reading. They should tell students about their favorite books and authors so that the students realize that adults do read for enjoyment.

Skill 4.3   Identify strategies for using context to define words and strategies to learn and extend word meanings

See Skill 2.5

Skill 4.4   Demonstrate an understanding of techniques for teaching understanding and learning skills, such as Directed Reading/Thinking Activities (DR-TA); what we know, what we want to know, what we learned (KWL); Survey, Question, Read, Recite, (SQ3R); graphic organizers; test-taking strategies; varying reading rate

See other skills.

Skill 4.5   Identify techniques that enable students to connect prior knowledge with new information

See Competency 2.0

Skill 4.6   Identify techniques to develop comprehension strategies in the content areas

See Competency 2.0

Skill 4.7   Demonstrate an understanding of ways to develop fluency in students' reading and its link to comprehension

See Skills 1.4 and 1.8

COMPETENCY 5.0 VOCABULARY, SPELLING AND WORD STUDY

Skill 5.1 Demonstrate an understanding of strategies and skills (phonemic awareness, print concepts, conceptual vocabulary, experience with print, and stories) contributing to the development of reading

See Skill 1.8

Skill 5.2 Demonstrate an understanding of word study strategies, as well as effective use of phonics (graphophonic cues), context (syntactic and semantic cues), and sight words (instant recognition)

See Skill 1.8

Skill 5.3 Demonstrate an understanding of the use of phonics, along with other awareness and cues in text, e.g., phonemes, morphemes, endings, prefixes, suffixes, to analyze and decode words that are not recognized instantly

See Skill 1.8

Skill 5.4 Demonstrate an understanding of the role that spelling plays in enhancing and informing instruction

Concentration in this section will be on spelling plurals and possessives. The multiplicity and complexity of spelling rules based on phonics, letter doubling, etc. and the exceptions to these rules make a good dictionary an essential tool.

Most plurals of nouns that end in hard consonants or hard consonant sounds followed by a silent *e* are made by adding *s*. Some words ending in vowels only add *s*.

 fingers, numerals, banks, bugs, riots, homes, gates, radios, bananas

Nouns that end in soft consonant sounds *s, j, x, z, ch,* and *sh,* add *es*. Some nouns ending in *o* add es.

 dresses, waxes, churches, brushes, tomatoes, potatoes

Nouns ending in *y* preceded by a vowel just add *s*.

 boys, alleys

Nouns ending in *y* preceded by a consonant change the *y* to *i* and add *es*.

>babies, corollaries, frugalities, poppies

Some nouns plurals are formed irregularly or remain the same.

>sheep, deer, children, leaves, oxen

Some nouns derived from foreign words, especially Latin, may make their plurals in two different ways, one of them Anglicized. Sometimes the meanings are the same; other times, the two plurals are used in slightly different contexts. It is always wise to consult the dictionary.

>appendices, appendixes   criterion, criteria
>indexes, indices   crisis, crises

Make the plurals of closed (solid) compound words in the usual wayd.
>timelines, hairpins, cupfuls

Make the plurals of open or hyphenated compounds by adding the change in inflection to the word that changes in number.

>fathers-in-law, courts-martial, masters of art, doctors of medicine

Make the plurals of letters, numbers, and abbreviations by adding *s*.

>fives and tens, IBMs, 1990s, *p*s and *q*s (Note that letters are italicized.)

Skill 5.5   Demonstrate strategies for teaching vocabulary (roots, affixes, context, word origins) and helping students use these strategies to enhance their reading comprehension

See Skill 1.7

COMPETENCY 6.0 APPLICATION OF THEORETICAL KNOWLEDGE BASES OF READING IN DIAGNOSIS AND ASSESSMENT

Skill 6.1 Identify appropriate strategies to assess students' awareness of letter-sound correspondences, of vocabulary, and of reading comprehension

See Skills 1.7 and 2.6

Skill 6.2 Understand formal and informal assessments such as criterion and norm referenced tests, running records, anecdotal records, work samples, Informal Reading Inventories (IRIs) portfolios, and self-assessment

The Use of Data and Ongoing Reading Assessment to Adjust Instruction to Meet Students' Reading Needs

Assessment is the practice of collecting information about children's progress, and evaluation is the process of judging children's responses to determine how well they are achieving particular goals or demonstrating reading skills.

Assessment and evaluation are intricately connected in the literacy classroom. Assessment is necessary because teachers need ways to determine what students are learning and how they are progressing. In addition, assessment can be a tool which can also help students take ownership of their own learning and become partners in their ongoing development as readers and writers. In this day of public accountability, clear, definite and reliable assessment creates confidence in public education.

There are two broad categories of assessment:

Informal assessment utilizes observations and other non-standardized procedures to compile anecdotal and observation data/evidence of children's progress. It includes but is not limited to checklists, observations, and performance tasks. Formal assessment is composed of standardized tests and procedures carried out under circumscribed conditions. Formal Assessments include state tests, standardized achievement tests, NAEP tests, and the like.

To be effective, assessment should have the following characteristics:

It should be an ongoing process with the teacher making informal or formal assessments on an ongoing basis. The assessment should be a natural part of the instruction and not intrusive.

The most effective assessment is integrated into ongoing instruction. Throughout the teaching and learning day, the child's written, spoken and reading contributions to the class or lack thereof need to and can be continually noted.

Assessment should reflect the child's actual reading and writing experiences. The child should be able to show that he or she can read and explain or react to a similar literary or expository work.

Assessment needs to be a collaborative and reflective process. Teachers can learn from what the children reveal about their own individual assessments. Children, even as early as Grade 2, should be supported by their teacher to continually and routinely ask themselves questions assessing their reading. They might ask: "Am I understanding what the author wanted to say?" "What can I do to improve my reading?" and "How can I use what I have read to learn more about this topic?" Teachers need to be informed by their own professional observation AND by children's comments as they assess and customize instruction.

Quality assessment is multidimensional and may include but not be limited to samples of writings, student retellings, running records, anecdotal teacher observations, self-evaluations, and records of independent reading. From this multidimensional data, the teacher can derive a consistent level of performance and design additional instruction that will enhance the child's reading performance.

Assessment must take into account children's age and ethnic/cultural patterns of learning.

Assess to teach children from their strengths, not their weaknesses. Find out what reading behaviors children demonstrate well and then design instruction to support those behaviors.

Assessment should be part of children's learning process and not done TO them, but rather done WITH them.

Characteristics and Uses of Criterion-referenced and Norm-referenced Tests to Assess Reading Development and Identify Reading Difficulties

Criterion-referenced – tests in which the children are measured against criteria or guidelines which are uniform for all test-takers. Therefore, by definition, no special questions, formats or considerations are made for the test-taker who is either from a different linguistic/cultural background or is already identified as a struggling reader/writer. On a criterion-referenced test, it is possible that a child test-taker can score 100% because the child may have actually been exposed to all of the concepts taught and mastered them. A child's score on such a test would indicate which of the concepts have already been taught and what he or she needs additional review or support to master.

Two criterion-referenced tests that are commonly used to assess children's reading achievement are the Diagnostic Indicators of Basic Early Literacy Skills (DIBELS) and the Stanford Achievement Test. DIBELS measures progress in literacy from kindergarten to Grade 3. It can be downloaded from the Internet free at dibels.uoregon.edu. The Stanford test is designed to measure individual children's achievement in key school subjects. Subtests covering various reading skills are part of this test. Both DIBELS and the Stanford Achievement Test are group-administered.

DEGREES OF READING POWER (DRP) – This test is targeted to assess how well children understand the meaning of written text in real life situations. This test is supposed to measure the process of children's reading, not the products of reading such as identifying the main idea and author's purpose.

CTPIII- This is a criterion-referenced test which measures verbal and quantitative ability in Grades 3-12. It is targeted to help differentiate among the most capable students, i.e., those who rank above the 80th percentile on other standardized tests. This is a test that emphasizes higher-order thinking skills and process-related reading comprehension questions.

Norm-referenced – test in which the children are measured against one another. Scores on this test are reported in percentiles. Each percentile indicates the percent of the testing population whose scores were lower than or the same as a particular child's score. Percentile is defined as a score on a scale of 100 showing the percentage of a distribution that is equal to it or below it. This type of state standardized norm-referenced test is being used in most districts today in response to the No Child Left Behind Act. While this type of test does not help track the individual reader's progress in his or her ongoing reading development, it does permit comparisons across groups.

There are many more standardized norm-referenced tests to assess children's reading than there are criterion-referenced. In these tests, scores are based on how well a child does compared to others, usually on the local, state and national level. IF the norming groups on the tests are reflective of the children being tested (e.g., same spread of minority, low income, gifted students), the results are more trustworthy.

One of the best-known norm-referenced test is the Iowa Test of Basic Skills. It assesses student achievement in various school subjects and has several subtests in reading. Other examples of norm-referenced tests used around the country are the Metropolitan Achievement Tests, the Terra Nova-2, and the Stanford Diagnostic Reading Test-4. These are all group tests. An individual test that reading specialists use with students is the Woodcock Reading Mastery Test.

The Characteristics and Uses of Formal and Informal Assessments

Informal Assessments

A running record of children's oral reading progress in the early Grades K-3 is a pivotal informal assessment. It supports the teacher in deciding whether a book a child is reading is matched to his or her stage of reading development. In addition, this assessment allows the teacher to analyze a child's miscues to see which cueing systems and strategies the child uses and to determine which other systems the child might use more effectively. Finally, the running record offers a graphic account of a child's oral reading.

Generally, a teacher should maintain an annotated class notebook with pages set aside for all the children or individual notebooks for each child. One of the benefits of using running records as an informal assessment is that they can be used with any text and can serve as a tool for teaching rather than an instrument to report on children's status in class.

Another good point about using running records is that they can be taken repeatedly and frequently by the teacher, so that the educator can truly observe a pattern of errors. This in turn provides the educator with sufficient information to analyze the child's reading over time. As any mathematician or scientist knows, the more samples of a process you gather over time, the more likely the teacher you are to get an accurate picture—in this case, a picture of the child's reading needs.

Using the notations which Marie Clay developed and shared in her *An Observation Study of Early Literacy Achievement*, Sharon Taberski offers in her *On Solid Ground* a lengthy walk through keeping a running record of children's reading. She writes in the child's miscue on the top line of her running record above the text word. Indeed, she records all of the child's miscue attempts on the line above the text word. Sharon advises the teacher to make all the miscue notations as the child reads, since this allows the teacher to get additional information about how and why the child makes miscue choices. Additionally, the teacher should note, self-corrections (coded SC) when the child is monitoring his or her own reading, crosschecks information, and uses additional information.

As part of the informal assessment of primary grade reading, it is important to record the child's word insertions, omissions, requests for help, and attempts to get the word. In informal assessment the rate of accuracy can be estimated by dividing the child's errors by the total words read.

Results of a running record assessment can be used to select the best setting for the child's reading. If a child reads from 95% to 100% correct, the child is ready for independent reading. If the child reads from 92% to 97% right, the child is ready for guided reading. Below 92% the child needs a read-aloud or shared reading activity. Note that these percentages are slightly different from those one would use to match books to readers.

One of the increasingly popular and meaningful forms of informal assessment is the compilation of the literacy portfolio. What is particularly compelling about this type of informal portfolio is that artists, television directors, authors, architects and photographers use portfolios in their careers and jobs. This is a most authentic format for documenting children's literacy growth over time. The portfolio is not only a significant professional informal assessment tool for the teacher, but a vehicle and format for the child reader to take ownership of his or her progress over time. It models a way of compiling one's reading and writing products as a lifelong learner, which is the ultimate goal of reading instruction.

Portfolios can include the following six categories of materials:

Work samples: These can include children's story maps, webs, K-W-L charts, pictures, illustrations, storyboards, and writings about the stories which they have read.

Records of independent Reading and Writing: These can include the children's journals, notebooks or logs of books read with the names of the authors, titles of the books, date completed, and pieces related to books completed or in progress.

Checklists and Surveys: These include checklists designed by the teacher for reading development, writing development, ownership checklists, and general interest surveys.

Self-Evaluation Forms: These are the children's own evaluations of their reading and writing process framed in their own words. They can be simple templates with starting sentences such as the following:

I am really proud of the way I _____

I feel one of my strengths as a reader is _____

To improve the way I read aloud I need to _____

To improve my reading I should _____

Generally, at the beginning of a child's portfolio in Grade 3 or above there is a letter to the reader explaining the work that will be found in the portfolio and from fourth grade level up, children write a brief reflection detailing their feelings and judgments about their growth as readers and writers.

When teachers are maintaining the portfolios for mandated school administrative review, district review, or even for their own research, they often prepare portfolio summary sheets. These provide identifying data on the children and then a timeline of their review of the portfolio contents plus professional comments on the extent to which the portfolio documents satisfactory and ongoing growth in reading.

Portfolios can be used beneficially for child-teacher, and of course parent/teacher, conversations to review the child's progress, discuss areas of strength, set future goals, make plans for future learning activities and evaluate what should remain in the portfolio and what needs to be cleared out for new materials.

Rubrics

Holistic scoring involves assessing a child's ability to construct meaning through writing. It uses a scale called a RUBRIC which can range from 0 to 4.

0. This indicates the piece cannot be scored. It does not respond to the topic or is illegible.
1. The writing does respond to the topic, but does not cover it accurately.
2. This piece of writing does respond to the topic but lacks sufficient details or elaboration.
3. This piece fulfills the purpose of the writing assignment and has sufficient development (which refers to details, examples, and elaboration of ideas).
4. This response has the most details, best organization, and presents a well-expressed reaction to the original writer's piece.

Miscue Analysis

This is a procedure that allows the teacher a look at the reading process. By definition, the miscue is an oral response different from the text being read. Sometimes miscues are also called unexpected responses or errors. By studying a student's miscues from an oral reading sample, the teacher can determine which cues and strategies the student is correctly using or not using in constructing meaning. Of course, the teacher can customize instruction to meet the needs of this particular student.

Informal Reading Inventories (IRI)

These are a series of samples of texts prearranged in stages of increasing difficulty. Listening to children read through these inventories, the teacher can pinpoint their skill level and the additional concepts they need to work on.

Characteristics and uses of Group versus Individual Reading Assessments

In assessment, tests are used for different purposes. They have different dimensions or characteristics whether they are given individually or in a group and whether they are standardized or teacher-made. The chart below shows the relationships of these elements.

	Standardized	**Teacher-made**
Individual	*Characteristics* • is uniformly administered *Uses* • is best for younger children • helps with placement for special services	*Characteristics* • has more flexibility *Uses* • assists teaching decisions • used for diagnostic purposes
Group	*Characteristics* • is uniformly administered • is time efficient *Uses* • permits comparisons across groups • used for policy decisions by administrators	*Characteristics* • has high face validity • is time efficient *Uses* • informs teach-reteach & enrichment decisions • documents students' learning

Techniques for Assessing Particular Reading Skills

Sharon Taberski recommends that the teacher build in one-on-one time for supporting individual children as needed in considering what makes sense, sounds right and matches the letters.

She has noted that emergent and early readers tend to focus on meaning without adequate attention to graphophonic cues. She suggests using the following prompts for children who are having problems with graphophonic cues:

Does what you said match the letters?

If the word were what you said ___, what would it have to start with?
Look carefully at the first letters, then look at the middle letters, then look at the last letters. What could it be?

If it were ___, what would it end with?

Oral retellings can be used to test children's comprehension.

Children who are retelling a story to be tested for comprehension should be told that that is the purpose when they sit down with the teacher. It is a good idea to let the child start the retelling on his or her own because then the teacher can see whether he or she needs prompts to retell the story. Often more experienced readers summarize what they have read. This summary usually flows out along with the characters, the problem of the story and other details.

Other signs that children understand what they are reading when they give an oral retelling include their use of illustrations to support the retelling, references to the exact text in the retelling, emotional reaction to the text, making connections between the text and other stories or experiences they have had, and giving information about the text without the teacher's asking for it.

Skill 6.3 Demonstrate an understanding of basic measurement concepts (e.g., reliability, validity)

Concepts of Validity, Reliability, and Bias in Testing

Validity is how well a test measures what it is supposed to measure. Teacher-made tests are therefore not generally extremely valid, although they may be an appropriate measure for the validity of the concept the teacher wants to assess for his or her own children's achievement.

Reliability is the consistency of the test. This is measured by whether the test will indicate the same score for the child who takes it more than once.

Bias in testing occurs when the information within the test or the information required to respond to a multiple choice question or constructed response (essay question on the test) is not available to some test-takers who come from a different cultural, ethnic, linguistic or socio-economic background than do the majority of the test-takers. Since they have not had the same prior linguistic, social or cultural experiences that the majority of test-takers have had, these test-takers are at a disadvantage in taking the test and no matter what their actual mastery of the material taught by the teacher, cannot address the "biased" questions. Generally other "non-biased" questions are given to them and eventually the biased questions are removed from the examination.

To solidify what might be abstract to the reader, on a recent reading test in a school system, the Grade 4 reading-comprehension multiple choice had some questions about the well-known fairy tale of the Gingerbread Boy. These questions were simple and accessible for most of the children in the class. But two children who were recent new arrivals from the Dominican Republic had learned English there. They were reading on Grade 4 level, but in their Dominican grade school, the story of the Gingerbread Boy was not a major one. So the question about this story on the standardized reading test did demonstrate examiner bias and was not fair to these test-takers.

Skill 6.4 Demonstrate an understanding of how to collaborate with classroom teachers to use assessment results to evaluate and modify reading instruction

Any assessment of students must be documented and samples kept so that the parents and other teachers can understand what you mean. Communicating the findings of assessment is not something that has to wait for parent-teacher interviews or the report card. It is something that teachers should report to parents on a regular basis, such as in monthly notes or telephone calls, arranged meetings or even simple chats.

Guidance and speech counselors should communicate the results of assessments to teachers and parents as soon as possible after the testing is complete. In many districts this is called a debriefing and takes the form of an arranged meeting. In this meeting the counselor discusses the findings and makes suggestions as to how best meet the needs of the child.

Skill 6.5 **Demonstrate an understanding of how to effectively communicate the findings of reading assessment data with all stakeholders (e.g., students, parents, classroom teachers, guidance counselors, speech teachers and other personnel.**

Quite often the only communication between the school and parents takes the form of end of term reports and parent-teacher interviews. Parents are sometimes reluctant to come to the school because they feel that the teachers are more knowledgeable than they are. In order to have good literacy communication between the school and parents, teachers and reading specialists can employ different techniques. These include:

- Holding a curriculum night during the first two weeks of school. At this time the teacher can explain how the children will be taught and the textbooks and materials that will be used.
- Having an open door policy in which parents can feel free to come into the classroom and observe what is happening.
- Telephoning or emailing parents on a regular basis. Parents dread getting a call from the teacher because it usually means that their children have been in trouble or are experiencing problems in school. When you make these phone calls to report progress parents become an ally in helping their children at home.
- Notes to parents in the child's agenda are also helpful in keeping them informed about how to help at home and about how well their children are doing.
- Inviting parents or members of the community into the classroom to help with literacy centers gives those outside the school a chance to experience what is happening in the classroom. This could be listening to children read, helping them revise and edit writing or even helping them choose books to take home.

Skill 6.6 **Demonstrate an understanding of how to effectively communicate and collaborate with families in children's reading development**

See Skills 6.4 and 6.5

COMPETENCY 7.0 READING LEADERSHIP

Skill 7.1 Demonstrate an understanding of how to develop and adapt reading programs to meet student needs within the framework of guidelines and regulations at the classroom, building, district, state and federal levels

In every classroom across the country, there are students at different reading levels. There is no such thing as one reading program to meet the needs of all students. Therefore, a reading specialist within the school must adapt and develop reading programs so that each child will experience success and develop further in reading skills. For some students, the reading material in the program is beyond their level, while for others it may be too easy.

One way to assure that all students are reading at their individual levels is to implement a guided reading program. The Fountas and Pinnel method of guided reading is one that has been accepted widely and is evincing major success with teaching children to read fluently and accurately. In this method, students are assessed at the beginning of the year to see where they fit on the letter grade scale. Each letter in the guided reading system refers to the manner in which a book is written (e.g. Level A books have one word on a page, with pictures that correspond to the word).

Once the students are assessed, the teacher gathers each group together on a regular basis to instruct them in a specific learning strategy. The classroom must be rich in print materials and students should know exactly where to go to get the books they can read. Assessment takes place on a regular basis as well and students progress as they grasp the strategies. The groups are constantly changing so that students will not get the idea they are in the slow group or the smart group.

Within the content areas, the reading material may have to be rewritten so that it is in words that students can understand. The explanations may have to be more detailed, especially if the student does not have the appropriate background knowledge. Evaluations and tests may also have to be different for those students, thus allowing them to experience success.

Skill 7.2 Demonstrate an awareness of how to access literacy research and disseminate it across grade levels

Educational journals are full of literacy research. These are often available at the school if the district has a subscription. As the reading specialist you should have a subscription to these, which includes:

- The Reading Teacher
- Educational Leadership
- Adolescent Learning

In addition, experts are writing about the findings of research into literacy and there are many published books on the subject. Consider the writings of the following authors:

- Marie Clay
- Donald Graves
- Regi Routman
- Susan Taberski

Skill 7.3 Demonstrate an understanding of how to use school-wide initiatives and other services to students to improve instruction

Reading specialists, administrators and teachers should take a critical look at the policies in place within the school for meeting the reading needs of all students. Part of this should include a school-wide reading initiative such as 15 minutes of silent reading in every classroom every day. During this time the teacher can be reading as a model for the students or can be conferencing with individual students about what they are reading. This can take the form of listening to students read or asking them questions to ensure they comprehend what they are reading.

Guided Reading materials should be in place in every classroom with books at the students' reading levels. The teacher or reading specialist can work with small groups of students on a particular reading strategy and provide them with the opportunity to practice various strategies.

Students from Grades 1 to 6 can also participate in a weekly rotation in which they work with students of the same reading ability. Within this group students can work on projects related to the reading material, engage in writing activities or crafts demonstrating comprehension.

Literacy centers in the classroom allow students to work on different projects, as does a Reading/Writing workshop. Conferencing with students on a regular basis helps to ensure that students understand what they are reading as well as to employ various strategies to help them become fluent readers.

Skill 7.4 Demonstrate an understanding of culturally relevant curricular approaches to improve instruction

The standards mandated by the state should be the beginning point for any instructional design. These are what the students need to know in order to progress to the next level or grade. The curriculum guide, not the textbook or reading programs, is the bible of teaching. The standards should be communicated to students in words they understand so that they know exactly what they have to learn. By employing "assessment for learning" teachers can assess the students before instruction to find out exactly where their deficiencies lie and gear the instruction toward them.

When planning for instruction, teachers should begin with the end in mind. This may mean deconstructing the outcomes to make them more manageable. Assessment should also be in the forefront. For example, ask yourself what students will have to do to demonstrate they have achieved the objective of the lesson. Once you know what you want students to do, then you can plan accordingly.

Skill 7.5 Demonstrate an understanding of how standards and their assessment define curriculum, impact the reading program and influence instruction

Teachers have a critical role to play in encouraging multicultural experiences. They have an opportunity to incorporate activities that reflect our nation's increasing diversity and allow students to share their similarities, develop a positive cultural identity, and appreciate the unique contributions of all cultures. The best way to incorporate multicultural literature depicting African-American, Asian, Arabic, Native American, and Hispanic heritage is to integrate it into the established reading program rather than as a separate or distinct area of study.

Reading Workshops
In reading workshops, students select from a variety of reading materials such as books, biographies, encyclopedias, and magazines. Students share their responses to the literature by writing or talking with teachers and classmates. This allows students to take ownership of their reading by choosing their own reading material. Teachers should have a large supply of multicultural literature to choose from that is sensitive to and reflective of students' diverse cultural backgrounds. When reading these materials, students can learn that most people have similar emotions, needs and dreams. During reading workshops, students usually engage in reading, responding, sharing, and reading aloud.

Reading

Students may spend an hour independently reading books and other written materials that include diverse cultural material. Classrooms should have a variety of instructional materials representing diverse cultures.

Responding

After students read a multicultural storybook, teachers should direct the students to reflect on the meaning of the story in their own lives. In this process, students interpret meanings and draw inferences based upon their own cultural perspectives and experiences. Students might keep journals in which they write their initial responses to the materials they are reading. They may also talk with the teacher about their books. Teachers should help students move beyond simply writing summaries and toward reflecting and making connections between literature and their own lives.

Sharing

Sharing differences of diverse families heightens a child's sensitivity to issues involving prejudice, racism, and intolerance toward students of different cultures. Exposing students to culturally diverse literature provides them with a means to become global citizens who can perform more effectively in a culturally diverse society.

Reading Aloud

Teachers read aloud when they wish to present literature that students might not be able to read themselves. Students should participate in class discussion about the book, share the reading experience, and respond to the story together as a community of learners, not as individuals.

Writing Workshops

It is important for teachers to encourage students to write a story depicting the lives of persons around the world. In a writing workshop, students can make a box containing cultural items of a country or several countries such as ornaments, clothing, pictures, or music tapes associated with the story line they create.

Another way of integrating multicultural activities in writing workshop is to involve students in a multicultural pen-pal project. Students can compose group letters to partner classes in other nations about their school, their lives, or the books they have read about the partner's country. Copies of these books and thank you notes from partner classes can be displayed in the school by posting them on bulletin boards. From this activity, students learn that there are interesting books to read from different countries and nice kids to share ideas with all around the world. As students engage in these writing activities, they expand their views about other cultures by sharing language, beliefs, religion, heritage, and their school and home life.

Teachers can also invite guest speakers from their local area by contacting a minority community center. Speakers might be a director of an international program at a local university, a minister, or a person from the community with knowledge of a different culture. It is useful for the students to prepare questions in advance. Students should write the invitation and follow-up letter of appreciation to the speaker.

Skill 7.6 **Demonstrate an understanding of how to critically analyze school-wide reading programs and initiatives in relation to reading goals and student needs**

See Skill 7.3

Skill 7.7 **Demonstrate an understanding of how to serve as a resource within a school**

As a reading specialist within a school, you will likely serve as a resource for the rest of the teachers. There are several ways that this job can be accomplished, such as:

- Working with teachers in the classroom to organize the classroom setting
- Working with small groups of students in the classroom
- Helping organize professional development in the field of reading
- Preparing the Individual Program Plans for students needing extra reading assistance
- Creating inclusive classrooms
- Helping the teachers with learning about and employing the different learning theories and ways students learn in the classroom
- Performing the testing on students to determine their reading levels for guided reading
- Tracking the progress of students in reading
- Determining strategies to help students develop as readers
- Identifying the individual needs of students with reading difficulties or those that need more challenges

- Analyzing the assessments and evaluations to provide assistance to the teachers in reporting to parents
- Establishing enrichment programs for students identified as reading beyond grade level

Skill 7.8 Demonstrate an understanding of how to promote collaboration among colleagues (e.g., classroom teachers, paraprofessionals, volunteers) for the literacy development of all students

Providing time for teachers to get together to plan instructional activities geared towards reading contributes to a spirit of collaboration in the school. One way to accomplish this is to provide the teachers with time to visit other schools and observe what is happening in another classroom in the district. Teachers within the same division or teachers of one grade in the school can get together on a regular basis to discuss how they are teaching various concepts and to discuss how to best help students that are struggling with reading. The Reading Specialist should be part of this team, as well as the teacher giving support to the struggling readers. These meetings might take place after-school or during days when the school is not in operation. Administrators can also schedule the timetable in such a way that these teachers have time off during the school day for this purpose.

Skill 7.9 Demonstrate an understanding of how to engage in, promote and provide professional development opportunities

Reading specialists, administrators and teachers are always on the lookout for professional development opportunities that will help them in teaching reading. Most school districts offer professional development and provide an outline of these opportunities to the schools at the beginning of the year. However, this often involves travel and for schools that manage their own budgets, this is something that has to be looked at carefully.

With the many demands placed on teachers, it is often not feasible to hold PD sessions after school hours on a regular basis. Teachers do not mind if this is scheduled into the timetable at the beginning of the year and the sessions are kept relatively short. Using the PD time allowable by the school district to close schools for a half or full day is one way of bringing appropriate professional development to the staff. Schools within close proximity to one another can work together to share the cost of bringing in guest speakers and experts in the field of reading.

Another method that has seen success is to add 15 minutes to the school day from Monday to Thursday and give teachers Friday afternoons for professional development. When this becomes a district-wide policy, teachers know exactly what is expected of them on Friday. Some of these sessions can be school PD where the teachers get time to plan together, discussing how best to teach and how to make sure they are teaching state-mandated outcomes. Some of these Fridays can be a chance for teachers to get together with those from other schools. For example, there could be a PD for Grade 1 teachers, those in middle literacy, high school English teachers, etc. When small groups are formed in this way, professional learning communities within the school district are strengthened.

Skill 7.10 Demonstrate an understanding of the importance of school and community when promoting home-school connections

The home and community play an important part in the reading development of children. "It takes a village to raise a child" is an old adage that has great ramifications for a successful school. At the beginning of the year, teachers should hold an information session for parents explaining how they can help their children at home. Some of the suggestions teachers can make include:

- Having children write out the grocery list
- Writing thank you cards or letters for gifts
- Writing notes to the child
- Reading to children at home
- Listening to children reading
- Discussing what was learned at school
- Reading the newspaper

People from the community can become active volunteers in school by reading to small groups of children and listening to them read. They can also help children in writing groups or lead craft activities.

Skill 7.11 Demonstrate an understanding of how to promote positive and effective literacy connections between the home and the school and between the school and the community

See Skill 6.6

GLOSSARY

These definitions are critical for success on all multiple choice questions on examinations. Proper use of these terms is crucial for success in tackling a constructed response involving balanced literacy.

ABILITY GROUPING- grouping of children with similar needs for instructional purposes. Ability groups do not remain constant throughout the year, but change as the children's needs within them change.

ALLITERATION- occurs when words begin with the same consonant sound, as in *Peter Piper picked a pair of pickled peppers*.

ALPHABETIC PRINCIPLE- the idea that written spellings represent spoken words.

ANCHOR BOOK- a balanced literacy term for a book that is purposely read repeatedly and used as part of both the reading and writing workshop.

It is a good idea to use certain books that become the children's familiar and cherished favorites for both reading and then to inspire children's writing.

ASSONANCE- Occurs when words begin with the same vowel sound.

AUTHENTIC ASSESSMENT- assessment activities which reflect the actual workplace, family, community and school curriculum.

BALANCED LITERACY LESSON FORMAT- the Balanced Literacy Approach has its own specific format for the delivery of the literacy lesson, whether it is a reading or writing workshop lesson. The format begins with a 10-15 minute mini-lesson which the teacher delivers to the whole class. This mini-lesson is then followed by a 30-minute small group lesson in which the children break up into small groups. It concludes with a 10-minute share in which the whole class reconvenes to share what has happened in the small groups.

One can refer to this format as the whole-small-whole group approach.

BENCHMARKS- school, state or nationally mandated statements of the expectations for student learning and achievement in various content areas.

BICS-BASIC INTERPERSONAL COMMUNICATION SKILLS (ELL term-Bilingual Education)- learning second language skills and becoming proficient in a second language through face-to-face interaction-translation through speaking, listening, and viewing.

BLENDING- the process of hearing separate phonemes and being able to merge them to read the word.

BOOK FEATURES- children need to be familiar with the following book features: front and back cover, title and half-title page, dedication page, table of contents, prologue and epilogue, and foreword and after notes. For factual books, children need to be familiar with terms such as labels, captions, glossary, index, headings and subheadings of chapters, charts and diagrams, and sidebars.

CHECKLIST- an assessment form which lists targeted learning and social behaviors as indicators of achievement, knowledge or skill. They can be professionally or teacher-prepared.

CINQUAIN- a five-line poem that can be read and then used as a model for writing. Generally, line one of this format is a single word, line two has two words which describe the title of line one, line three is comprised of three words which are movement words, line four has four words which express feeling and line five has a single word which is a synonym for line one's single word.

COMPREHENSION- this occurs when the reader correctly interprets the print on the page and constructs meaning from it. Comprehension depends on activating prior knowledge, cultural and social background of the reader, and the reader's ability to use comprehension-monitoring strategies.

CONCEPTS ABOUT PRINT- these include how to handle books, how to look at print, directionality, sequencing, locating skills, punctuation, and concepts of letters and words.

CONSONANT DIGRAPHS- two consecutive consonants that represent one new speech sound. In the word "digraph" the *ph* which sounds like /f/ is a digraph.

CONTEXTS- sentences deliberately prepared by the teacher which include sufficient contextual clues for children to decipher meaning.

CONTEXTUAL REDEFINITION- using context to determine word meaning.

COOPERATIVE READING- Children read with a partner or buddy. It can be silent or oral reading.

CRISSCROSSERS- an ELL term for second language learners who have a positive attitude toward both first language and second language learning. These second language learners, children from ELL backgrounds, are comfortable navigating between the two languages as they learn.

CUES- as they self-monitor their reading comprehensions, readers have to integrate various sources of information or cues to help them construct meaning from text and graphic illustrations.

DECODING- sounding out a printed sequence of letters based on knowledge of letter-sound correspondences.

DIPHTHONGS- two vowels in one syllable where the two sounds are heard. For instance in the word *house* both the "o" and the "u" are heard.

DIRECTIONALITY- children use their fingers to indicate left to right direction and return sweep to the next line.

DIFFERENTIATED INSTRUCTION- The need for the teacher to provide modified instruction and alternative strategies or activities based on observation of individual student's work, progress, test results, fluency, and other reading/literacy behaviors. These activities are specifically developed by the teacher to address individual students' different needs.

EARLY READERS- recognize most high frequency words and many simple words. They use pictures to confirm meaning. Using meaning, syntax, and phonics, they can figure out most simple words. They use spelling patterns to figure out new words. They are gaining control of reading strategies. They use their own experiences and background knowledge to predict meanings. They occasionally use story language in their writing. This stage follows emergent reading.

EMERGENT READERS- the stage of reading in which the reader understands that print contains a consistent message. The reader can recognize some high frequency words, names, and simple words in context. Pictures can be used to predict meaning. The emergent reader begins to attend to left to right directionality and features of print and may identify some initial sounds and ending sounds in words.

ENCODE- to change a message into symbols. For example, readers encode oral language into writing.

ENGLISH as a SECOND LANGUAGE- a way of teaching English to speakers of other languages using English as the language of instruction.

EXPOSITORY TEXT- non-fiction that provides information and facts. This text type is what newspapers, science, mathematics and history texts use. Currently there is much focus, even in elementary schools, on teaching children how to comprehend and author expository texts. They must produce brochures, guides, recipes, and procedural accounts on most elementary grade levels. The teaching of reading of expository texts requires working with a particular vocabulary and concept structure that is very different from that of the narrative text. Therefore, time must be taken to teach the reading of expository texts and contrast it with the reading of narrative texts.

FIRST LANGUAGE- an ELL term for the language any child acquires in the first few years of life. It is through this acquired language that the child acquires phonological and phonemic awareness.

FLUENT READERS- identify most words automatically. They can read chapter books with good comprehension. They consistently monitor, cross-check, and self-correct when reading. They can offer their own interpretations of text based on personal experiences and prior reading experiences. Fluent readers are capable of reading a variety of genres independently. Furthermore, they can respond to texts or stories by sharing pertinent examples from their lives. They can also readily make connections to other books which they have read. Finally, they are capable of beginning to create spoken and written writings which are in the style of a particular author.

FORMAL ASSESSMENT- a test or an observation of a performance task which is done under controlled and regulated conditions.

FUNCTIONAL READING- the reading of instructions, recipes, coupons, classified ads, notices, signs, and other documents which we have to read and correctly interpret in school and in society.

GRADE EQUIVALENT/GRADE SCORE- a score transformed from a raw score on a standardized test into the equivalent score earned by an average student in the norming group.

GRAPHIC ORGANIZERS- graphic organizers express relationships among various ideas in visual form, including sequence, timelines, character traits, fact and opinion, main idea and details, differences and likenesses. Graphic organizers are particularly helpful for visual learners.

GUIDED READING- one of the key modes of instruction in the balanced literacy theory approach. During guided reading, the teacher "guides" the child through silent reading of a text by giving him or her prompts, target questions, and even helping to start an answer to a specific prompt or question. At the end of each guided reading section or excerpt of the text, the child stops to talk with the teacher about the text. By definition, guided reading is an interactive discussion between the child and the teacher. This mode of reading instruction is generally used when children need extra support in constructing meaning because the text is complex or because their current independent reading capacities are still limited.

HIGH FREQUENCY- frequently used words. These words appear many more times than do other words in ordinary reading material. Examples of such words include *as, in, of,* and *the*. These words are also sometimes called service words and are also part of sight vocabulary words. A classic best-known high frequency word list was generated by Dolch (1936).

INDEPENDENT READING- a set period of time within the daily literacy block when children read books with 95%-100% accuracy on their own. This reading of books by themselves which they can understand without teacher support promotes lifelong literacy and love of learning, which enhances reading mileage, builds fluency, and helps children orchestrate integrated cue strategies.

INFORMAL ASSESSMENT- observations of children made under informal conditions; these can include kid watching, checklists, and individual child/teacher conversations.

INFORMAL READING INVENTORY (IRI) - a series of reading excerpts that can be used to determine a child's reading strengths and needs in comprehension and decoding. Many published reading series have an IRI to go with their series.

JUSTIFIED PRINT- the positioning of print on the page so that each line ends either a sentence or a phrase.

KID WATCHING- term used within the balanced literacy approach for the teacher's deliberate, detailed, and recorded observations of individual student and class literacy behaviors, often done during small group work. The teacher then reconfigures lessons on experiences to meet the students' individual and group needs.

KINESTHETIC- learning that is tactile, as contrasted with an activity in which the learner sits still or attempts to sit still in one place. Cutting and moving syllable or word strips or using sandpaper letters are kinesthetic activities.

LANGUAGE EXPERIENCE- Children giving dictation to the teacher who writes their words on a chart or their drawings. This shows children that words can be written down.

LEARNING LOGS- daily records of what students have learned.

LISTENING POST- sets of headphones attached to a single tape player. Children can go to centers where they listen to audiotapes of books while reading the print book. These posts exist in many libraries as well.

LITERATURE CIRCLES- a group discussion involving four to six children who have read the same work of literature (narrative or expository text). They talk about key parts of the work, relate it to their own experience, listen to the responses of others, and discuss how parts of the text relate to the whole.

MANIPULATION- moving around or switching sounds within a word or words within a phrase or sentence.

MEANING VOCABULARY- words whose meanings children understand and can use.

MISCUE- an oral reading error made by a child which differs from the actual printed text.

MISCUE ANALYSIS- the teacher keeps a detailed recording of the errors or inaccurate attempts of a child reader during a reading assessment. These are recorded in a running record. This helps the teacher see if the cues the child is using, whether syntactic, semantic, or graphophonemic, are accurate.

MONITORING READING- various strategies that children use to monitor their readings. Some examples include maintaining fluency by bringing prior knowledge to the story to make predictions, using these predictions to do further checking, searching, and self-correcting as the story progresses, and using problem-solving word study skills to make links from known words to unknown words.

MORPHEMES- the smallest units of meaning in words. There are two types of morphemes; free morphemes, which can stand alone, such as *love,* and bound morphemes, which must be attached to another morpheme to carry meaning such as *ed* in *loved*.

NARRATIVE TEXT- one of two basic text structures. The narrative text tells or communicates a story. Narrative texts are novels, short stories and plays. Some poems are narratives as well. The narrative text needs to be taught differently than the expository text because of its structure.

ONE TO ONE MATCHING- matching one spoken word with one written word.

ONSET-RIME BLENDING- Everything before the vowel and RIME (the vowel and everything after it). For example, the word "sleep" can be broken into /sl/ and /eep/. Word families are built using rimes. The /eep/ word family would include *jeep, keep* and *weep*.

ORTHOGRAPHY- a method of representing spoken language through letters and diacritics.

PERCENTILE- if a child scores at the 56th percentile for his or her grade level, his or her score is equal to or above that of 56 percent of the children taking that standardized test and below that of 46 percent of the children on whose scores the test was normed.

PERFORMANCE ASSESSMENT- having children do a task that demonstrates their knowledge, skills and competency. Having children author their own alphabet book on a particular topic would be a performance assessment for knowledge of the alphabet.

PHONEME- The speech sound units that make a difference in meaning. The word "rope" has three phonemes /r/, /o/, and /p/. Change one phoneme, say /r/, to /n/, and you have a different word: *nope*.

PHONEMIC AWARENESS- the understanding that words are composed of sounds. Phonemic awareness is a specific type of phonological awareness dealing only with phonemes in a spoken word.

PHONICS- the study of relationships between phonemes (speech sounds) and graphemes (letters) that represent phonemes. It is also decoding or the sounding out of unknown words.

PHONOLOGICAL AWARENESS- the ability to recognize the sounds of spoken language and how they can be blended together, segmented, and switched/manipulated to form new combinations and words.

PHONOLOGICAL CUES- readers use their knowledge of letter/sound and sound/letter relationships to predict and confirm reading.

PHONOLOGY- the study of speech structure in language that includes both the patterns of basic speech units (phonemes) and the tacit rules of pronunciation.

PORTFOLIOS- collections of a child's work over time. They include a cover letter, reflections from the child and teacher, and other supportive documents including standards, performance task examples, prompts and sometimes peer comments.

PRIMARY LANGUAGE (ELL term)- the language in which an individual is most fluent or at ease. This is usually, but not always, the individual's first language.

PROMPTS- when the teacher intervenes in the child's independent reading to help the child pronounce or comprehend a specific word or prompt. On a reading record, the teacher notes the prompt. When the teacher wants to match a child with a particular book or determine the child's stage of reading/level, the teacher does not use prompts.

QUESTION GENERATING STRATEGY FOR AN EXPOSITORY TEXT- first the child previews the text by reading titles, subheads, looking at pictures or illustrations, and reading the first paragraph. Next the child asks a "think" question which he or she records. Then the child reads to find information that might answer the "think" question. The child may write down the information found or think about another question that is answered by what the child is reading. The child continues to read using this strategy.

READING FOR INFORMATION- Reading with the purpose of extracting facts and expert opinion from the text. Children should be introduced to the following information reading resources: web resources that are age and grade appropriate for children, the concept of the table of contents, chapter headings, glossaries, pictures, maps, charts, diagrams and text structures in an information text. They should be taught to use notes, graphs, organizers, and mind maps to share information extracted from a text.

RECODE- To change information from one code into another, as recoding writing into oral speech.

RECOGNITION VOCABULARY- the group of words which children are able to correctly pronounce, read orally and understand on sight.

RECORD OF READING BEHAVIOR – (running record) an objective observation during which the teacher records, using a standard set of symbols, everything the child reader says as the child reads a book selected by the teacher.

REFLECTION- to analyze, discuss, and react to one's learning on any grade or age level.

RETELLING- retelling can be written or oral. Children are expected and encouraged to tell as much of a story as they can remember. Retelling is far more extensive than just summarizing. Children should include the beginning, middle and end plot lines and should be able to tell about the book's characters.

RUBRIC- a set of guidelines or acceptable responses for the completion of any task. Usually a rubric ranges from 0 to 4 with 4 being the most detailed response and 0 indicating a response to the task which lacked detail or was in other ways insufficient.

SCAFFOLDING- refers to the teacher support necessary for the child to accomplish a task or to achieve a goal which the child could not accomplish on his or her own. Vygotsky termed this window of opportunity the "zone of proximal development." Ultimately, as the child becomes more proficient or capable, the scaffold is withdrawn. The goal of scaffolding is to help the child to perform the reading task independently and internalize the behavior. During SHARED READING, the task is scaffolded by the teacher reading to the children aloud. As the teacher reads, he or she scaffolds the initial decoding and helps with the meaning making/construction.

SEARCHING- children pause to search in the picture, print, or their memory for known information. This can happen as the child tackles an unknown word or after an error.

SECOND LANGUAGE (ELL term)- A language acquired or learned simultaneously with or after a child's acquisition of a first language.

SEGMENTING- the process of hearing a spoken word and identifying its separate phonemes or syllables.

SELF-CORRECTION- children begin to correct some of their own reading errors. Generally this behavior is accompanied by the re-reading of the previous phrase or sentence.

SEMANTIC CUES- children use their prior knowledge, sense of the story, and pictures to support their predicting and confirming the meaning of the text.

SEMANTIC WEB- a visual graphic organizer that the teacher can use to introduce a reading on a specific topic. It visually represents many other words associated with a target word. The web can help activate the children's prior knowledge and extend or clarify it. It can also serve to check new learning after guided or independent reading.

SPATIAL LEARNING- Using images, color, or layout to help readers whose learning style is spatial.

STANDARD SCORE- how far a child's grade on a standardized test is from the average score (mean) in terms of the standard deviation. If a child scores 70 on a standardized test and the standard deviation is 5 and the average (mean) score is 65, the child is one standard deviation above the average.

STANDARDIZED TEST- a test given under specified conditions allowing comparisons to be made. A set of norms or average scores on this test will be used for comparisons.

STOP AND THINK STRATEGY- a balanced literacy strategy for constructing meaning. As the text is being read, the child asks himself or herself, does this make sense to me? If it does not make sense to me, I should then try to re-read it or read ahead. I can also look up words that I don't know or ask for help. Generally the teacher models this strategy with the whole class as a mini-lesson and then it is posted prominently in the classroom for continued reference by the children.

STRATEGIC READERS- as defined by researchers Marie Clay and Sharon Taberski, strategic readers are self-improving and do the following as they read:

(A lengthy glossary explanation of this term has been provided because it can appear in a variety of multiple choice questions on the examination as well as part of a constructed response question).

- Monitor their reading to see if it makes sense semantically, syntactically, and visually.
- Look for and use semantic, syntactic, and visual clues.
- Uncover and identify new things about the text.
- Cross check and use one cueing system against another.
- Self-correct reading when what was first read does not match the semantic, syntactic and visual clues
- Solve for and identify new words using multiple cueing systems

Beyond these behaviors, a strategic or self-improving reader uses many strategies to construct meaning. When their reading experience is going well—i.e., they know the words and understand the text or story—they are working continuously (even if they are not conscious of it) at maintaining meaning. If and when the strategic or self-improving reader runs into an unfamiliar word, then the reader has many strategies to identify that word. Becoming a successful strategic reader is a goal that can and should be shared with children as early as the middle of the first grade, although the term "self-improving reader" might be used at that point.

TEXT FEATURES- children need to be alerted to the following text features which may initially appear strange to them. The features of text include a period which marks the end of a "telling sentence"; a question mark at the end of a sentence that asks a question; an exclamation mark used to express surprise or excitement at the end of a sentence; capital letters which begin a sentence and the names of persons, places, and things; bold italicized or underlined text to highlight key ideas; quotation marks which show dialogue, a hyphen used to break up a long word into its syllables; a dash used to show a break in an idea, or to indicate a parenthetical element or an omission; an ellipse, which shows an omission or break in the text; and a paragraph in nonfiction, which shows a new point being made.

TRANSITIONAL READERS- recognize an increasing number of "hard" words that are content-related. They can provide summaries of the stories that they read. They are more at ease with handling longer, more complex, connected text with short chapters. Transitional readers can read independent level texts with correct phrasing, expression, and fluency. When they encounter unfamiliar words, they have a variety of strategies to figure out the unfamiliar words. Their reading demonstrates that they are able to integrate meaning, syntax and phonics in a consistent manner so that they can understand the texts they are reading.

VENN DIAGRAM- a diagram consisting of two or three intersecting circles to visually represent similarities and differences for texts, characters and topics. No author study is complete without VENN DIAGRAMS comparing different author's works. This is the most commonly used graphic organizer in elementary schools today. It can be used effectively as part of an answer to a constructed response question.

VISUAL CUES- readers use their knowledge of graphemes to predict and confirm text. The graphemes may be words, syllables or letters.

WORD ANALYSIS- analysis of words employing letters, phonic structures, contextual clues, or dictionary skills.

WORD IDENTIFICATION- how the reader determines the pronunciation and the meaning of an unknown word.

WORD RECOGNITION- The process of determining the pronunciation and some degree of meaning of an unknown word.

WORD WORK- the term that the balanced literacy approach uses for the study of vocabulary.

Directory of Theorists and Researchers

Introduction

Many questions on the teacher certification examinations can only be correctly answered if you know the theorist or the research that is referenced. The teaching of reading owes much to the work, principles and guidelines of teacher educators and university field researchers who have changed the style, methods and practice of teaching reading. While those listed in this directory are by no means all the major researchers (page constraints would make a complete listing impossible), the individuals listed below are those whose contributions are frequently referenced on the certification tests and whose work is evident in today's elementary classroom teaching and learning of reading.

PHONICS CENTERED APPROACH

In 1955 Rudolph Flesch gained national prominence when he published *Why Johnny Can't Read*. This book went on to become a bestseller and has now become a classic which is readable and speaks to current concerns. Flesch became the spokesperson for a war that periodically resurfaces in the reading world.

Flesch, Chall (1967) Stahl (1992), Adams (1990), and Johnson and Bauman (1984) believe that a phonics-based approach is crucial for reading success. Flesch and others feel that the balanced literacy advocates are seriously undermining the crucial role that phonics plays in children's development as successful decoding readers. However, it must be noted that while balanced literacy does emphasize the use of literature-based reading programs, it in no way dismisses phonics from its reading program; indeed, phonics is included in the crucial "word work" component of the reading and writing workshop.

Phonics advocates point to the fact that most research shows that early and systematic instruction in phonics skills results in superior reading achievement in elementary school and beyond.

Adams (1990) detailed what type of phonics instruction is needed.

To learn to read skillfully, children need practice in seeing and understanding decodable words in real reading situations and with connected text. Phonics instruction needs to be part of a reading program that provides ample practice in reading and writing. Encouraging children with connected text can also show them the importance of what they are learning and make the lessons in phonics relevant and sensible. Phonics-centered advocates believe that children should begin to learn letter associations in kindergarten with most useful phonics skills being taught by first grade. These basic skills should then be reviewed in second grade and beyond.

Consonant sounds should be taught first, since they are more reliable in their letter-sound associations.

Short vowel sounds appear more frequently in beginning reading materials, so they should be introduced before long vowels. Phonics advocates believe that most beginning readers need to be taught letter-sound associations explicitly. Phonics advocates also believe that beginning readers need to read stories that have words to which phonics skills apply. This allows them to practice their phonics skills as they write and spell words. They should also play lots of letter-sound association games.

Phonics advocates claim that when phonics is abandoned reading scores drop and balanced literacy advocates counter with the fact that they have never advocated abandoning the teaching of phonics.

As Jeanne Chall, a professor at Harvard's Graduate School of Education, notes, "a beginning reading program that does not give children knowledge and skill in recognizing and decoding words will have poor results."

Theorists and Researchers

Adams, Marilyn Jager
Noted for her research on early reading, Adams lists five basic types of phonemic awareness tasks which should be covered by the end of first grade. These include ability to hear rhymes and alliterations, ability to do oddity tasks, ability to orally blend words, ability to orally segment words, ability to do phonemic manipulation tasks.

Clay, Marie M.
A New Zealand born researcher in the field of special needs emergent literacy and in the development of assessment tools for these children. Her research in this field is felt throughout the Reading Recovery movement and involves the use of her *Reading Recovery: A Guidebook for Teachers in Training* in the majority of graduate emergent literacy courses and in many classrooms in the US, including those that do not have a Reading Recovery teacher.

Her doctoral thesis focused on what was to become her life's work—emergent reading behavior. At the crux of her research for the dissertation, Clay reviewed and detailed the progress week by week of one hundred children during their first year of school (1966). An important outcome of the dissertation was her development of reliable observation tools for the assessment and analysis of changes over time in children's literacy learning. These assessments are the crux of *An Observation Survey of Early Literacy Achievement* (1993), which is an essential work for the primary school educator. The assessments have been validated and reconstructed for learners from the Spanish, Maori and French languages. A special appendix in this guide includes the *Record of Reading Behavior* tool she created with Kenneth Goodman.

Reading Recovery is a key Clay contribution to the field of foundations of reading teaching. The movement, which is discussed in detail in this section, was born out of the concerns of classroom educators who were upset that even with excellent programs and expert teaching, they were not able to positively influence the literacy progress of some of their young children. Clay posed the idea of investigating what would happen if the design and delivery of traditional reading education were changed for these struggling young learners.

The whole thrust of the Reading Recovery movement has been to improve the early identification and instructional delivery for these struggling young readers. Her goal was to develop a system which would bring those children scoring the lowest in assessment measures to the level of the average readers within their classes.

With the support of Barbara Watson and others, the program was developed in three years. The first field tests of the program took place in the late 1970s in Auckland schools. To date, circa 2005, the program is operating in most English-speaking countries and has been reconstructed for use in Spanish and French.

Janet S. Gaffey and Billie Askew have said of Marie Clay (1991) that her contribution "has been to change what is possible for individual learners when teaching permits different routes to be taken for desired outcomes."

Reading Recovery has been identified by the International Reading Association as a program that not only teaches children how to read, but also reduces the number of children who are labeled as "learning disabled." It further lowers the number of children who are placed in remedial reading programs and classes.

Clay Reading Recovery lessons are designed to promote accelerated learning so that children can catch up to their peers and continue to learn independently.

The hallmark of the Reading Recovery program is that the Reading Recovery teacher works with one student at a time over a 12- to 20-week period. Each daily 30-minute lesson is tailored to address the needs of the individual student. Therefore, Reading Recovery teachers generally teach no more than four or five students per day in individual lessons.

The Clay Observation of Early Childhood Achievement (1993) is used to assess children's strengths and weaknesses. Reading Recovery teachers devote the first ten minutes of their sessions with individual children to assessment as the children engage in reading and writing. A running record of the child's progress is taken every day and is used to plan future lessons.

The lessons themselves include the use of familiar stories. Children engage in assembling and in sequencing cut-up stories. They work with letters or write a story. Teaching style involves the teacher demonstrating strategies and the child then developing effective strategies to continue reading independently. Key components of each lesson include phonemic awareness, phonics, spelling, and comprehension study. Much time is devoted to problem solving so that the children's decoding is purposeful. Children are given time to practice and demonstrate fluency skills.

Ultimately, what sets Reading Recovery apart is the fact that it is one-to-one tutoring. This is also what makes it effective for children and, of course, raises the issue of costs for the school systems which may want to adopt it. Obviously, districts and education systems have to decide whether they want to pay the costs of this and other individualized tutoring systems now in the primary school years or pay later as these children become adults whose literacy skills are not sufficient for proactive citizenship.

Fountas, Irene C. and Gay Su Pinnell
These two researchers have developed a leveling system for reading texts which arranges them by level of difficulty. Beyond a specific analysis of set titles, the theorists have explained in several published works how to use their leveling system to meet and assess the progress of various readers. They also provide detailed explanations and support for reading teachers of young children K-3 in using reading records and benchmark texts.

They are the key articulators of the balanced literacy model that includes reading and writing workshop. Among their other contributions to the field are guidelines for creating sets of leveled books, assessment rubrics, strategies for fostering "word solver" skills in child readers, and methods for teaching phonics and spelling in the literacy classroom.

Routman, Regie
Routman's contributions to Reading Foundations are the result of over three decades of experience as an elementary school teacher, a reading specialist, a learning disabilities tutor, a Reading Recovery teacher, a language arts and mentor teacher and a staff developer. Due to these various experiences, her insights into reading resonate with a broad spectrum of school community members.

Routman's works are conversational, teacher-to-teacher sharings of her daily experiences in classrooms. In her published books on the teaching of reading (e.g. *Reading Essentials*, Heinemann, 2002), Routman shows teachers how to teach consistent with the findings in reading research, yet also with highly practical "scripted lessons" and teaching tips which make the classroom come alive. She advocates literature-based teaching and meaning-centered approaches for learning.

In addition, she is a strong advocate of using poetry from Grade 1 and beyond as an integral thread for a reading program. She is the author of *Kids' Poems: Teaching Children to Love Writing Poetry* (Scholastic, 2000) which includes separate volumes of poetry for Grades K-4.

Routman believes in teaching reading to meet specific children's needs regardless of the particular reading program in place. She is a strong advocate for the use of small guided reading groups and reading for understanding. Phonics and other word analysis strategies are part of her reading framework, but not at its core. Her focus for the reading classroom is on the development and use of the classroom library as the center for an independent reading program, shared reading and reading aloud.

Routman has designed informal reading evaluations on books/texts her students are reading (her published works are known for their appendices replete with templates for evaluations, projects, reports, book lists, suggested texts by topics, etc.). Her classroom model includes matching children with specific library books as well as linking assessment with instruction. Finally, she is a researcher who sees reading as intimately linked to writing.

Routman is also involved with the politics of literacy. This vision of literacy involves the image of the teacher as an informed professional who regularly reads the latest professional books, collaborates with colleagues in school and beyond, and deals with the most recent research developments. Interestingly, Routman is one researcher who also feels that an informed professional can and should know when to question research. Other aspects of the politics of literacy as Routman conceptualizes them are communicating effectively with parents and dealing with testing and standards mandates.

Two of her published works, *Conversations: Strategies for Teaching, Learning, and Evaluating* (Heinemann, 2000) and *Invitations: Changing as Teachers and Learners K-12* (Heinemann, 1991 and 1994), are essential for the elementary reading teacher's bookshelf and can take the teacher through several years of work.

Taberski, Sharon

Taberski is an experienced elementary teacher educator who is also a member of the Primary Literacy Standards Committee run by the National Center on Education and the Economy and the University of Pittsburgh. Her works in the field are served up as wonderfully accessible and necessary advice from "the veteran teacher across the hall" who loves her students and is delighted to help a new colleague.

Unlike many theorists in the field of reading, Taberski's work is not focused around a prescribed set of skills, but rather around a series of interconnected interactions with the learner.

These interactions, which are detailed and clearly communicated in her book *On Solid Ground* (Heinemann, 2000), include the following:

- Assessment- Procedures for assessing children's reading and to inform teaching, scheduling and managing reading conferences, taking oral reading records, and using retellings as discussion tools.
- Demonstration- Taberski developed and field tested strategies for using shared reading and read-alouds as platforms for figuring out words and comprehending texts. She is a strong advocate of small group work- guided reading, word-study groups and teaching children one-on-one.
- Practice- In the Taberski framework, independent reading is used as a time for practice. Students play key roles in this practice and Taberski has a set of detailed and easily adaptable guidelines for matching children with books for independent reading. Her work includes booklists and ready to use information that is available for reproduction.
- Response- It's important for students to know that they are doing well and where they must focus their efforts to improve skills. Taberski explains how her students use writing and dialogue as tools for independent reading.

Vail, Priscilla

Noted for her research in the study of dyslexia and its myths, Vail has articulated ways in which children can develop their reading skills as they cope with this disorder and techniques parents and educators can use to support reading development. She has also worked on specific test-taking skills for children coping with dyslexia and other special needs. Her strategies can be included in the regular education program to enhance all students' reading achievement schools. She is a proponent of phonics instruction and skills within the context of an integrated whole language approach (once called integrated language arts).

Another focus of Vail's research is the link between language and thinking. She is concerned with how a child's receptive language, expressive language and meta-cognition can be fostered. She has developed assessment methods for each of these capacities and activities to help strengthen them in children Grades K-4.

TEACHER CERTIFICATION STUDY GUIDE

BIBLIOGRAPHY OF PRINT RESOURCES

PROFESSIONAL BOOKS

Adams, M. (1990). *Beginning to Read: Thinking and Learning about Print.* Cambridge, MA: MIT Press.

Anders, P., & Bos, C. (l986). Semantic Feature Analysis: An Interactive Strategy for Vocabulary Development and Reading Comprehension, *Journal of Reading*, 29, 610-616.

Blevins, W. (l997). *Phonemic Awareness Activities for Early Reading Success.* New York: Scholastic.

Boyd-Bastone, P. (2004). Focused Anecdotal Record Assessment (ARA): A Tool for Standards Based Authentic Assessment. *Reading Teacher, 58* (3), pp. 230-239.

Calkins, Lucy McCormick. (2001). *The Art of Teaching Reading.* New York: Longman.
   Beautifully explains the reading workshop and its relationship to the writing workshop and includes wonderful snapshots of mini-lessons, conferring, conferencing, independent reading, guided reading, book talks, prompts, coaching, and classroom library use. Exceedingly readable and direct.

Campbell, Robin. (2004). *Reading and Writing for Real Purposes.* Portsmouth, NH: Heinemann.
   This work focuses on how children who deftly absorb and interconnect symbols and sounds of their universes can be supported in K-1 classes to extend this ability into phonics learning. Campbell demonstrates how immersion in a highly literate classroom filled with print and language stimuli allows kids to build accurate letter-sound relationships. The book provides a framework for teaching phonics using proven field-tested Campbell strategies.

   Among these strategies are early mark-making, read-alouds, playing with language in rhyme and song, writing and reading in a variety of genres, exploring environmental and classroom print, and using students' own names. Samples of student work are included.

Chancey, C. (l994). Language development, metalinguistic awareness, and emergent literacy skills of 3-year-old children in relation to social class. *Applied Psycholinguistics*, 15, 371-394.

Clay, Marie M. (1993). *An Observation Survey of Early Literacy Achievement.* Portsmouth, NH: Heinemann.

Clay, Marie M. (1993). *Reading Recovery: A Guidebook for Teachers in Training.* Portsmouth, NH: Heinemann.

Cooper, J. David. (2004). *Literacy: Helping Children Construct Meaning.* Boston, MA: Houghton Mifflin. (5th Edition).
This book explains the balanced literacy approach to the teaching of reading and writing using numerous charts, tables, templates, and excerpts from actual texts. It offers the new teacher exact schedules, strategies, guidelines, assessment tools, bibliographies, research, and even scripts for conferring with children.

Cooper is a clear and crisp writer who does not overwhelm the reader, but rather engages her. Even veteran teachers would return again and again to this text for support and refreshing insights.

Cox, Carole. (2005). *Teaching Language Arts.* Boston, MA: Pearson.
A compendium of state of the art lesson plans, web resources, online case studies, teaching ideas and extensive templates. All of these materials are aligned to the balanced literacy reading and writing workshop model.

The book also includes teaching ideas for the ELL reader, children with learning disabilities, and speakers of non- standard dialects. The book also features snapshots of second language learners as well as bi-literacy web resources.

Cullinan, Bernice E. (1998). *Three Voices: An Invitation to Poetry Across the Curriculum.* New York: Stenhouse. K-6 and beyond.
Two classroom educators and a noted researcher in children's literature demonstrate how poetry can be used in the classroom to teach various aspects of reading and to nurture lifelong literacy. Includes 33 grade- and age-appropriate strategies which have been field tested in classrooms across the country.

Ezell, H. K., & Justice, L. M. (2000). Increasing the Print Focus of Adult -Child Shared Book Reading through Observational Learning. *American Journal of Speech Pathology*, 9, 36-37.

Flesch, Rudolf. (1985). *Why Johnny Can't Read.* New York: Harper and Row.

Fountas, Irene C., & Gay Su Pinnell. (2001). *Guiding Readers and Writers 3-6.* Portsmouth, NH: Heinemann.
This work includes 1000 leveled books with guidelines for using them as part of a reading and writing workshop. The book explains how to use various genres in the classroom and how to use visual graphic organizers for the teaching of reading and writing.

Fountas, Irene. C., & Gay Su Pinnell. (1999). *Matching Books to Readers Using Leveled Books in Guided Reading K-3.* Portsmouth, NH: Heinemann.
> This major contribution to the field has a list of 7,500 grade- and age-appropriate books. In addition, the authors include word counts to be used for keeping running records, text characteristics, guidelines for leveling of additional books and suggestions for developing classroom library collections.

> Other works by these researchers also published by Heinemann include *Voices on Word Matters: Learning about Phonics and Spelling in the Literacy Classroom* (1999) and *Word Matters: Teaching Phonics and Spelling in the Reading/Writing Classroom* (1998).

Fry, Edward Bernard, Kress, Jacqueline, Fountakidis, Dona Lee. (2000). *The Reading Teacher's Book of Lists.* San Francisco, CA: Wiley Press.
> This book is an invaluable one for the working classroom educator. It includes ready to use lists that cover a multiplicity of teacher needs. Among them are spelling demons, readability graphs, phonics, useful words, reading math, vowel lists, anagrams, portmanteaus (do you know what they are and how well they can work in word study?), websites, classic children's literature, etc. Even a veteran teacher educator will find useful and new resources. Also wonderful for developing independent word study investigations and literature explorations.

Ganske, Kathy. (2000). *Word Journeys: Assessment-Guided Phonics, Spelling, and Vocabulary Instruction.* New York, NY: Guilford Press.
> This book offers a practical approach for assessing children's spelling. The author has created a DSA (Development Spelling Analysis) tool which teachers can use to evaluate individual children's spelling progress and to differentiate instruction. The book includes snapshots of children at different levels of spelling development.

Hall, Susan. (1994). *Using Picture Books to Teach Literary Devices.* Westport, CT: Oryx Press.

How to Help Every Child Become a Reader. Just Publishing. K-6 and beyond.
> This accessible text draws on materials developed by the US Department of Education to share research, resources, referrals and suggestions for supporting all children to become lifelong and engaged readers. It offers specific suggestions and resources for assisting struggling readers, including those with special needs and those from ELL backgrounds.

Labov, L. (2003). When Ordinary Children Fail to Read. *Reading Research Quarterly*, 38, 128-31.

Macmillan, B. M. (2002). Rhyme and Reading. A Critical Review of the Research Methodology. *Journal of Research in Reading,* 25(1), 4-42.

Makor, Barbara. *Primary Phonics Readers.*
    Short storybooks that K-2 can own and read independently.
They feature phonetically controlled texts, sounds and spellings that are grade- and age-appropriate and have high interest child-centered themes. As children progress through the series of 20 titles, they review and enhance their mastery of phonetic elements, sight words, and sequences at a more rapid pace. This material is compatible with the majority of phonics programs.

Munro, J. (1998). Phonological and Phonemic Awareness: Their Impact on Learning to Read Prose and Spell. *Australian Journal of Learning Disabilities*, 3, 2, 15-21.
    Paperback Nursery Rhyme Sampler, Whispering Coyote Press. Essential for a Pre-K-1 classroom and useful even in Grades 1 and 2; these classic nursery rhymes promote phonemic and phonological awareness and children's ownership of their reading through song and movement.

Routman, Regie. (2000). *Conversations: Strategies for Teaching, Learning, and Evaluating.* Portsmouth, NH: Heinemann.

Routman, Regie. (1994). *Invitations: Changing as Teachers and Learners K-12.* Portsmouth, NH. Heinemann.

Routman, Regie. (1996). *Literacy at the Crossroads: Crucial Talk About Reading, Writing, and Other Teaching Dilemmas.* Portsmouth, NH: Heinemann.

Routman, Regie. (2002). *Reading Essentials.* Portsmouth, NH: Heinemann.

Statman, Ann. *Handprints:Leveled Storybooks for Early Readers Educators Publishing Service*, Grades K-2.
    These 50 titles which come with five teachers' guides were leveled using the Fountas and Pinnell Guided Reading Leveling System. The stories reflect real world situations and people young readers know. They include sentence structure and pictures and cues that focus strategic reading. Print size, sentence positioning, and word spacing is appropriate for the level of the particular storybook. The titles build a strong sight vocabulary through the use of high frequency words. Language used within the series progresses from natural to formal book language.

Schumm, Heanne Shay. *The Reading Tutor's Handbook*. Free Spirit. K-6 and beyond.
> This guide offers step-by-step instructions, templates and handouts for providing children with differentiated reading support. It is not only helpful for teachers, but also can be shared with paraprofessionals, teachers, interns, and parents as a support framework for the classroom reading program.

Taberski, Sharon. (2000). *On Solid Ground: Creating a Literacy Environment in Your K-3 Classroom*. Portsmouth, NH: Heinemann.

Terban, Marvin. *Time to Rhyme: A Rhyming Dictionary*. Boyd Mills Press. Grades 1-3.
> This book is easily enough formatted so that it can be used to introduce children in the early elementary grades to the use of a rhyming dictionary as a reference tool. Its simple word groupings encourage writing which can also reinforce and reciprocally enhance reading skills through the reading and writing workshop.

Vail, Patricia. *Reading Comprehension: Students Needs and Teacher's Tools*. Educators Publishers Service. K-6 and beyond.
> This is a compendium of explanations of specific instructional practices, terms, student projects, learning games and resources which are critical for successfully teaching reading.

ALPHABET BOOKS

A major genre of fiction and non-fiction for the teacher of reading is the alphabet book. These books' appeal, concepts, and efficiency as models for reading and writing merit them a special section in this bibliography. Even those whose text is simple enough for Pre-K-2 can serve as anchor books and models for writing workshop in Grades 3-6.

Aigner-Clark, Julie. (2002). *Baby Einstein: The ABCs of Art*. Illustrations by Nadeen Zaidi. New York: Hyperion Books.

Beaton, Clare. *Zoe and Her Zebra*. Barefoot Books. Pre-K-1.
> This board book features a character young children can identify with named Zoe. Her adventures are told in a simple, repetitive text with a soft, literally "touchy," felt art.

Bunting, Eve. *Girls A to Z*. Boyd Mills Press. Pre-K-1.
> This book uses the alphabetic format to promote the opportunity for girls to select various professions and careers ranging from astronaut to zookeeper. Bunting's text is breezy and rhymes.

Cheney, Lynne. (2002). *America: A Patriotic Primer.* New York: Simon and Schuster Books. Illustrated by Robin Priess Glasser.

Cheney, Lynne. *A Is For Abigail: An Almanac of Amazing American Women.* New York: Simon and Schuster Books. Ages 4-8.

Glaser, Milton. (2003). *The Alphazeds.* Miramax. Ages 4-8.

Grimes, Nikki. *C is for City.* Illustrated by Pat Cummings. Boyd Mill Press. K-3.
    This alphabet rhyme book doubles as a guide to city activities. With its built-in invitations to readers to search for alphabetical items, it is perfect for use as an informal assessment tool or an interactive/paired reading anchor text.

Inkpen, Mick. (2000). *Kipper's A to Z.* San Diego: Harcourt. Ages 3-7.

Isadora, Rachel. (1999). *ABC Pops! (Picture Books).* Disney Press. Ages 4-8.

Johnson, Stephen. (1995). *Alphabet City.* Penguin Books. All ages.

Kelley, Marty. *Summer Stinks.* Zino Press. Pre-K-1.
    This work describes the summer season in terms of things which "stink" about it, including ants, bugs, and sweat. Fun to read and add to as the alphabet letters are learned and vocabulary is built up.

Martin, Mary Jane. *From Anne to Zach.* Boyd Mills Press.
    In this captivating book which can serve as a touchstone text for model collaborative authoring, children learn the letters of the alphabet through other children's names.

Melmed, Laura Krauss and Frane, Lesser. (2003) *Capital! Washington DC from A to Z.* New York: Harper Collins.

Musgrove, Margaret. (1976). Illustrated by Leo and Diane Dillon. *Ashanti to Zulu: African Traditions.* New York: Dial Books for Young Readers.
    This is a Caldecott-winning book which uses the alphabetic format for a richly detailed and researched study of 26 African Peoples. It includes a map and pronunciation guide and illustrations that were researched in the Schomberg Center and the American Museum of Natural History. Even the frame design for each illustration reflects the African Kano knot which signifies endless searching.

Paratore, Colleen. *26 Big Things Hands Do*. Minneapolis, MN: Free Spirit.
   What is delightful about this alphabet book is that it presents the alphabet letters as positive actions children can perform with their own small hands to help others. These actions include applauding, giving gifts, planting, and volunteering. Of course, alphabet study can continue with adding other "helping actions" to the word wall or substituting them in the text.

Pelham, David, (1991). *A Is for Animals*. New York: Simon and Schuster

Seeley, Lorna. *The Book of Shadow Boxes*. Peachtree.
   Within the shadow of each letter's shadow box lies a hidden treasure for the young reader to find. The book is intricately and exquisitely designed and conceptualized by Ms. Seeley. Its visual fascination extends well beyond the elementary grades as it fosters not only the alphabetic principle, but also reading comprehension and literacy response.

Sneed, Brad. (2002). *Picture a Letter*. New York: Penguin Books.

Seuss. *ABC*. Random House. Ages 2-up.

Thornhill, Jim. *The Wildlife ABC and 123: A Nature Alphabet and Counting Book*. Maple Tree Press. K-1 with additional nature notes on the species for the teacher/parent.
   In addition to fostering the alphabetic principle, the book nicely mixes geographic, multicultural, and scientific knowledge into a beautifully designed text. It uses children's fascination with nature to foster reading and math literacy.

Zschock, Martha and Heather. (2002). *Journey Around New York from A to Z*. Beverly Mass: Commonwealth Editions

Zschock, Martha. (2001). *Journey Around Boston from A to Z*. Beverly Mass: Commonwealth Editions.

TRADE BOOKS

These books foster particular aspects of reading skills, fluencies and competencies.

Blackstone, Stella. *Where's the Cat?* Barefoot Books. Pre-K.
   Focuses its primary school readers on searching for a lost cat and provides excellent use of repetitive language while encouraging interactive reading.

Campbell, Bebe Moore. (2003). *Sometimes My Mommy Gets Angry.* New York, New York: G. P. Putnam's Sons.

This is a moving story about a young girl whose mother suffers from mental illness. It is told in a way that is easy to read, along with beautiful illustrations. The main character is Annie. Sometimes her mother is very happy and other times very angry and sad. Annie has learned what to do when her mom is having a bad episode. She has books to read, a special stuffed animal and some secret snacks. Annie also has a strong support system in place with friends, neighbors, her teacher and grandmother. This book is a good introduction to the issue of mental illness. It is especially important in that students see how a young girl is able to cope with this difficult part of her life. "Sometimes by mommy has a dark cloud inside of her. I can't stop the rain from falling, but I can find sunshine in my mind."

Teachers can introduce students to a complicated issue with this poignant book. Students can brainstorm different scenarios and discuss how they can be resolved. They can discuss who their support network includes and what it takes for a person to be strong enough to weather such a storm.

The book is a much needed resource for children in times in which Annie's situation is far more common than is generally known. Annie's capacity to make effective, affirming social decisions makes the work an inspirational touchstone for other peers who need to confront their parents' emotional crises. Children might be inspired to author poetry or create deliberately fictionalized narrative accounts about how they have confronted various crises.

In offering an upper elementary grade- and age-appropriate narrative of a peer dealing with an emotionally ill parent, this book provides readers confronting similar family and caregiver issues with an opening for discussion and for hopeful outreach. Just reading this account may well be the first step necessary to assist a youngster in acknowledging a "hidden problem" and getting crucial adult assistance in dealing with the crisis.

Garza, Carmen Lomas. (1990). *Family Pictures/Cuadros de familia*. Children's Book Press.

This book tells the story of the author growing up in a Hispanic community in Texas. The book is written in both Spanish and English, accompanied by the author's incredible paintings. The paintings are unique, somewhat folksy, colorful, and totally entrancing. They bring you into Carmen's world. Once inside it, you don't want to leave.

There is so much to explore in this book; it works well with the study of "myself and family," community, communities around the world, Mexico, family traditions and customs. It emphasizes social and emotional learning and how a young girl can find her way in the world. The traditions followed by her community and family are not necessarily accepted or understood by white America. Yet these values give her the strength to be her own person and to rely on both her relationships and rich inner life to express herself.

There are so many activities that this book inspires. Children can study the origins of the piñata and then make one. They can make a cookbook of recipes from Mexico or from their own homes. Children can also be encouraged to design their own book of family pictures. They can emphasize special occasions that they celebrate or focus on family traditions which reflect their cultural backgrounds. The richness and lushness of the paintings invites the readers to construct meaning and to create their own narratives, procedural accounts, poetry, and dialogues inspired by one or more of the paintings.

Picture-walk through the illustrations. Given the Spanish/English text, this strategy can be an engaging spatial entry point for descriptive and narrative spoken and written presentations. The lushly detailed illustrations of family rites and celebrations can be springboards for children's literary and artistic renditions of equivalent family pictures and events which are prompted by Carmen's selections.

Use of dual language text for the book validates children's and family member's responses in languages other than English. Obviously, this book and its format are inspirational for ELL/Bilingual learners and for special needs learners who can be captivated by the paintings.

The power of this book lies in its accessing and modeling the magic of family rites and rituals for a broad spectrum of linguistics, intrapersonal, spatial, and kinesthetic learners from monolingual, bilingual and special needs backgrounds. Common to all of its audience members are the social and emotionally celebratory components of family pictures.

Glaser, Shirley, & Glaser, Milton. (2003). *The Alphazeds Words*. Hyperion Books.

This book is incredible in so many ways! It is an alphabet book that can be read by or to little ones and not so little ones. It starts with an empty room. One by one, each letter of the alphabet enters the room, each with its own distinct look and fantastic illustrations and typography by the designer Milton Glaser. Each of these letters also has its own distinct personality. A is angry, B is bashful, J is jealous, and so on. The room gets quite crowded. How do all of these different personalities manage to get along and coexist? Not too well, apparently, as there is shouting, pushing, hitting and kicking. In the midst of all the chaos, the light in the room goes out and there is silence.

> "When the light came back on, something extraordinary had happened. Four letters had gotten together to comfort one another. Together they had managed to create something larger and more important than themselves.
> *"They had made the first word."*

This is a great lesson on how each of us can be an individual, yet when we work together, something wonderful can happen. This book illustrates an incredible lesson in social and emotional maturity, and helps the child realize that it isn't just about "me."

There are many different activities that a teacher can use with this book. The children can work in groups to make their own alphabet book of emotions. They can then present the book as a group, discussing the roles each of them played, and how they each used their unique talents to make the book.

Older children Grades 3 and up can research and present as a group some important discoveries that were made more special because they involved people working together. They can also work on a project about cooperative learning, perhaps surveying class and schoolmates on how they feel they learn the best.

Hest, Amy. (1985). *The Purple Coat*. New York: Macmillan Publishing Co.

In the autumn of every year, Gabrielle travels with her mother to New York City to visit her Grandpa who owns a tailor shop. Once there, he always makes her a new coat, but this year Gabrielle decides the usual navy blue coat won't do. The Purple Coat follows Gabrielle in her attempt to establish her own identity.

Lionni, Leo. (1980). *Inch by Inch*. Astor-Honor Publishing Co., Inc.

In *Inch by Inch*, an inchworm (a caterpillar, or larval stage, of the fall cankerworm, which becomes a moth) keeps itself from being eaten by various birds by proving its worth as a measuring device.

Lupton, Hugh. *The Story Tree: Tales to Read Aloud.* Barefoot Books. K-3
These seven multicultural stories are accessible enough to children to encourage their eventually taking over the read-aloud sharing on their own. This book is also a good one for family literacy sessions and for parent volunteers to read aloud in the classroom.

Martin Jr., Bill, & John Archambault. (1966). *Knots on a Counting Rope.* New York, New York: Henry Holt and Company.

This beautifully illustrated book reaches out in so many different directions and we can all learn so much from it. Knots on a Counting Rope is the story of a Native American boy who is blind and is learning from his grandfather how to survive in this world. Boy-Strength-of-Blue-Horses insists on hearing the story of his birth over and over again.

Every time his grandfather retells the story of the boy's birth, he adds a knot to his counting rope. Each time he hears the story, Boy-Strength-of-Blue-Horses gains more confidence in himself. The story emphasizes the Native-American tradition of storytelling and there are numerous art, math and social studies lessons that could be offshoots from this book.

The telling and retelling of the story celebrate the young blind hero's strengths and weaknesses and ability to set goals with optimism. Stories of one's birth related by others are powerful demonstrations of social skills of the highest order.

This book also deals extensively with social and emotional learning. Children learn that those with disabilities need to be treated with sensitivity while learning to find their place in the world. One way in which children's social and emotional learning is strengthened is by understanding themselves and those around them. In order to facilitate this, each child could interview at least one family member about when he or she was born. The accounts collected with appropriate photos or memorabilia can then be shared in class and perhaps even authored into a *Knots on a Counting Rope* style book format.

Children can also retell the story of the boy using the counting system of cultures other than Native American. This literary response will incorporate cultural study, respect and empathy into ongoing reading and writing workshop efforts.

McCully, Emily Arnold. (1992). *Mirette on the High Wire*. G.P. Putnam's & Sons.

Mirette helps her mother run a boardinghouse for acrobats, jugglers, actors and mimes. Her life changes when she discovers a boarder crossing the courtyard on air. She begs him to teach her how he does it. He refuses to teach her, but she begins practicing on her own. As she improves, he begins to help her. In the end she helps him overcome his fear of the high wire.

Rabe, Bernice. (1981). *The Balancing Girl*. E.P. Dutton.

Margaret, a girl who uses a wheelchair, is excellent at balancing all kinds of objects. Margaret shows her friend Tommy how good she is at balancing at the school carnival.

Ringgold, Faith. (1991). *Tar Beach*. New York, New York: Crown Publishers.

This book is one of my favorites and it is moving in its words, art, and the beautiful story it tells. This is an effective book to use for younger grades to connect with myself, my family and my community. It can also be used in connection with a mapmaking unit. The children can be encouraged to make a map of their neighborhood from an aerial view.

A starting point for a discussion would be why the author portrayed New York from such a vantage point. In this beautiful book, the narrator, Cassie Louise Lightfoot, lets her dreams and ambitions take her to places in New York City that she ordinarily would not be able to be part of because of her circumstances. As a result of her self-motivation and self-awareness, Cassie is able to go as far as her dreams will let her. In this book Cassie also shows strengths in the areas of emotional sensitivity as well as inter- and intra-personal relationships.

Children can author their own Tar Beach equivalent night fantasies and then share them with one another through an exhibit or Big Books. Although Cassie's family is obviously poor (since they have to picnic on their roof), Cassie's dreamlike, lushly illustrated flight over Harlem validates the beauty of their family life and of the city landscape which is accessible to all. This is an invaluable lesson in the importance of the wealth inherent in the appreciation of family connections and the beauty of nature and public architectural designs. A song of family and of the city!

Schories, Pat. *Breakfast for Jack/Jack and the Missing Piece*. Front Street.

> These wordless stories help pre-literate children, ELL learners new to this country and special needs children explore the basic elements of story-character, setting and plot. The lack of words allows the children to construct their own meaning and create their own different stories which "fit" the illustrations.

Steinberg, Laya. *Thesaurus Rex*. Barefoot Books.

> This book introduces a dinosaur with an interest in words whose story is told through a wonderful rhyming text which can be used for fostering phonemic awareness and for choral readings.

Uhlberg, Myron. *The Printer*. Peachtree.

> This story celebrates the conventions of print in that the boy narrator's father is a deaf man who speaks with his hands and as a job chooses to turn lead-type letters into words and sentences. An excellent book to support family literacy and an appreciation for the conventions of print.

Van Allsburg, Chris. (1988). *Two Bad Ants*. Houghton Mifflin Co.

> In *Two Bad Ants*, news comes to the ant world of a great discovery in a faraway place. A delicious crystal has been found. A group of ants set out to bring back this crystal to their queen. Two ants are overwhelmed by the treasure and stay behind in this dangerous alien world. It is a tale of choices, consequences and the discovery of life's real treasures.

Walter, Mildred Pitts. (2004). Illustrated by Larry Johnson. *Alec's Primer*. Lebanon, NH: University Press of New England.

> This is the true account of a Virginian slave who was taught to read by his owner's daughter. He later fought in the Civil War on the Union side and became a landowner himself in Vermont. The beautifully written narrative is complemented by the vibrant paintings of Larry Johnson, which include authentic period details.

Webliography

Reading Online
http://www.readingonline.org
This online web resource which is sponsored by the International Reading Association is full of specific reading teaching ideas, lessons and new research. It includes summaries of conference presentations and even tips on how to use technology to teach reading.

Balanced Literacy
http://www.thekcrew.net/balancedliteracy.html
Established in 1996, this site is organized according to the components of the balanced literacy approach. It also has an excellent listing of professional books that can assist with various aspects of teaching reading.

Carol Hurst
http://www.carolhurst.com/index.html
This is a terrific resource for exploring the children's literature works which are at the crux of author and genre study. It can be used for material to supplement period studies and discussions of authors' lives. Older children will be able to explore it on their own.

Read, Write, Think
http://www.readwritethink.org/lessons/
This resource maintained by the National Council of Teachers of English (NCTE), has a growing database of age- and grade-specific literacy lesson plans. It also includes all the graphic organizers cited in this book and many more, ready to download.

Inspiration Software
http://www.inspiration.com
http://www.inspiration.com/freetrial/index.cfm
This is the home site for the Inspiration and Kidspiration mind mapping software. These online templates and capacities assist the reading teacher with customizing the various graphic organizers discussed throughout the book and with gaining the ability to design customized graphic organizers for a particular theme, study or student group. A free trial version of this child-friendly resource can be downloaded.

Visual Thesaurus
http://www.visualthesaurus.com/online/
This is really both an online dictionary and a thesaurus.

Resources for Read Aloud, Shared Reading, and Independent Reading available on the Internet include the following:

http:// www.mightybook.com/library_4to6.htm.
This is a library of books read aloud by the computer. Children can listen to these books or practice reading with a buddy as the computer broadcasts the text. Of course, this type of read-aloud would only be used in addition to the vibrant read-aloud of the teacher.

http://www.enchantedlearning.com/Rhymes.html
These are online nursery rhymes ready for reading to children and posting throughout for room or for literacy center display.

SEDL-RCI Framework of Reading
http://www.sedl.org/reading/framework/assessment.html
This is an excellent resource for readings in the theories and methods of foundations. There are topic-aligned links to specific theorists which can be included at the close of your lesson planning and may be reviewed before certification tests.

TEACHER CERTIFICATION STUDY GUIDE

TOOLS TO HELP YOU TEACH THE FOUNDATIONS OF READING AND FOR SUCCEEDING IN CONSTRUCTED-RESPONSE CERTIFICATION EXAMINATIONS

Appendix One: The Record of Reading Behavior. A close-up look at a key assessment tool.

Often in the constructed-response question on a foundations of education certification test or on a general elementary certification test the educator is asked to analyze a record of reading behavior or to construct an appropriate one from data given in an anecdote. In the current climate of accountability, it is a good idea for new teachers and for career changers to examine closely the basic elements of recording reading behavior.

While there are various acceptable formats for emergent literacy assessment used throughout the country, the one selected for use here is based on the work of Marie Clay and Kenneth Goodman. These two are key researchers in the close observation and documentation of children's early reading miscues (reading mistakes).

It is important to emphasize that the teacher should not just take a Record of Reading Behavior and begin filling it out as the child reads from a random book prior to beginning observation. There are specific steps for taking the record and analyzing its results.

Select a text
If you want to see if the child is reading on the instructional level, choose a book that the child has already read. If the purpose of the test is to see whether the child is ready to advance to the next level, choose a book from that level which the child has not yet seen.

Introduce the text
If the book is one that has been read, you do not need to introduce the text other than by saying the title. But if the book is new to the child, you should briefly share the title and tell the child a bit about the plot and style of the book.

Take the record
Generally, with emergent readers' Grades 1-2, there are only 100-150 words in a passage used to take a record. Make certain that the child is seated beside you, so that you can see the text as the child reads it.

If desired, you may want to photocopy the text in advance for yourself, so you can make direct notations on your text while the child reads from the book. After you introduce the text make certain that the child has the chance to read the text independently. Be certain that you do not "teach" or help the child with the text other than to supply an unknown word that the child requests you supply. The purpose of the record is to see what the child does on his or her own. As the child reads the text, you must be certain to record the reading behaviors the child exhibits using the following notations.

Allow enough time for the child to work independently on a problem before telling or supplying the word. If you wait too long, you could run the risk of having the child lose the meaning and his or her interest in the story as he or she tries to identify the unknown word.

It is recommended that when a child is way off track, you tell him or her to "Try that again" (TTA). If a whole phrase is troubling, note it in square brackets and score it as only one error.

The notation for filling out the Record of Reading behavior involves noting the child's response with the actual text below it.

Comprehension Check
This can and should be done by inviting the child to retell the story. This retelling can then be used to ask further questions about characters, plot, setting and purpose which allow you to observe and to record the child's level of comprehension.

Calculating Reading Level and Self-correction Rate

Calculating the reading level lets you know if the book is at the level on which the child can read it independently or comfortably with guidance or if the book is at a level where reading it frustrates the child.

Generally, an accuracy score of 95-100% suggests that the child can read the text and other books or texts on the same level.

An accuracy score of 90-94% indicates that the text and texts likely will present challenges to the child, but with guidance from you, a tutor or parent, the child will be able to master these texts and enjoy them. This is instructional level.

However, an accuracy score of less than 89% tells you that the material you have selected is too hard for the child to control alone. Such material needs to be introduced to the child in a shared reading situation or read to the child.

KEEPING SCORE ON THE RECORD

Insertions, omissions, substitutions, and teacher-told responses all count as errors. Repetitions are not scored as errors. Corrected responses are scored as self-corrections.

No penalty is given for a child's attempts at self-correction that results in a finally incorrect response but the attempts should be noted. Multiple unsuccessful attempts at a word are scored as one error only.

The lowest score for any page is zero. If a child omits a line or lines, each word omitted is counted as an error. If the child omits a page, deduct the number of words omitted from the total number of words which you have used for the record.

Calculating the Reading Level

Note the number of errors made on each line on the Record of Reading Behavior in the column marked E (Error).

Total the number of errors in the text and divide this number into the number of words that the child has read. This will give you the error rate.

If a child read a passage of 100 words and made 10 errors, the error rate would be 1 in 10. Convert this to an accuracy percentage, or 90%.

Calculating the Self-Correction Rate

Total all the self-corrections. Then add the number of errors to the number of self-corrections and divide by the number of self-corrections.

A self-correction rate of 1 in 3 to 1 in 5 is considered good. This rate indicates that the child is able to help himself or herself as problems are encountered in reading.

Analyzing the Record

This record should assist the educator in developing a detailed date-specific picture of the child's progress in reading behavior. It should be used to help the educator individualize instruction for the specific child.

As the errors are reviewed, consider whether the child made the error because of semantics (cues from meaning), syntactic (language structure), or visual information difficulties.

As self-corrections are analyzed, consider what led the child to make that self-correction. Check out and consider what cues the child does use effectively and which the child does not use well.

Consider the ways in which the child tackles a word which is unknown. Characterize that behavior and consider how the teacher can assist the child with this issue.

If a child can retell at least three-quarters of a story, this is considered adequate for retelling.

Analysis of reading behavior records can and should support the educator in designing appropriate mini-lessons and strategies to help the child with his or her recorded errors and miscues.

Sample Test

1) Classrooms generally contain a diverse population of students. Assessments presented to students need to reflect that diversity. Methods to ensure diversity needs are being addressed include which of the following?
   (Average Rigor) (Skill 1.1)

   A) Create a climate that fosters diversity.

   B) Use printed materials that reflect a variety of cultural backgrounds.

   C) Disaggregate data so that it reflects various cultural groups.

   D) All of the above.

2) Mr. Mark is a brand new teacher who is not from the neighborhood where his school is located. He is a bit nervous as this is his first teaching assignment. He does not yet know how to relax enough to get his students to activate prior experience. He should:
   (Average Rigor) (Skill 1.2)

   A) Try a free recall question: Tell us what you know about...

   B) Try an unstructured Question: Let's talk About...

   C) Use word association: What do you associate X with?

   D) All of the above.

3) Among the literary strategies that teachers can use to activate prior knowledge are:
   (Easy) (Skill 1.2)

   A) Predicting and previewing a story.

   B) Story mapping.

   C) Venn diagramming.

   D) Linear arrays.

READING

4) Reading expression, appropriate phrasing, and good inflection are characteristics of:
(Rigorous) (Skill 1.3)

A) Prosody

B) Fluency

C) Modeling

D) Accuracy

5) Young children often spell words they write according to the way the letters sound. This is called:
(Average Rigor) (Skill 1.4)

A) Spelling lists

B) Incorrect spelling

C) Developmental spelling

D) Invented spelling

6) Adolescent literature covers a wide range of reading levels and topic. A 5th grader reading at a high level has selected a book that is at the appropriate reading level, but the content is somewhat inappropriate. The student should be guided to:
(Average Rigor) (Skill 1.5)

A) select a more appropriate book.

B) read the book.

C) turn the book into the library media specialist so that it may be removed from the shelf.

D) read the book, but select as second book as an alternate

7) Understanding and interpreting visual communications that are conveyed nonverbally refers to:
(Easy) (Skill 1.6)

A) Reading

B) Writing

C) Listening

D) Viewing

8) As a parent walked through the first grade floor of her school, she kept hearing repeated clapping. Most likely the children were: *(Average Rigor) (Skill 1.7)*

   A) Clapping to show respect for one another.

   B) Rehearsing for how they would clap at a play.

   C) Clapping out syllables of multi-syllabic words.

   D) All of the above.

9) Greg Ball went to an author signing where Faith Ringgold gave a talk about one of her many books. He was so inspired by her presence and by his reading of her book *TAR BEACH,* that he used the book for his reading and writing workshop activities. His supervisor wrote in his plan book, that he was pleased that Greg had used the book as an/a _____ book.
   (Average Rigor) (Skill 1.7)

   A) Basic book.

   B) Feature book.

   C) Anchor book.

   D) Focus book.

10) An observer enters Julia's first grade classroom. Children are working with oaktag strips and placing the word letters on these strips on a sentence strip holder. Then they seem to be involved in some kind of counting. The observer is confused. This activity is taking place during the reading block. Julia explains: *(Rigorous) (Skill 1.7)*

    A) The children are counting letters.

    B) This is word sorting and the children are grouping words by length, common letters and sound.

    C) The children are combining mathematics counting and word study.

    D) The children are doing a strategy sheet based on a particular word family

11) As he walks up and down the hallway, Mr. Adams, the new Assistant Principal, continually hears Ms. Brown telling her children to go to the wall. Mr. Adams looks briefly at the literacy block schedule and continues on his walk through the building. He realizes that Ms. Brown's children are at work on:
(Rigorous) (Skill 1.7)

A) A new hall display.

B) Taking down an old display and then redoing it for a new theme.

C) Adding words to their spelling word wall.

D) Measuring the height of plants for a mathematics lesson.

12) If children are engaged in creating a museum within classroom project to exhibit their work, they are:
(Average Rigor) (Skill 1.7)

A) Not doing any reading or writing.

B) Doing many authentic reading, writing, and researching tasks.

C) Not likely to visit a real museum.

D) All of the above.

13) Based on individual conferences with many children, the teacher realizes that although they are all self-Improving readers, they need help in better use of the context to define words. The teacher decided to try the use of:
(Rigorous) (Skill 1.7)

A) A dictionary to look up words.

B) A thesaurus to use with the dictionary.

C) Contextual redefinition training.

D) Instruction in how to effectively use a dictionary.

14) Two steps a teacher might take before selecting words for study are:
(Rigorous) (Skill 1.7)

A) Reading the story and story mapping.

B) Asking advice from a veteran teacher and the grade leader.

C) Looking in a teacher's guide and copying out the words listed there.

D) All of the above are Correct

15) A teacher discovers after considering his class's prior knowledge of the story material that he would need to teach 12 words at least before he starts teaching the story to the whole group. This indicates:
 (Rigorous) (Skill 1.7)

 A) The children will need a read-aloud.

 B) The children will need independent reading.

 C) The children will need guided reading.

 D) The children will need shared reading.

16) Vocabulary should be introduced after reading if:
 (Average Rigor) (Skill 1.7)

 A) The children have identified words from their reading which were difficult and which they need explained.

 B) The text is appropriate for vocabulary building.

 C) The teacher would like to teach vocabulary after the reading.

 D) a and b

17) Taking responsibility for a child's own learning, will usually involve the child in:
 (Average Rigor) (Skill 1.7)

 A) Reading and writing on his/her own.

 B) Developing a personal literacy project which will later be shared with the teacher and peers and family.

 C) Putting away books and materials when directed.

 D) a and b.

18) The major difference between phonemic and phonological awareness is:
 (Average Rigor) (Skill 1.8)

 A) One deals with a series of discrete sounds and the other with sound-spelling relationships.

 B) One is involved with teaching and learning alliteration and rhymes.

 C) Phonemic awareness is a specific type of phonological awareness that deals with separate phonemes within a given word.

 D) Phonological awareness is associated with printed words.

19) The theorist in early reading (emergent reading) who has identified five tasks for phonemic awareness is:
(Average Rigor) (Skill 1.8)

A) John Munro

B) Brian Cambourne

C) Marilyn Jager Adams

D) Lucy Calkins

20) **An oddity task is one in which children:**
(Rigorous) (Skill 1.8)

A) Identify the odd number in a mathematical series and talk about how they did it.

B) Perform a creative exercise designed for differentiated learning styles.

C) Recognize which sound is odd in a series of like sounds.

D) Design a different activity for themselves.

21) All of the following are true about phonological awareness EXCEPT:
(Average Rigor) (Skill 1.8)

A) It may involve print.

B) It is a prerequisite for spelling and phonics.

C) Activities can be done by the children with their eyes closed.

D) It starts before letter recognition is taught.

22) "Beautiful Beth is the Best Girl in the Bradley Bay area." This sentence could be used to help children learn about:
(Easy) (Skill 1.8)

A) Assonance.

B) Alliteration.

C) Rhyming pairs.

D) None of the above

23) Phonological awareness includes all of the following skills except:
(Average Rigor) (Skill 1.8)

A) Rhyming and syllabification

B) Blending sounds into words

C) Understanding the meaning of the root word

D) Removing initial sounds and substituting others

24) Paul is a new teacher. He has just started his logs and assessments for his children's phonemic awareness. He asks a reading teacher to look over his log, but the log is returned to him:
(Average Rigor) (Skill 1.8)

A) Paul gave the log to the wrong colleague.

B) The colleague would not help him out by reviewing it.

C) The log did not have the dates the child's behavior was observed and had no stated performance standards.

D) The log didn't have a cover letter from Paul.

25) The work of Chard and Osborn (1999) in establishing guidelines for children with reading disabilities has shown that it is essential for them to:
(Rigorous) (Skill 1.8)

A) Read wordless picture books.

B) Learn at least 10 sight words.

C) Work intensely on the alphabetic principle.

D) Focus on using syntactic clues.

26) As Ms. Maxwell enters a first grade class, the teacher is busily writing down what the children are saying. The teacher is probably doing this to:
(Easy) (Skill 1.8)

A) Demonstrate how to copy down speech.

B) Make a connection and promote awareness of the relationship between spoken and written language.

C) Authenticate the children's comments.

D) Raise the children's self esteem.

27) **The best way for a primary grade teacher to model directionality and one to one word matching would be:**
(Easy) (Skill 1.8)

A) Using a regular library or classroom text book.

B) Using her own person reading book.

C) Using a big book.

D) Using a book dummy.

28) **Two consonants placed together in a word to make a unique sound is a :**
(Easy) (Skill 1.8)

A) Consonant digraph

B) Consonant blend

C) Morpheme

D) Phoneme

29) **By definition, which children in a classroom will have trouble with syntactic cues?**
(Rigorous) (Skill 1.8)

A) Those from families who do not have household libraries.

B) Those not in a top reading group.

C) Those from ELL backgrounds.

D) All of the above.

30) **In a balanced literacy classroom, new vocabulary would most likely appear on:**
(Easy) (Skill 1.8)

A) An experiential chart.

B) A class newspaper.

C) The word wall.

D) Outside the room on a bulletin board.

31) **Andrew is just starting school, but it looks like he will be successful in reading because:**
(Average Rigor) (Skill 1.8)

A) He comes from a family which cares about his progress.

B) He is phonemically aware and knows his alphabet.

C) He has been in pre-school.

D) He is well behaved.

32) **Historical Fiction, Mythology, Folklore, Realistic Fiction, Mystery, and Legends are known as:**
(Easy) (Skill 1.8)

A) Reading styles

B) Young Adult topics

C) Genres

D) Booklists

33) The work of Chard and Osborn (1999) in establishing guidelines for children with reading disabilities has shown that it is essential for them to:
(Rigorous) (Skill 1.8)

A) Read wordless picture books.

B) Learn at least 10 sight words.

C) Work intensely on the alphabetic principle.

D) Focus on using syntactic clues.

34) Book handling skills include ALL of the following except:
(Easy) (Skill 1.8)

A) Putting a cellophane or plastic cover on a book.

B) Identifying the back cover of the book.

C) Reading the book jacket.

D) Reading dedication page and the title page of the book.

35) A "decodable text" is:
(Average Rigor) (Skill 1.9)

A) A text that a child can read aloud with correct pronunciations.

B) A text that a child can answer comprehension questions about with a high percentage of accuracy.

C) Text written to match the sequence of letter-sound relationships that have been taught.

D) None of the above.

36) To help students develop as readers it is important to do all of the following except:
(Average Rigor) (Skill 1.10)

A) Surround children with books

B) Have students participate in daily read aloud activities

C) Have students read only the books that have been picked out for them by the teacher

D) Have students read their favorite books over and over

37) Strategies for educating parents and family include providing:
(Average Rigor) (Skill 1.11)

A) Workshops

B) Newsletters

C) Parent Nights

D) All of the above

38) To help children with "main idea" questions, the teacher should:
(Rigorous) (Skill 2.1)

A) Give out a strategy sheet on the main idea for children to place in their reader's notebooks.

B) Model responding to such a question as part of guided reading.

C) Have children create "main idea questions" to go with their writings.

D) All of the above.

39) Specific outcomes that will be taught during a lesson are known as:
(Easy) (Skill 2.2)

A) Goals

B) Objectives

C) Procedures

D) Assessment

40) There are two basic types of text structure:
(Easy) (Skill 2.3)

A) Fiction and non-fiction.

B) Primary and pre-k.

C) Expository and narrative.

D) Wordless and text rich.

41) A district observer notes that fifth graders are showing younger peers in the third grade how to hold a book and walk around with it, they assume:
(Rigorous) (Skill 2.3)

A) That the fifth graders are particularly theatrical.

B) That the fifth graders are proud of how they read stories aloud.

C) That the fifth graders are training the younger children in book holding.

D) That this has nothing to do with instruction.

42) A theorist who believes that there is a finite body of approved literature children should be taught on various grade levels and has produced books about what everyone needs to know to be literate on various grade levels is:
(Rigorous) (Skill 2.3)

A) Rudolf Flesch

B) J. David Cooper

C) John Dewey

D) E. D. Hirsch

43) Three general types of critical thinking skills include all except:
(Average Recall) (Skill 2.4)

A) Analysis

B) Evaluation

C) Recall

D) Synthesis

44) Most of the children in first-year teacher Ms. James's class are really doing well in their phonemic awareness assessments. However, Ms. James is very concerned about three children who do not seem to be able to distinguish between spoken words that "sound alike," but are different. Since she is a first year teacher, she feels her inexperience may be to blame. In truth, the reason these three children have not yet demonstrated phonemic awareness is most likely that:
(Rigorous) (Skill 2.5)

A) They are not capable of becoming good readers.

B) They are bored in class.

C) They may be from an ELL background.

D) Ms. James does not pronounce the different phonemes clearly enough.

45) As the child is reading and has made an incorrect attempt, the teacher prompts:
(Average Rigor) (Skill 2.5)

A) That is a mistake, do it again.

B) No, you are stupid. .. why can't you get it?

C) Does that make sense to you?

D) Forget it, this is too hard for you.

46) Ms. Clark is seen by outside observers from her district, seated in front of her class of sixth graders with a notebook in her lap and an easel. She reads aloud from a book and then writes down a series of questions. As she reads along, she sometimes writes down the answers to her own questions. This is most likely:
(Rigorous) (Skill 2.6)

A) A sign that Ms. Clark is uncertain of her own comprehension capacity.

B) She is modeling self questioning for the children.

C) She is aware that she is being watched and wants to make a good impression.

D) All of the above.

47) A second grader is writing his first book review. He has conferred with his teacher several times while he was writing the book review. Now he is rehearsing it with the teacher before he reads it aloud to the class. The child's learning of how to compose and deliver a book review has been:
(Rigorous) (Skill 2.7)

A) Done independently.

B) Assisted by family support.

C) Done in a cooperative group setting.

D) Scaffolded by the teacher.

48) The teacher is very concerned about identifying a book that is "just right" for Jay to read independently. This means that Jay should be able to read this book with:
(Average Rigor) (Skill 2.8)

A) Below 92% accuracy

B) 100% accuracy

C) 95-100% accuracy

D) 92-97% accuracy

49) Jay really wants to read a book that he can only read with 94% accuracy. He could get to read this book as:
(Average Rigor) (Skill 2.8)

A) An independent reading.

B) A guided reading.

C) A shared reading.

D) All of the above.

50) When you ask a child, if what he or she has just read "sounds right" to him or her, you are trying to get that child to use:
(Average Rigor) (Skill 2.9)

A) Phonics cues.

B) Syntactic cues.

C) Semantic cues.

D) Prior knowledge.

51) Ms. Angel has to be certain that her fourth graders know the characteristics of the historical fiction genre. She can best support them in becoming comfortable with this genre by:
(Rigorous) (Skill 2.10)

A) Providing sequel and prequel writing opportunities using that genre.

B) Reading them many different works from that genre.

C) A and B.

D) Having them look up the definition of that genre in a literary encyclopedia.

52) Historical Fiction, Mythology, Folklore, Realistic Fiction, Mystery, and Legends are known as:
(Easy) (Skill 2.11)

A) Reading styles

B) Young Adult topics

C) Genres

D) Booklists

53) A fifth grade teacher as subscribed to an online version of a local newspaper. She can help the students examine this resource and how it compares to the print version by noting which of the following differences:
(Rigorous) (Skill 2.12)

A) Use of video to document events.

B) Use of sound clips in addition to written text

C) Links to other web resources

D) all of the above

54) When determining the audience for a piece of writing, students need to consider which of the following factors?
(Average Rigor) (Skill 2.13)

A) Values

B) Constraints

C) Needs

D) All of the above.

55) The Stop and Think Strategy means that the child reader will:
(Rigorous) (Skill 2.14)

A) Read through until the end of the story or text.

B) Ask himself or herself if what he or she has read makes sense to him or her.

C) Stop after reading some text and write down his/her concerns.

D) All of the above

56) Making inferences from the text means that the reader:
(Average Rigor) (Skil 2.14)

A) Is making informed judgments based on available evidence.

B) Is making a guess based on prior experiences.

C) Is making a guess based on what the reader would like to be true of the text.

D) All of the above.

57) In order to get children to compile specialized vocabulary, they can use: *(Rigorous) (Skill 2.15)*

   A) Newspapers.

   B) Internet resources and approved web-sites that focus on the special interest.

   C) Experts they can interview.

   D) All of the above.

58) Most of the children in first-year teacher Ms. James's class are really doing well in their phonemic awareness assessments. However, Ms. James is very concerned about three children who do not seem to be able to distinguish between spoken words that "sound alike," but are different. Since she is a first year teacher, she feels her inexperience may be to blame. In truth, the reason these three children have not yet demonstrated phonemic awareness is most likely that: *(Rigorous) (Skill 2.16)*

   A) They are not capable of becoming good readers.

   B) They are bored in class.

   C) They may be from an ELL background.

   D) Ms. James does not pronounce the different phonemes clearly enough.

59) The Developing Readers Assessment System for leveling books was developed by: *(Rigorous) (Skill 2.17)*

   A) Calkins and Clay

   B) Fountas and Pinnell

   C) Wylie and Durrell

   D) Flesch and Clay

60) Ability grouping means: *(Rigorous) (Skill 2.18)*

   A) Grouping of children according to the results of an IQ test.

   B) Grouping of children with similar test results for instructional purposes.

   C) Grouping of children according to their oral reading accuracy rate.

   D) Grouping of children wit similar needs for instructional purposes

61) Features of safe and caring schools include which of the following:
(Average Rigor) (Skill 2.19)

A) low morale

B) a clear mission

C) some communication between parents and teachers

D) acknowledgement of student mistakes

62) Monthly book clubs, book fairs, read-a-thons, and the class library are all examples of:
(Rigorous) (Skill 2.20)

A) Ways to foster reading outside class

B) Ways to raise money for the school library

C) Ways to raise money for the classroom library

D) None of the above

63) Mrs. Young is a first grade teacher trying to select a books that are "just right" for her students to read independently. She needs to consider which of the following:
(Rigorous) (Skill 3.1)

A) Illustrations should support the meaning of the text.

B) Content that relates to student interest and experiences

C) Predictable text structures and language patterns

D) All of the above

64) Nonfiction genres include all of the following except:
(Easy) (Skill 3.2)

A) Essays

B) Poetry

C) Speech

D) Biography

65) Historical Fiction, Mythology, Folklore, Realistic Fiction, Mystery, and Legends are known as:
(Easy) (Skill 3.3)

A) Reading styles

B) Young Adult topics

C) Genres

D) Booklists

66) A small group of students choose a book to read. Each person in the group is assigned a role, which changes so that each person gets to play each role is called a:
(Rigorous) (Skill 3.4)

A) Literature circle

B) Workshop

C) Reading Center

D) None of the above.

67) It is important for students to have an opportunity to read silently or on their own:
(Average Rigor) (Skill 3.4)

A) hourly.

B) daily.

C) weekly.

D) monthly

68) Prose fiction includes which of the following types of literature:
(Average Rigor) (Skill 3.6)

A) Essays

B) Biographies

C) Novels

D) None of the above.

69) Dictionary study:
(Average Rigor) (Skill 3.6)

A) can begin in grades 1 or 2.

B) can begin in pre-K using the lush picture dictionaries.

C) should start on grade three level.

D) a and b.

70) Author's viewpoint questions stump Gary. His teacher can help him by asking him during their reading conferences:
(Average Rigor) (Skill 3.7)

A) If Gary-feels the book he is reading, is it just right for him.

B) What the author would say about what the character is doing in the story.

C) How the story can be changed to another genre.

D) If Gary-wants to read more books by this author.

71) One of the many ways in which a child can demonstrate comprehension of a story is by:
(Average Rigor) (Skill 3.9)

A) Filling in a strategy sheet.

B) Retelling the story orally.

C) Retelling the story in writing.

D) All of the above.

72) To promote word study, children can:
(Average Rigor) (Skill 3.10)

A) Be required to go to the dictionary at least once or twice a day.

B) Collect and share words of interest they find in their readings.

C) Do vocabulary work sheets from a basal reader or commercial vocabulary book.

D) Do all of the above.

73) Structural analysis is:
(Rigorous) (Skill 3.10)

A) the "sounding out" a printed sequence of letters based on knowledge of letter sound correspondences

B) when the teacher keeps a detailed recording of the errors or inaccurate attempts of a child reader during a reading assessment

C) the process of hearing a spoken word and identifying its separate phonemes or syllables.

D) the process of examining the words in the text for meaningful word units (affixes, base words, inflected endings).

74) A delegation from the United Kingdom has come to the United States and since they are considering adapting the balanced literacy approach, they are very interested in seeing the small group demonstrated. Mr. Adams knows that he should bring them into Greg's room when Greg is doing which activity? *(Rigorous) (Skill 3.11)*

A) A mini lesson.

B) A conference with individual students.

C) A time when children are divided into small and independent study groups.

D) A read-aloud.

75) It is 4 PM, yet Francine is still in her classroom. The seats in her classroom are filled with adults of various ages who are holding books. They are seated two by two with both holding copies of the same book. Francine probably is: *(Rigorous) (Skill 3.13)*

A) Explaining to parents how she will teach a particular story.

B) Demonstrating shared reading with a buddy for volunteer parents.

C) Hosting a parents organization meeting for her grade level.

D) Distributing old books from the class library to parents.

76) Ms. James is seated with a child by her side. The child is reading aloud from an open book. Ms. James is teaching in a school that has embraced the Balanced Literacy Approach. Therefore it is most likely that Ms. James is writing and recording:
(Average Rigor) (Skill 3.14)

A) The child's use of expression in reading aloud.

B) The child's errors and miscues.

C) Her observations of the child's attitude toward reading.

D) The child's feelings about the particular passage being read.

77) "Self correct" in reading means:
(Easy) (Skill 3.14)

A) The teacher corrects on the record the errors the child makes.

B) The child goes back and corrects errors made in a running record.

C) The reading specialist teaches this to the child.

D) a and b.

78) When taking a child's running record, the kinds of self corrections the child makes: (Average Rigor) (Skill 3.14)

A) Are not important, but the percentage of accuracy is important.

B) May show something about which cueing systems the child relies on.

C) Can be meaningful if analyzed over several records.

D) Both b and c

79) Miscue analysis assists the teacher in determining which of the following:
(Average Rigor) (Skill 3.14)

A) Methods a student uses to figure out unknown words

B) Student ability to monitor their own reading

C) Strategies that students are using with the greatest success

D) All of the above

80) **In terms of a balanced literacy classroom, a "leveled bin" indicates:**
(Easy) (Skill 3.15)

A) A plant set at child's eye level for descriptive writing purposes.

B) A bin with books the child has selected.

C) A bin with books leveled by the teacher.

D) A bin with all kinds of reading materials including magazines and packaging on a child's level.

81) **Direct teaching of a concept or strategy means:**
(Average Rigor) (Skill 3.15)

A) The teacher teaches the concept or strategy as part of a genre lesson.

B) The teacher teaches the concept as part of the writing workshop.

C) The teacher explicitly announces to the class that this strategy will be taught.

D) The teacher teaches the strategy to a small group of children or to an individual child.

82) **The theorist who believes children should not be "taught" vocabulary and structural analysis is:**
(Rigorous) (Skill 3.16)

A) Cooper

B) Flesch

C) Hirsch

D) Calkins

83) **A key theorist who supports a phonics centered approach is:**
(Rigorous) (Skill 3.16)

A) Marie Clay.

B) Sharon Taberski.

C) Shelley Harwayne.

D) Rudolf Flesch.

84) **D.E.A.R. stands for**
(Easy) (Skill 4.2)

A) Day Everyone Around Reads

B) Drop Everything and Read

C) Drop Everyone and Read

D) Daily Events and Reading

85) Asking a child if what he or she has read makes sense to him or her, is prompting the child to use:
(Easy) (Skill 4.2)

A) Phonics cues.

B) Syntactic cues.

C) Semantic cues.

D) Prior knowledge.

86) The strategy in which a graphic organizer is used to help identify what students know, what they want to know, and what they learned is referred to as:
(Easy) (Skill 4.3)

A) A bubble map

B) A reading log

C) A K-W-L- chart

D) A Venn Diagram

87) Reader's Theater is:
(Average Rigor) (Skill 4.4)

A) Reading as a group or with the teacher

B) When students use scripts that have different parts for different characters

C) When students read aloud daily

D) When students work together to provide instruction for each other

88) A natural role for a highly proficient reader would be:
(Rigorous) (Skill 4.5)

A) To assist the teacher with cleaning the classroom and organizing the student folders.

B) To develop charts for the teacher by copying needed poems for full class study.

C) Tutor and support struggling readers.

D) Work on his/her own interests while the teacher works with the rest of the class.

89) The term graphophenemic awareness refers to:
(Easy) (Skill 4.6)

A) Handwriting skills.

B) Letter to sound recognition.

C) Alphabetic principle.

D) Phonemic awareness

90) Gracie seems to be struggling with her reading, even in first grade, although her mother works at a publishing firm and her dad is an editor. Her speech is also full of mispronunciations although her parents were born in the school neighborhood. Gracie should be checked by: *(Average Rigor) (Skill 4.7)*

A) A reading specialist.

B) A speech therapist or an audiologist

C) A pediatrician.

D) A psychologist.

91) Environmental print is available at all of the following except: *(Easy) (Skill 4.7)*

A) Within a newspaper.

B) On the page of a library book.

C) On a supermarket circular.

D) In a commercial flyer.

92) The best way for a teacher to track a student's progress in demonstrating the alphabetic principal/ graphophonemic awareness is to: *(Rigorous) (Skill 5.1)*

A) Provide group assessments

B) Maintain individual records

C) Assess with standardized tests

D) Have the student assessed by a team of teachers

93) Cues in reading are: *(Easy) (Skill 5.1)*

A) Vowel sounds.

B) Digraphs.

C) Sources of information used by readers to help them construct meaning.

D) None of the above

94) A teacher is asking children to look at the beginning letters of words. She then asks the child to connect the beginning letter to the text and story and to think about what word would make sense there. This is an example of: *(Average Rigor) (Skill 5.2)*

A) A balanced literacy approach.

B) A phonemic approach.

C) A phonic approach.

D) AN ELL differentiated approach.

95) To encode means that you: *(Average Rigor) (Skill 5.3)*

A) Decode a second time.

B) Construct meaning from a code.

C) Tell someone a message.

D) None of the above.

96) Dictionary study: *(Average Rigor) (Skill 5.3)*

A) can begin in grades 1 or 2.

B) can begin in pre-K using the lush picture dictionaries.

C) should start on grade three level.

D) a and b.

97) The best ways to select words students need to learn to spell include all of the following except: *(Rigorous) (Skill 5.4)*

A) Misspelled words from student writing

B) Lists of theme words

C) Lists from a spelling textbook

D) Lists of words from content areas

98) Children "own" words when all of the following happen except: *(Average Rigor) (Skill 5.4)*

A) They find these words on their own.

B) The teacher provides a mandated word list.

C) They use the words in their own writings.

D) The words appear in literature that interests them.

99) "Ballgame" is a _____ word. Its meaning is derived from the combination of "Ball" and "Game":
(Easy) (Skill 5.4)

   A) Contraction.

   B) Compound.

   C) Portmanteau.

   D) Palindrome.

100) The word "bat" is a ___ word for "batter-up":
(Easy) (Skill 5.4)

   A) Suffix.

   B) Prefix.

   C) Root word.

   D) Inflectional ending.

101) Four of Ms. Wolmark's students have lived in other countries. She is particularly pleased to be studying Sumerian proverbs with them as part of the sixth grade unit in analyzing the sayings of other cultures because:
(Rigorous) (Skill 5.5)

   A) This gives her a break from teaching and the children can share sayings from other cultures they and their families have experienced.

   B) This validates the experiences and expertise of ELL learners in her classroom.

   C) This provides her children from the US with a lens on other cultural values.

   D) All of the above.

102) An effective way to build vocabulary and to make connections with mandated science and mathematics material is to teach Greek and Latin roots using:
(Average Rigor) (Skill 5.5)

   A) Semantic maps.

   B) Hierarchical arrays.

   C) Linear arrays.

   D) Word webs.

103) A bound morpheme is:
(Easy) (Skill 5.5)

A) A prefix.

B) A contraction.

C) An inflectional ending that can be added to a base word to change its case, gender, number, tense or form.

D) A root word.

104) Teachers should select at least ___ words for pre-reading vocabulary discussion:
(Rigorous) (Skill 5.5)

A) 12.

B) 15.

C) 2-3.

D) 8-10.

105) Among the literary strategies that teachers can use to activate prior knowledge are:
(Average Rigor) (Skill 6.1)

A) Predicting and previewing a story.

B) Story mapping.

C) Venn diagramming.

D) Linear arrays.

106) A key theorist whose work has helped teacher's document children's oral reading progress throughout the school year is:
(Average Rigor) (Skill 6.1)

A) Jerome Bruner.

B) Daniel J. Chard.

C) J. David Cooper.

D) Marie Clay.

107) Bill has been called up to the teacher for an individual conference. She asks him to retell one of the books he has listed on his weekly log. He begins and is still talking 7 minutes later. Most probably, Bill:
(Average Rigor) (Skill 6.2)

A) Told the entire story with all its details and minor characters.

B) May or may not have really gotten the main points and perspectives of the story.

C) May have really liked the Story.

D) None of the above.

108) When taking a child's running record, the kinds of self corrections the child makes:
(Average Rigor) (Skill 6.2)

A) Are not important, but the percentage of accuracy is important.

B) May show something about which cueing systems the child relies on.

C) Can be meaningful if analyzed over several records.

D) Both b and c

109) Once a teacher has carefully recorded and documented a running record:
(Rigorous) (Skill 6.2)

A) There is nothing further to do as long as the teacher keeps the running record for conferences and documentation of grades.

B) The teacher should review the running record and other subsequent ones taken for growth over time.

C) The teacher should differentiate instruction for that particular student as indicated by growth over time and evidence of other needs.

D) Both b and c

110) "Sounds right" can sound wrong to:
(Rigorous) (Skill 6.2)

A) Any reader who is not a fluent or early reader.

B) AN ELL reader.

C) A struggling reader.

D) None of the above.

111) Sometimes children can be asked to demonstrate their understanding of a text in a non-written format. This might include all of the following except:
(Average Rigor) (Skill 6.2)

A) A story map.

B) A Venn diagram.

C) Storyboarding a part of the story with dialogue bubbles.

D) Retelling or paraphrasing.

112) Norm-referenced tests:
(Average rigor) (Skill 6.2)

A) Give information only about the local samples results.

B) Provide information about the local test takers did compared to a representative sampling of national test takers.

C) Make no comparisons to national test takers.

D) None of the above.

113) The reliability of a test is measured by:
(Rigorous) (Skill 6.3)

A) The number of children who can pass it.

B) The number of children who fail it.

C) The degree to which it measures what it is supposed to measure over time.

D) None of the above

114) A quartile on a test is:
(Average Rigor) (Skill 6.3)

A) A quarter of the grades grouped.

B) The division of the percentiles into four segments each of which is called a quartile.

C) 25 of the tests scored.

D) b and c

115) Validity in assessment means:
(Rigorous) (Skill 6.3)

A) The test went off without any previewing of the questions or leaks on its contents.

B) The majority of test takers passed.

C) The correct time was allowed for the children to complete the test.

D) The test assessed what it was supposed to assess and measure.

116) "Bias" in testing occurs when:
(Rigorous) (Skill 6.3)

A) The assessment instrument is not an objective, fair and impartial one for a given cultural, ethnic, or special needs participant.

B) The testing administrator is biased.

C) The same test is given with no time considerations or provisions for those in need of more time or those who have handicapping conditions.

D) All of the above

117) Communication with parents needs to occur:
(Average Rigor) (Skill 6.4)

A) at the end of each grading period only.

B) several times during the grading period.

C) at the end of the school year.

D) It is not important to communicate with parents.

118) Tasks a reading specialist can use to determine student's level of comprehension include:
(Rigorous) (Skill 6.5)

A) Listening to passages.

B) Oral Reading

C) Written Response

D) All of the above.

119) To keep abreast of reading trends and research, a reading specialist should subscribe to which of the following periodicals:
(Rigorous) (Skill 7.2)

A) *The Reading Teacher*

B) *Educational Leadership*

C) *Reading Research Quarterly*

D) All of the above

120) A strategy is:
(Rigorous) (Skill 7.3)

A) A practice or routine the teacher can continually refer to.

B) A practice or routine a child can continually refer to or use.

C) A sheet or template for a practice the child can continually fill out.

D) All of the above.

121) To assist in the integration of various cultures within the reading program, it helps to employ a variety of strategies including:
(Rigorous) (Skill 7.4)

A) Reading Workshop

B) Writing Workshop

C) Responding

D) All of the above

122) The phrase "begin with the end in mind" when planning instruction implies teachers need to start the planning process with which of the following at the forefront:
(Rigorous) (Skill 7.5)

A) Assessment

B) Goals

C) Objectives

D) Procedures

123) To enhance reading instruction it is recommended that schools to provide at least how many minutes of silent reading per day?
(Rigorous) (Skill 7.6)

A) 10

B) 15

C) 30

D) 60

124) Reading specialists play a key role in the enhancement of reading instruction within a school. Which of the following demonstrates ways in which this can occur?
(Rigorous) (Skill 7.7)

A) Working with groups of students

B) Track student progress in reading

C) Establish reading enrichment programs.

D) All of the above.

125) Collaboration is a key part of reading instruction. To foster a collaborative environment within a school which of the following factors is key?
(Rigorous) (Skill 7.8)

A) Working individually to assess classroom teacher's progress

B) Allow time to visit other schools

C) Allow time to visit other classrooms

D) Both B and C

Answer Key:

1. D	45. C	89. C
2. B	46. B	90. B
3. A	47. D	91. B
4. A	48. D	92. B
5. D	49. A	93. C
6. A	50. B	94. C
7. D	51. C	95. B
8. C	52. C	96. D
9. C	53. D	97. C
10. B	54. D	98. B
11. C	55. B	99. B
12. B	56. A	100. C
13. C	57. D	101. D
14. D	58. C	102. D
15. C	59. B	103. C
16. D	60. D	104. C
17. D	61. B	105. A
18. C	62. A	106. D
19. C	63. D	107. A
20. C	64. B	108. D
21. A	65. C	109. C
22. B	66. C	110. B
23. C	67. B	111. D
24. C	68. C	112. B
25. C	69. D	113. C
26. B	70. B	114. B
27. C	71. D	115. D
28. A	72. D	116. D
29. C	73. D	117. B
30. C	74. C	118. D
31. B	75. B	119. D
32. C	76. B	120. D
33. C	77. B	121. D
34. A	78. D	122. A
35. A	79. D	123. B
36. C	80. C	124. D
37. D	81. D	125. D
38. D	82. A	
39. B	83. D	
40. C	84. B	
41. C	85. C	
42. B	86. C	
43. C	87. B	
44. C	88. C	

Rigor Table

	Easy %20	Average Rigor %40	Rigorous %40
Question #	3, 7, 22, 26, 27, 28, 30, 32, 34, 39, 40, 52, 64, 65, 77, 80, 84, 85, 86, 89, 90, 91, 93, 99, 100, 103	1, 2, 5, 6, 8, 9, 12, 16, 17, 18, 19, 21, 23, 24, 31, 35, 36, 37, 43, 45, 48, 49, 50, 54, 56, 61, 68, 69, 70, 71, 72, 76, 78, 79, 81, 87, 90, 94, 95, 96, 98, 102, 105, 106, 107, 107, 111, 112, 114, 117	4, 10, 11, 13, 14, 15, 20, 25, 29, 33, 38, 41, 42, 44, 46, 47, 51, 53, 55, 57, 58, 59, 60, 62, 63, 66, 67, 73, 74, 75, 82, 83, 88, 92, 97, 101, 104, 109, 110, 113, 115, 116, 118, 119, 120, 121, 122, 123, 124, 125

Rationales with Sample Questions

1) **Classrooms generally contain a diverse population of students. Assessments presented to students need to reflect that diversity. Methods to ensure diversity needs are being addressed include which of the following?**
(Average Rigor) (Skill 1.1)

   A) Create a climate that fosters diversity.

   B) Use printed materials that reflect a variety of cultural backgrounds.

   C) Disaggregate data so that it reflects various cultural groups.

   D) All of the above.

Answer: D) All of the above

Some methods of displaying sensitivity to diversity include:

- Student portfolios reflecting multicultural/multiethnic perspectives
- Journals and reflections from field trips/ guest speakers from diverse cultural backgrounds
- Printed materials and wall displays from multicultural perspectives
- Parent/guardian letters in a variety of languages reflecting cultural diversity
- Projects that include cultural history and diverse inclusions
- Disaggregated student data reflecting cultural groups
- Classroom climate of professionalism that fosters diversity and cultural inclusion

2) Mr. Mark is a brand new teacher who is not from the neighborhood where his school is located. He is a bit nervous as this is his first teaching assignment. He does not yet know how to relax enough to get his students to activate prior experience. He should: (Average Rigor) (Skill 1.2)

   A) Try a free recall question: Tell us what you know about...

   B) Try an unstructured Question: Let's talk About...

   C) Use word association: What do you associate X with?

   D) All of the above.

Answer: B) Try and unstructured question: Let's talk about...

An unstructured question is open-ended and can lead to great discussion. This type of question can also provide the teacher with more insight into the student's thoughts.

3) Among the literary strategies that teachers can use to activate prior knowledge are:
(Easy) (Skill 1.2)

   A) Predicting and previewing a story.

   B) Story mapping.

   C) Venn diagramming.

   D) Linear arrays.

Answer: A) Predicting and previewing a story.

By predicting the events or preview a story the teacher can help students connect with and not only activate prior knowledge, but build vocabulary as well.

4) Reading expression, appropriate phrasing, and good inflection are characteristics of:
   (Rigorous) (Skill 1.3)

   A) Prosody

   B) Fluency

   C) Modeling

   D) Accuracy

Answer: A) Prosody

Prosody is defined as the stress and intonation in a language.

5) Young children often spell words they write according to the way the letters sound. This is called:
   (Average Rigor) (Skill 1.4)

   A) Spelling lists

   B) Incorrect spelling

   C) Developmental spelling

   D) Invented spelling

Answer: D) Invented spelling

Spelling is of utmost importance in the writing process. At first young children will use invented spelling in which they write the words according to letter sounds.

6) Adolescent literature covers a wide range of reading levels and topic. A 5th grader reading at a high level has selected a book that is at the appropriate reading level, but the content is somewhat inappropriate. The student should be guided to:
(Average Rigor) (Skill 1.5)

   A) select a more appropriate book.

   B) read the book.

   C) turn the book into the library media specialist so that it may be removed from the shelf.

   D) read the book, but select as second book as an alternate

Answer: A) select a more appropriate book

Just because a student is able to read the words on the page, does not mean the content is appropriate for the student. In cases such as this it is important to guide a student towards literature that is on both a proper reading level and contains appropriate content.

7) Understanding and interpreting visual communications that are conveyed nonverbally refers to:
(Easy) (Skill 1.6)

   A) Reading

   B) Writing

   C) Listening

   D) Viewing

Answer: D) Viewing

Because society is flooded with media of various types, teachers must help students become critical viewers and consumers of media. *Viewing* refers to understanding and interpreting visual communications that are conveyed non-verbally.

8) **As a parent walked through the first grade floor of her school, she kept hearing repeated clapping. Most likely the children were:**
(Average Rigor) (Skill 1.7)

   A) Clapping to show respect for one another.

   B) Rehearsing for how they would clap at a play.

   C) Clapping out syllables of multi-syllabic words.

   D) All of the above.

Answer: C) Clapping out syllables of multi-syllabic words.

The objective of this activity is for children to understand that there are every syllable in a polysyllabic word can be studied for its spelling patterns in the same way that monosyllabic words are studied for their spelling patterns.

First the teacher reads the poem with the children. As they are reading it aloud, the children clap the beats of the poem and the teacher uses a colored marker to place a tic (/) above each syllable.

9) **Greg Ball went to an author signing where Faith Ringgold gave a talk about one of her many books. He was so inspired by her presence and by his reading of her book *TAR BEACH*, that he used the book for his reading and writing workshop activities. His supervisor wrote in his plan book, that he was pleased that Greg had used the book as an/a _____ book.**
(Average Rigor) (Skill1.7)

   A) Basic book.

   B) Feature book.

   C) Anchor book.

   D) Focus book.

Answer: C) Anchor book.

ANCHOR BOOK- a balanced literacy term for a book that is purposely read repeatedly and used as part of both the reading and writing workshop.

10) An observer enters Julia's first grade classroom. Children are working with oaktag strips and placing the word letters on these strips on a sentence strip holder. Then they seem to be involved in some kind of counting. The observer is confused. This activity is taking place during the reading block. Julia explains:
(Rigorous) (Skill 1.7)

A) The children are counting letters.

B) This is word sorting and the children are grouping words by length, common letters and sound.

C) The children are combining mathematics counting and word study.

D) The children are doing a strategy sheet based on a particular word family

Answer: B) This is word sorting and the children are grouping words by length, common letters and sound.

This activity allows children to focus closely on the specific features of words and to begin to understand the basic elements of letter sound relationships. Start with one syllable (monosyllabic) words. Have the children group them by their length, common letters, sound, and/or spelling pattern.

11) As he walks up and down the hallway, Mr. Adams, the new Assistant Principal, continually hears Ms. Brown telling her children to go to the wall. Mr. Adams looks briefly at the literacy block schedule and continues on his walk through the building. He realizes that Ms. Brown's children are at work on:
(Rigorous) (Skill 1.7)

A) A new hall display.

B) Taking down an old display and then redoing it for a new theme.

C) Adding words to their spelling word wall.

D) Measuring the height of plants for a mathematics lesson.

Answer: C) Adding words to their spelling word wall.

Teachers often use a word wall to reinforce new vocabulary and assist with writing. A teacher would have a child go to the wall to add new words or to use the wall to help with spelling words during writing.

12) If children are engaged in creating a museum within classroom project to exhibit their work, they are:
(Average Rigor) (Skill 1.7)

   A) Not doing any reading or writing.

   B) Doing many authentic reading, writing, and researching tasks.

   C) Not likely to visit a real museum.

   D) All of the above.

Answer: B) Doing many authentic reading, writing, and researching tasks.

By creating a museum within the classroom students take ownership in the creation of their project. The project would generally involve a topic meaningful to the student. The student would be more motivated to create a quality product.

13) Based on individual conferences with many children, the teacher realizes that although they are all self-improving readers, they need help in better use of the context to define words. The teacher decided to try the use of:
(Rigorous) (Skill 1.7)

   A) A dictionary to look up words.

   B) A thesaurus to use with the dictionary.

   C) Contextual redefinition training.

   D) Instruction in how to effectively use a dictionary.

Answer: C) Contextual redefinition training.

This strategy encourages children to use the context more effectively by presenting them with sufficient context BEFORE they begin reading. It models for the children the use of contextual clues to make informed guesses about word meanings.

14) Two steps a teacher might take before selecting words for study are: (Rigorous) (Skill 1.7)

   A) Reading the story and story mapping.

   B) Asking advice from a veteran teacher and the grade leader.

   C) Looking in a teacher's guide and copying out the words listed there.

   D) All of the above are correct

Answer: D) All of the above are correct.

It may be beneficial for the teacher to utilize all of these resources when planning reading instruction.

15) A teacher discovers after considering his class's prior knowledge of the story material that he would need to teach 12 words at least before he starts teaching the story to the whole group. This indicates: (Rigorous) (Skill 1.7)

   A) The children will need a read-aloud.

   B) The children will need independent reading.

   C) The children will need guided reading.

   D) The children will need shared reading.

Answer: C) The children need guided reading.

Stories that include so many words to be taught may prove difficult for a student to read independently. They would need assistance in attacking these words. The best way to complete this lesson is through guided reading.

16) Vocabulary should be introduced after reading if:
(Average Rigor) (Skill 1.7)

   A) The children have identified words from their reading which were difficult and which they need explained.

   B) The text is appropriate for vocabulary building.

   C) The teacher would like to teach vocabulary after the reading.

   D) a and b

Answer: D) a and b

Introduce vocabulary AFTER READING if. . .
- The children themselves have shared words which they found difficult or interesting
- The children need to expand their vocabulary
- The text itself is one that is particularly suited for vocabulary building.

17) Taking responsibility for a child's own learning, will usually involve the child in:
(Average Rigor) (Skill 1.7)

   A) Reading and writing on his/her own.

   B) Developing a personal literacy project which will later be shared with the teacher and peers and family.

   C) Putting away books and materials when directed.

   D) A and B.

Answer: D) A and B

While keeping ones area neat and tidy is important, it does not directly engage students in taking responsibility for their own learning. When students are involved in they are able to select meaningful projects and take and active role in planning their leaning.

18) The major difference between phonemic and phonological awareness is:
(Average Rigor) (Skill 1.8)

- A) One deals with a series of discrete sounds and the other with sound-spelling relationships.

- B) One is involved with teaching and learning alliteration and rhymes.

- C) Phonemic awareness is a specific type of phonological awareness that deals with separate phonemes within a given word.

- D) Phonological awareness is associated with printed words.

Answer: C) Phonemic awareness is a specific type of phonological awareness that deals with separate phonemes within a given word.

Phonemic awareness is a specific type of phonological awareness which focuses on the ability to distinguish, manipulate and blend specific sounds or phonemes within an individual word.

19) The theorist in early reading (emergent reading) who has identified five tasks for phonemic awareness is:
(Average Rigor) (Skill 1.8)

- A) John Munro

- B) Brian Cambourne

- C) Marilyn Jager Adams

- D) Lucy Calkins

Answer: C) Marilyn Jager Adams

Theorist Marilyn Jager Adams who researches early reading has outlined five basic types of phonemic awareness tasks. Task 1- Ability to hear rhymes and alliteration. Task 2- Ability to do oddity tasks (recognize the member of a set that is different.) Task 3 –The ability to orally blend words and split syllables. Task 4 –The ability to orally segment word. Task 5- The ability to do phonics manipulation tasks

20) An oddity task is one in which children:
(Rigorous) (Skill 1.8)

A) Identify the odd number in a mathematical series and talk about how they did it.

B) Perform a creative exercise designed for differentiated learning styles.

C) Recognize which sound is odd in a series of like sounds.

D) Design a different activity for themselves.

Answer: C) Recognize which sound is odd in a series of like sounds.

The ability to detect an oddity is the ability to recognize the member of a set that is different [odd] among the group. For example, the children would look at the pictures of grass, a garden and a rose, answering, Which one starts with a different sound?

21) All of the following are true about phonological awareness EXCEPT:
(Average Rigor) (Skill 1.8)

A) It may involve print.

B) It is a prerequisite for spelling and phonics.

C) Activities can be done by the children with their eyes closed.

D) It starts before letter recognition is taught.

Answer: A) It may involve print.

PHONOLOGICAL AWARENESS- the ability to recognize the sounds of spoken language and how they can be blended together, segmented, and switched/manipulated to form new combinations and words.

22) "Beautiful Beth is the Best Girl in the Bradley Bay area." This sentence could be used to help children learn about:
(Easy) (Skill 1.8)

   A) Assonance.

   B) Alliteration.

   C) Rhyming pairs.

   D) None of the above

Answer: B) Alliteration

Alliteration is the term for a series of words that begin with the same sound as in "Beautiful Beth is the Best Girl in the Bradley Bay area."

23) **Phonological awareness includes all of the following skills except:**
(Average Rigor) (Skill 1.8)

   A) Rhyming and syllabification

   B) Blending sounds into words

   C) Understanding the meaning of the root word

   D) Removing initial sounds and substituting others

Answers: C) Understanding the meaning of the root word

Phonological awareness involves the recognition that spoken words are composed of a set of smaller units such as onsets and rimes, syllables, and sounds.

24) Paul is a new teacher. He has just started his logs and assessments for his children's phonemic awareness. He asks a reading teacher to look over his log, but the log is returned to him:
(Average Rigor) (Skill 1.8)

A) Paul gave the log to the wrong colleague.

B) The colleague would not help him out by reviewing it.

C) The log did not have the dates the child's behavior was observed and had no stated performance standards.

D) The log didn't have a cover letter from Paul.

Answer: C. The log did not have the dates the child's behavior was observed and had no stated performance standards.

Records of independent Reading and Writing: These can include the children's journals, notebooks or logs of books read with the names of the authors, titles of the books, date completed, and pieces related to books completed or in progress.

25) The work of Chard and Osborn (1999) in establishing guidelines for children with reading disabilities has shown that it is essential for them to:
(Rigorous) (Skill 1.8)

A) Read wordless picture books.

B) Learn at least 10 sight words.

C) Work intensely on the alphabetic principle.

D) Focus on using syntactic clues.

Answer: C) Work intensely on the alphabetic principle.

David J. Chard and Jean Osborn (1999) have reflected on the guidelines necessary for teachers to use in selecting supplemental phonics and word-recognition materials for addressing students with learning disabilities.
They note that an important way to help children with reading disabilities figure out the system underlying the printed word is leading them to understand the alphabetic principle.

26) As Ms. Maxwell enters a first grade class, the teacher is busily writing down what the children are saying. The teacher is probably doing this to:
(Easy) (Skill 1.8)

A) Demonstrate how to copy down speech.

B) Make a connection and promote awareness of the relationship between spoken and written language.

C) Authenticate the children's comments.

D) Raise the children's self esteem.

Answer: B) Make a connection and promote awareness of the relationship between spoken and written language.

By writing down what the children are saying, the teacher promotes the awareness of the relationship between the spoken and written word. Other strategies include:
- Reading together big-print and oversized books to teach print conventions such as directionality.
- Practicing how to handle a book: How to turn pages, to find the top and bottom of pages, and how to tell the difference between the front and back covers.
- Discussing and comparing with children the length, appearance and boundaries of specific words. For example, children can see that

27) The best way for a primary grade teacher to model directionality and one to one word matching would be:
(Easy) (Skill 1.8)

A) Using a regular library or classroom text book.

B) Using her own person reading book.

C) Using a big book.

D) Using a book dummy.

Answer: C) Using a big book.

Teachers often use big books to model reading skills for children. Teaching directionality and one to one word matching are just two of the skills that can be taught.

28) Two consonants placed together in a word to make a unique sound is a :
(Easy) (Skill 1.8)

A) Consonant digraph

B) Consonant blend

C) Morpheme

D) Phoneme

Answer: A) Consonant digraph

Consonant Digraph – a consonant digraph are two consonants of the English language who when placed together in a word make a unique sound, neither makes when alone. Examples: ch, th, sh, and wh.

29) By definition, which children in a classroom will have trouble with syntactic cues?
(Rigorous) (Skill 1.8)

A) Those from families who do not have household libraries.

B) Those not in a top reading group.

C) Those from ELL backgrounds.

D) All of the above.

Answer: C) Those from ELL backgrounds.

By definition a child from an ELL background does not have a strong accurate sense of what "sounds right" in English. Not all English phonemes are present in various ELL native languages; for example, the sound of /th/ does not appear in Spanish. Some native language phonemes may and do conflict with English phonemes.

30) In a balanced literacy classroom, new vocabulary would most likely appear on:
(Easy) (Skill 1.8)

   A) An experiential chart.

   B) A class newspaper.

   C) The word wall.

   D) Outside the room on a bulletin board.

Answer: C) The Word Wall

A word wall is a classroom display of high frequency and/or grade level specific words available for student reference.

31) Andrew is just starting school, but it looks like he will be successful in reading because:
(Average Rigor) (Skill 1.8)

   A) He comes from a family which cares about his progress.

   B) He is phonemically aware and knows his alphabet.

   C) He has been in pre-school.

   D) He is well behaved.

Answer: B) He is phonemically aware and knows his alphabet

Since the ability to distinguish between individual sounds, or phonemes, within words is a prerequisite to association of sounds with letters and manipulating sounds to blend words—a fancy way of saying "reading," the teaching of phonemic awareness is crucial to emergent literacy (early childhood K-2 reading instruction). Children need a strong background in phonemic awareness in order for phonics instruction (sound –spelling relationship-printed materials) to be effective.

32) **Historical Fiction, Mythology, Folklore, Realistic Fiction, Mystery, and Legends are known as:**
(Easy) (Skill 1.8)

   A) Reading styles

   B) Young Adult topics

   C) Genres

   D) Booklists

Answer: C) Genres

A genre is a particular category of literature.

33) **The work of Chard and Osborn (1999) in establishing guidelines for children with reading disabilities has shown that it is essential for them to:**
(Rigorous) (Skill 1.8)

   A) Read wordless picture books.

   B) Learn at least 10 sight words.

   C) Work intensely on the alphabetic principle.

   D) Focus on using syntactic clues.

Answer: C) Work intensely on the alphabetic principle.

David J. Chard and Jean Osborn (1999) have reflected on the guidelines necessary for teachers to use in selecting supplemental phonics and word-recognition materials for addressing students with learning disabilities. They note that an important way to help children with reading disabilities figure out the system underlying the printed word is leading them to understand the alphabetic principle.

34) Book handling skills include ALL of the following except:
(Easy) (Skill 1.8)

A) Putting a cellophane or plastic cover on a book.

B) Identifying the back cover of the book.

C) Reading the book jacket.

D) Reading dedication page and the title page of the book.

Answer: A) Putting a cellophane or plastic cover on a book.

While students need to learn book handling skills such as how to hold the book, identifying key parts and pages, and directionality, it is not necessary for them to be able to put cellophane or plastic book covers on a book.

35) A "decodable text" is:
(Average Rigor) (Skill 1.9)

A) A text that a child can read aloud with correct pronunciations.

B) A text that a child can answer comprehension questions about with a high percentage of accuracy.

C) Text written to match the sequence of letter-sound relationships that have been taught.

D) None of the above.

Answer: A) A text that a child can read aloud with correct pronunciations.

Decodable books are vocabulary-controlled using language from word families with high predictability. Thus we get sentences like "Nan has a tan fan." Reading is seen as skills-based, and the skills are taught one at a time.

36) To help students develop as readers it is important to do all of the following except:
(Average Rigor) (Skill 1.10)

   A) Surround children with books

   B) Have students participate in daily read aloud activities

   C) Have students read only the books that have been picked out for them by the teacher

   D) Have students read their favorite books over and over

Answer: C) Have students read only the books that have been picked out for them by the teacher

To develop a love of reading, it is important for students to be able to choose their own reading material as well as reading assigned texts.

37) Strategies for educating parents and family include providing:
(Average Rigor) (Skill 11.1)

   A) Workshops

   B) Newsletters

   C) Parent Nights

   D) All of the above

Answer: D) All of the above

It is important to keep parents informed of school and classroom happenings. All of the tools listed above can be used to communicate and educate parents

38) **To help children with "main idea" questions, the teacher should:** *(Rigorous) (Skill 2.1)*

   A) Give out a strategy sheet on the main idea for children to place in their reader's notebooks.

   B) Model responding to such a question as part of guided reading.

   C) Have children create "main idea questions" to go with their writings.

   D) All of the above.

Answer: D) All of the above

Identifying main ideas can be improved when the children have an explicit strategy for identifying important information. All of the above strategies can be beneficial in identifying the main idea.

39) **Specific outcomes that will be taught during a lesson are known as:** *(Easy) (Skill 2.2)*

   A) Goals

   B) Objectives

   C) Procedures

   D) Assessment

Answer: B) Objectives

Objectives These are the specific outcomes that you will teach in the lesson. The way you design the lesson will depend on your answers to these questions:

- What will the students do during this lesson?
- What will they have to do to accomplish the objective?
- What are the standards that you will use to determine whether or not students have achieved the objective?
- What assessment will you use to determine whether the objectives have been achieved?

Use Bloom's Taxonomy to deconstruct the objectives into what you expect the students to be able to do.

You have to look at the background knowledge that students must possess in order to accomplish the objectives. Do you need to reteach any concepts?

40) There are two basic types of text structure:
(Easy) (Skill 2.3)

   A) Fiction and non-fiction.

   B) Primary and pre-k.

   C) Expository and narrative.

   D) Wordless and text rich.

Answer: C) Expository and narrative.

EXPOSITORY TEXT-. is non-fiction that provides information and facts. This text type is what newspapers, science, mathematics and history texts use. Currently there is much focus, even in elementary schools, on teaching children how to comprehend and author expository texts. They must produce brochures, guides, recipes, and procedural accounts on most elementary grade levels. The teaching of reading of expository texts requires working with a particular vocabulary and concept structure that is very different from that of the narrative text. Therefore time must be taken to teach the reading of expository texts and contrast it with the reading of narrative texts.

NARRATIVE TEXT- one of the two basic text structures. The narrative text tells or communicates a story. Narrative texts are novels, short stories and plays. Some poems are narratives as well. The narrative text needs to be taught differently than the expository text because of its structure.

41) A district observer notes that fifth graders are showing younger peers in the third grade how to hold a book and walk around with it, they assume:
(Rigorous) (Skill 2.3)

   A) That the fifth graders are particularly theatrical.

   B) That the fifth graders are proud of how they read stories aloud.

   C) That the fifth graders are training the younger children in book holding.

   D) That this has nothing to do with instruction.

Answer: C) That the fifth graders are training the younger children in book holding.

Students often learn better from other students. It is important to provide opportunities for students of various ages or levels to work together to learn from each other.

42) A theorist who believes that there is a finite body of approved literature children should be taught on various grade levels and has produced books about what everyone needs to know to be literate on various grade levels is:
(Rigorous) (Skill 2.3)

   A) Rudolf Flesch

   B) J. David Cooper

   C) John Dewey

   D) E. D. Hirsch

Answer: B) J. David Cooper

J. David Cooper (2004) and other advocates of the Balanced Literacy Approach, feel that children become literate, effective communicators and able to comprehend, by learning phonics and other aspects of word identification through the use of engaging reading texts. Engaging text, as defined by the balanced literacy group, are those texts which contain highly predictable elements of rhyme, sound patterns, and plot.

43) Three general types of critical thinking skills include all except:
(Average Recall) (Skill 2.4)

   A) Analysis

   B) Evaluation

   C) Recall

   D) Synthesis

Answer: C) Recall

Higher order thinking skills or critical thinking skills are analysis, evaluation, and synthesis. Recall questions are generally pulled from rote memory and considered one of the simplest type of questions.

44) Most of the children in first-year teacher Ms. James's class are really doing well in their phonemic awareness assessments. However, Ms. James is very concerned about three children who do not seem to be able to distinguish between spoken words that "sound alike," but are different. Since she is a first year teacher, she feels her inexperience may be to blame. In truth, the reason these three children have not yet demonstrated phonemic awareness is most likely that:
(Rigorous) (Skill 2.5)

   A) They are not capable of becoming good readers.

   B) They are bored in class.

   C) They may be from an ELL background.

   D) Ms. James does not pronounce the different phonemes clearly enough.

Answer: C) They may be from an ELL background.

Not all English phonemes are present in various ELL native languages; for example, the sound of /th/ does not appear in Spanish. Some native language phonemes may and do conflict with English phonemes.

45) As the child is reading and has made an incorrect attempt, the teacher prompts:
    (Average Rigor) (Skill 2.5)

    A) That is a mistake, do it again.

    B) No, you are stupid. .. why can't you get it?

    C) Does that make sense to you?

    D) Forget it, this is too hard for you.

Answer: C) Does that make sense to you?

Students will need use their base knowledge of word meanings, semantics, to help them decipher unknown words or text as well as to clarify reading when it does not seem to make sense. Some prompts the teacher can use which will alert the children to semantic cues include:
- Does that sentence make sense?
- Which word in that sentence does not seem to fit?
- Why doesn't it fit?
- What word might make sense in that sentence?

46) Ms. Clark-is seen by outside observers from her district, seated in front of her class of sixth graders with a notebook in her lap and an easel. She reads aloud from a book and then writes down a series of questions. As she reads along, she sometimes writes down the answers to her own questions. This is most likely:
    (Rigorous) (Skill 2.6)

    A) A sign that Ms. Clark is uncertain of her own comprehension capacity.

    B) She is modeling self questioning for the children.

    C) She is aware that she is being watched and wants to make a good impression.

    D) All of the above.

Answer: B) She is modeling self questioning for the children.

One of the most effective ways to teach students how to use various strategies is through modeling.

47) A second grader is writing his first book review. He has conferred with his teacher several times while he was writing the book review. Now he is rehearsing it with the teacher before he reads it aloud to the class. The child's learning of how to compose and deliver a book review has been:
(Rigorous) (Skill 2.7)

A) Done independently.

B) Assisted by family support.

C) Done in a cooperative group setting.

D) Scaffolded by the teacher.

Answer: D) Scaffolded by the teacher.

SCAFFOLDING- refers to the teacher support necessary for the child to accomplish a task or to achieve a goal which the child could not accomplish on his/her own. Vygotsky termed this window of opportunity the "zone of proximal development." Ultimately as the child becomes more proficient or capable, the scaffold is withdrawn. The goal of scaffolding is to help the child to perform the reading task independently and internalize the behavior. During SHARED READING, the task is scaffolded by the teacher's reading to the children aloud. As the teacher reads, the teacher scaffolds the initial decoding and helps with the meaning making/construction.

48) The teacher is very concerned about identifying a book that is "just right" for Jay to read independently. This means that Jay should be able to read this book with:
(Average Rigor) (Skill 2.8)

A) Below 92% accuracy

B) 100% accuracy

C) 95-100% accuracy

D) 92-97% accuracy

Answer: D) 92-97% accuracy

For a book to be considered on a child's independent level the student must be able to read it with 92-97% accuracy. A higher percentage would be too easy and a lower percentage would mean the text was too difficult.

49) Jay really wants to read a book that he can only read with 94% accuracy. He could get to read this book as:
   (Average Rigor) (Skill 2.8)

   A) An independent reading.

   B) A guided reading.

   C) A shared reading.

   D) All of the above.

Answer: A) An independent reading.

For a book to be considered on a child's independent level the student must be able to read it with 92-97% accuracy. A higher percentage would be too easy and a lower percentage would mean the text was too difficult.

50) When you ask a child, if what he or she has just read "sounds right" to him or her, you are trying to get that child to use:
   (Average Rigor) (Skill 2.9)

   A) Phonics cues.

   B) Syntactic cues.

   C) Semantic cues.

   D) Prior knowledge.

Answer: B) Syntactic cues.

Syntactic cues use the order of words and the student's knowledge of the oral English language to help determine if what was read could be accurate.

51) Ms. Angel has to be certain that her fourth graders know the characteristics of the historical fiction genre. She can best support them in becoming comfortable with this genre by:
(Rigorous) (Skill 2.10)

    A) Providing sequel and prequel writing opportunities using that genre.

    B) Reading them many different works from that genre.

    C) A and B.

    D) Having them look up the definition of that genre in a literary encyclopedia.

Answer: C) A and B

Providing students with writing experiences based upon particular genres and reading various works are good ways to introduce a particular genre.

52) Historical Fiction, Mythology, Folklore, Realistic Fiction, Mystery, and Legends are known as:
(Easy) (Skill 2.11)

    A) Reading styles

    B) Young Adult topics

    C) Genres

    D) Booklists

Answer: C) Genres

A genre is a particular category of literature.

53) A fifth grade teacher as subscribed to an online version of a local newspaper. She can help the students examine this resource and how it compares to the print version by noting which of the following differences:
(Rigorous) (Skill 2.12)

A) Use of video to document events.

B) Use of sound clips in addition to written text

C) Links to other web resources

D) all of the above

Answer: D) All of the above

Online resources contain other forms of media that go beyond the printed word. Audio and video clips can be used to enhance the experience of the learner.

54) **When determining the audience for a piece of writing, students need to consider which of the following factors?**
(Average Rigor) (Skill 2.13)

   A) Values

   B) Constraints

   C) Needs

   D) All of the above.

Answer: D) All of the above.

Remind students that it is not necessary to identify all the specifics of the audience in the initial stage of the writing process but that at some point they must make some determinations about audience.

- **Values**- What is important to this group of people? What is their background and how will that affect their perception of your speech?
- **Needs**- Find out in advance what the audience's needs are. Why are they listening to you? Find a way to satisfy their needs.
- **Constraints**- What might hold the audience back from being fully engaged in what you are saying, or agreeing with your point of view, or processing what you are trying to say? These could be political reasons, which make them wary of your presentation's ideology from the start, or knowledge reasons, in which the audience lacks the appropriate background information to grasp your ideas. Avoid this last constraint by staying away from technical terminology, slang, or abbreviations that may be unclear to your audience.
- **Demographic Information**- Take the audience's size into account, as well as the location of the presentation.

TEACHER CERTIFICATION STUDY GUIDE

55) The Stop and Think Strategy means that the child reader will:
(Rigorous) (Skill 2.14)

A) Read through until the end of the story or text.

B) Ask himself or herself if what he or she has read makes sense to him or her.

C) Stop after reading some text and write down his/her concerns.

D) All of the above

Answer: B) Ask himself or herself if what he or she has read makes sense to him or her.

When a student is reading, it is helpful for them to periodically stop and question themselves to see if what that have just read makes sense.

56) Making inferences from the text means that the reader:
(Average Rigor) (Skill 2.14)

A) Is making informed judgments based on available evidence.

B) Is making a guess based on prior experiences.

C) Is making a guess based on what the reader would like to be true of the text.

D) All of the above.

Answer: A) Is making informed judgments based on available evidence.

Inferencing is a process that involves the reader making a reasonable judgment based on the information given and engages children to literally construct meaning.

57) In order to get children to compile specialized vocabulary, they can use:
(Rigorous) (Skill 2.15)

    A) Newspapers.

    B) Internet resources and approved web-sites that focus on the special interest.

    C) Experts they can interview.

    D) All of the above.

Answer: D) All of the above

Vocabulary lists can be compiled from just about any source possible.

58) Most of the children in first-year teacher Ms. James's class are really doing well in their phonemic awareness assessments. However, Ms. James is very concerned about three children who do not seem to be able to distinguish between spoken words that "sound alike," but are different. Since she is a first year teacher, she feels her inexperience may be to blame. In truth, the reason these three children have not yet demonstrated phonemic awareness is most likely that:
(Rigorous) (Skill 2.16)

    A) They are not capable of becoming good readers.

    B) They are bored in class.

    C) They may be from an ELL background.

    D) Ms. James does not pronounce the different phonemes clearly enough.

Answer: C) They may be from an ELL background.

Not all English phonemes are present in various ELL native languages; for example, the sound of /th/ does not appear in Spanish. Some native language phonemes may and do conflict with English phonemes.

59) **The Developing Readers Assessment System for leveling books was developed by:**
    (Rigorous) (Skill 2.17)

    A) Calkins and Clay

    B) Fountas and Pinnell

    C) Wylie and Durrell

    D) Flesch and Clay

Answer: B) Fountas and Pinnell

Fountas and Pinnell created a leveling system for books. Knowing these levels will be helpful in meeting the instructional needs of the students in a more efficient manner.

60) **Ability grouping means:**
    (Rigorous) (Skill 2.18)

    A) Grouping of children according to the results of an IQ test.

    B) Grouping of children with similar test results for instructional purposes.

    C) Grouping of children according to their oral reading accuracy rate.

    D) Grouping of children wit similar needs for instructional purposes.

Answer: D) Grouping of children with similar needs for instructional purposes.

It is often difficult to meet each child's needs individually in a large classroom. Therefore, teachers often group students with similar needs to make the most efficient use of time and to provide students with others to work with.

61) **Features of safe and caring schools include which of the following:**
    (Average Rigor) (Skill 2.19)

    A) low morale

    B) a clear mission

    C) some communication between parents and teachers

    D) acknowledgement of student mistakes

Answer: B) a clear mission

The features of a safe and caring school are:

- A healthy, safe, and organized environment
- High morale
- Positive school attitude
- A clear mission designed to promote student achievement
- Quality instruction in the classroom
- Respectful interactions between the students and teachers
- Communication to parents on a regular basis
- Acknowledgement that making mistakes is a part of learning

62) **Monthly book clubs, book fairs, read-a-thons, and the class library are all examples of:**
    (Rigorous) (Skill 2.20)

    A) Ways to foster reading outside class

    B) Ways to raise money for the school library

    C) Ways to raise money for the classroom library

    D) None of the above

Answer: A) Ways to foster reading outside class

Providing students with opportunities to read outside of class is a key component of reading success. These events allow students to build their own home libraries or to spend time reading with friends and family.

63) **Mrs. Young is a first grade teacher trying to select a books that are "just right" for her students to read independently. She needs to consider which of the following:**
(Rigorous) (Skill 3.1)

    A) Illustrations should support the meaning of the text.

    B) Content that relates to student interest and experiences

    C) Predictable text structures and language patterns

    D) All of the above

Answer: D) All of the above.

It is important that all of the above factors be considered when selecting books for young children.

64) **Nonfiction genres include all of the following except:**
(Easy) (Skill 3.2)

    A) Essays

    B) Poetry

    C) Speech

    D) Biography

Answer: B) Poetry

Nonfiction genres include:
- Essays
- Narrative Nonfiction
- Biography
- Speech
- Autobiographies

65) **Historical Fiction, Mythology, Folklore, Realistic Fiction, Mystery, and Legends are known as:**
(Easy) (Skill 3.3)

   A) Reading styles

   B) Young Adult topics

   C) Genres

   D) Booklists

Answer: C) Genres

A genre is a particular category of literature.

66) **A small group of students choose a book to read. Each person in the group is assigned a role, which changes so that each person gets to play each role is called a:**
(Rigorous) (Skill 3.4)

   A) Literature circle

   B) Workshop

   C) Reading Center

   D) None of the above.

Answer: C) Literature Circles.

Literature Circles.
A small group of students (no more than 5) choose a book that they will read. Each person in the group is assigned a role, which changes so that each person gets to play each role. The group is temporary depending on the book. The groups meet on a regular basis to discuss the reading and they use written notes or drawings to help guide their discussions. Once students become more familiar with literature circles, they may abandon the use of roles and have an open dynamic discussion. The teacher becomes a facilitator and although he/she does evaluate the group, the students also engage in self-assessment. Once the book is read and discussed, the group members share with the whole class and a different book is chosen.

67) **It is important for students to have an opportunity to read silently or on their own:**
    (Average Rigor) (Skill 3.4)

    A) hourly.

    B) daily.

    C) weekly.

    D) monthly

Answer: B) daily

Reading specialists, administrators and teachers should take a critical look at the policies in place within the school for meeting the reading needs of all students. Part of this should include a school-wide reading initiative such as 15 minutes of silent reading in every classroom every day. During this time, the teacher can be reading as a model for the students or can be conferencing with individual students about what they are reading. This can take the form of listening to students read or asking them questions to ensure they comprehend what they are reading.

68) **Prose fiction includes which of the following types of literature:**
    (Average Rigor) (Skill 3.6)

    A) Essays

    B) Biographies

    C) Novels

    D) None of the above.

Answer: C) Novels

Prose fiction is literature about imaginary people, places and events. This narrative genre can be used to stimulate students' imaginations while considering the author's view of the world. This genre includes novels, short stories and plays, each of which has its own distinctive characteristics. They all have a setting, conflict, plot, climax and resolution to varying degrees.

69) Dictionary study:
(Average Rigor) (Skill 3.6)

A) can begin in grades 1 or 2.

B) can begin in pre-K using the lush picture dictionaries.

C) should start on grade three level.

D) A and B.

Answer: D) A and B.

Dictionary skills should be taught at an early age to assist students in discovering meaning of words. The use of a dictionary is often used to support the reading of a particular text.

70) Author's viewpoint questions stump Gary. His teacher can help him by asking him during their reading conferences:
(Average Rigor) (Skill 3.7)

A) If Gary feels the book he is reading, is it just right for him.

B) What the author would say about what the character is doing in the story.

C) How the story can be changed to another genre.

D) If Gary wants to read more books by this author.

Answer: B) What the author would say about what the character is doing in the story.

Author's viewpoint refers to what the author was thinking or feeling as they wrote the book. Questions may include: What do you think the author meant by having the character say that statement?

71) One of the many ways in which a child can demonstrate comprehension of a story is by:
(Average Rigor) (Skill 3.9)

   A) Filling in a strategy sheet.

   B) Retelling the story orally.

   C) Retelling the story in writing.

   D) All of the above.

Answer: D) All of the above.

All are examples of ways a child can demonstrate that they understand what they have read.

72) To promote word study, children can:
(Average Rigor) (Skill 3.10)

   A) Be required to go to the dictionary at least once or twice a day.

   B) Collect and share words of interest they find in their readings.

   C) Do vocabulary work sheets from a basal reader or commercial vocabulary book.

   D) Do all of the above.

Answer: D) Do all of the above.

All of the answers listed could be used to promote word study in the classroom.

73) **Structural analysis is:**
    (Rigorous) (Skill 3.10)

    A) the "sounding out" a printed sequence of letters based on knowledge of letter sound correspondences

    B) when the teacher keeps a detailed recording of the errors or inaccurate attempts of a child reader during a reading assessment

    C) the process of hearing a spoken word and identifying its separate phonemes or syllables.

    D) the process of examining the words in the text for meaningful word units (affixes, base words, inflected endings).

Answer: D) the process of examining the words in the text for meaningful word units (affixes, base words, inflected endings).

Structural analysis of words as defined by J. David Cooper (2004) involves the study of significant word parts. This analysis can help the child with pronunciation and constructing meaning.

74) **A delegation from the United Kingdom has come to the United States and since they are considering adapting the balanced literacy approach, they are very interested in seeing the small group demonstrated. Mr. Adams knows that he should bring them into Greg's room when Greg is doing which activity?**
    (Rigorous) (Skill 3.11)

    A) A mini lesson.

    B) A conference with individual students.

    C) A time when children are divided into small and independent study groups.

    D) A read-aloud.

Answer: C) A time when children are divided into small and independent study groups.

In a balanced literacy approach, small group time is when small groups of students are pulled to work independently with focused direction from the teacher.

75) It is 4 PM, yet Francine is still in her classroom. The seats in her classroom are filled with adults of various ages who are holding books. They are seated two by two with both holding copies of the same book. Francine probably is:
(Rigorous) (Skill 3.13)

   A) Explaining to parents how she will teach a particular story.

   B) Demonstrating shared reading with a buddy for volunteer parents.

   C) Hosting a parents organization meeting for her grade level.

   D) Distributing old books from the class library to parents.

Answer: B) Demonstrating shared reading with a buddy for volunteer parents.

It is important to provide opportunities for the public to come into the school and participate in activities to encourage reading. During these incentive and fun programs, it is important to share tidbits of information about the methodologies and strategies being implemented. In this way, the public can begin to understand the differences in reading instruction today than perhaps what occurred when they attended school. Adults often comment on changes they see in current educational trends.

76) Ms. James is seated with a child by her side. The child is reading aloud from an open book. Ms. James is teaching in a school that has embraced the Balanced Literacy Approach. Therefore it is most likely that Ms. James is writing and recording:
(Average Rigor) (Skill 3.14)

   A) The child's use of expression in reading aloud.

   B) The child's errors and miscues.

   C) Her observations of the child's attitude toward reading.

   D) The child's feelings about the particular passage being read.

Answer: B) The child's errors and miscues.

Running records taken of children help the teacher learn about the cueing systems that children use. It is important for the teacher to adjust reading instruction based on the pattern of miscues gathered from several successive reading records. When the teacher carefully reviews a given student's substitutions and self corrections, certain patterns begin to surface

77) "Self correct" in reading means:
(Easy) (Skill 3.14)

A) The teacher corrects on the record the errors the child makes.

B) The child goes back and corrects errors made in a running record.

C) The reading specialist teaches this to the child.

D) a and b.

Answer: B) The child goes back and corrects errors made in a running record.

SELF-CORRECTION- children begin to correct some of their own reading errors. Generally this behavior is accompanied by the re-reading of the previous phrase or sentence.

78) When taking a child's running record, the kinds of self corrections the child makes:
(Average Rigor) (Skill 3.14)

A) Are not important, but the percentage of accuracy is important.

B) May show something about which cueing systems the child relies on.

C) Can be meaningful if analyzed over several records.

D) Both b and c

Answer: D) Both b and c

A running record provides the teacher with insight into what a child is thinking and how they are approaching a text as they read. Teachers are better able to understand a student's strengths and weaknesses.

79) **Miscue analysis assists the teacher in determining which of the following:**
    (Average Rigor) (Skill 3.14)

    A) Methods a student uses to figure out unknown words

    B) Student ability to monitor their own reading

    C) Strategies that students are using with the greatest success

    D) All of the above

Answer: D) All of the above

As a teacher observes a child's reading and analyzes the data, then can determine how a student attempts to figure out words, how students check for comprehension and the strengths and weaknesses of the child.

80) **In terms of a balanced literacy classroom, a "leveled bin" indicates:**
    (Easy) (Skill 3.15)

    A) A plant set at child's eye level for descriptive writing purposes.

    B) A bin with books the child has selected.

    C) A bin with books leveled by the teacher.

    D) A bin with all kinds of reading materials including magazines and packaging on a child's level.

Answer: C) A bin with books leveled by the teacher

The classroom library in the context of the balanced literacy approach to reading instruction is focused on leveled books. These are books which have been leveled with the support of Fountas and Pinnell's Guided Reading: *Good First Teaching for All Children* and *Matching Books to Readers: Using Leveled Reading in Guided Reading,* K-3.

81) **Direct teaching of a concept or strategy means:**
(Average Rigor) (Skill 3.15)

  A) The teacher teaches the concept or strategy as part of a genre lesson.

  B) The teacher teaches the concept as part of the writing workshop.

  C) The teacher explicitly announces to the class that this strategy will be taught.

  D) The teacher teaches the strategy to a small group of children or to an individual child.

Answer: D) The teacher teaches the strategy to a small group of children or to an individual child.

Direct teaching occurs when the teacher specifically teaches or explains a skill to a student or group of students.

82) **The theorist who believes children should not be "taught" vocabulary and structural analysis is:**
(Rigorous) (Skill 3.16)

  A) Cooper

  B) Flesch

  C) Hirsch

  D) Calkins

Answer: A) Cooper

Cooper (2004) believes that children should not be "taught" vocabulary and structural analysis skills.

83) **A key theorist who supports a phonics centered approach is:**
    (Rigorous) (Skill 3.16)

   A) Marie Clay.

   B) Sharon Taberski.

   C) Shelley Harwayne.

   D) Rudolf Flesch.

Answer: D) Rudolf Flesch

Researchers, such as Flesch (l981), support a phonics-centered foundation before the use of engaging reading texts. This is at the crux of the phonics versus whole language/ balanced literacy/ integrated language arts, teaching of reading controversy.

84) **D.E.A.R. stands for**
    (Easy) (Skill 4.2)

   A) Day Everyone Around Reads

   B) Drop Everything and Read

   C) Drop Everyone and Read

   D) Daily Events and Reading

Answer: B) Drop Everything and Read

Silent reading involves the students reading to themselves. Some teachers regularly have a silent reading period in the class, such as Drop Everything And Read (DEAR).

85) Asking a child if what he or she has read makes sense to him or her, is prompting the child to use:
(Easy) (Skill 4.2)

   A) Phonics cues.

   B) Syntactic cues.

   C) Semantic cues.

   D) Prior knowledge.

Answer: C) Semantic cues.

SEMANTIC CUES- children use their prior knowledge, sense of the story, and pictures to support their predicting and confirming the meaning of the text.

86) The strategy in which a graphic organizer is used to help identify what students know, what they want to know, and what they learned is referred to as:
(Easy) (Skill 4.3)

   A) A bubble map

   B) A reading log

   C) A K-W-L- chart

   D) A Venn Diagram

Answer: C) A K-W-L- chart

A K-W-L chart is a graphic organizer strategy which activates children's prior knowledge and also helps them to target their reading of expository texts. This focus is achieved through having the children reflect on three key questions

87) **Reader's Theater is:**
    (Average Rigor) (Skill 4.4)

    A) Reading as a group or with the teacher

    B) When students use scripts that have different parts for different characters

    C) When students read aloud daily

    D) When students work together to provide instruction for each other

Answer: B) When students use scripts that have different parts for different characters

Reader's theater is just as it sounds. It is when students act out a story.

88) **A natural role for a highly proficient reader would be:**
    (Rigorous) (Skill 4.5)

    A) To assist the teacher with cleaning the classroom and organizing the student folders.

    B) To develop charts for the teacher by copying needed poems for full class study.

    C) Tutor and support struggling readers.

    D) Work on his/her own interests while the teacher works with the rest of the class.

Answer: C) Tutor and support struggling readers.

Highly proficient readers can sometimes support early readers through a partner relationship. Some children, particularly the emergent and beginning early readers, benefit from reading books with partners. The partners sit side by side and each one takes turns reading the entire text.

89) The term graphophonemic awareness refers to:
(Easy) (Skill 4.6)

A) Handwriting skills.

B) Letter to sound recognition.

C) Alphabetic principle.

D) Phonemic awareness

Answer: C) Alphabetic principle

Graphophonemic involves:
- Match all consonant and short vowel sounds.
- Read one's own name.
- Read one syllable words and high frequency words.
- Demonstrate ability to read and understand that as letters in words change, so do the sounds.
- Generate the sounds from all letters including consonant blends and long vowel patterns. Blend those different sounds into recognizable words.
- Read common sight words.
- Read common word families.

90) Gracie seems to be struggling with her reading, even in first grade, although her mother works at a publishing firm and her dad is an editor. Her speech is also full of mispronunciations, although her parents were born in the school neighborhood. Gracie should be checked by:
(Average Rigor) (Skill 4.7)

A) A reading specialist.

B) A speech therapist or an audiologist

C) A pediatrician.

D) A psychologist.

Answer: B) A speech therapist or an audiologist.

A speech therapist or an audiologist works with students who show difficulties in pronouncing words to improve the quality of their speech.

91) Environmental print is available at all of the following except:
    (Easy) (Skill 4.7)

    A) Within a newspaper.

    B) On the page of a library book.

    C) On a supermarket circular.

    D) In a commercial flyer.

Answer: B) On the page of a library book.

Environmental print involves print from items such as signs, boxes, etc. Magazines and catalogues are another source of environmental print that is accessible with ads for child centered products. Supermarket circulars and coupons from the newspaper are also excellent for engaging children in using environmental print as reading, especially when combined with dramatic play centers or prop boxes.

92) The best way for a teacher to track a student's progress in demonstrating the alphabetic principal/ graphophonemic awareness is to:
    (Rigorous) (Skill 5.1)

    A) Provide group assessments

    B) Maintain individual records

    C) Assess with standardized tests

    D) Have the student assessed by a team of teachers

Answer: B) Maintain individual records

The teacher will want to maintain individual records of children's reading behaviors demonstrating alphabetic principle/graphophonemic awareness

93) **Cues in reading are:**
(Easy) (Skill 5.1)

- A) Vowel sounds.

- B) Digraphs.

- C) Sources of information used by readers to help them construct meaning.

- D) None of the above.

Answer: C) Sources of information used by readers to help them construct meaning.

Cuing systems assist readers to construct meaning. These include: Syntactic and Semantic.

94) **A teacher is asking children to look at the beginning letters of words. She then asks the child to connect the beginning letter to the text and story and to think about what word would make sense there. This is an example of:**
(Average Rigor) (Skill 5.2)

- A) A balanced literacy approach.

- B) A phonemic approach.

- C) A phonic approach.

- D) AN ELL differentiated approach.

Answer: C) A phonic approach.

Instruction begins with a strong phonics approach, learning letter-sound relationships and often using basal readers or *decodable books*.

95) **To encode means that you:**
    (Average Rigor) (Skill 5.3)

    A) Decode a second time.

    B) Construct meaning from a code.

    C) Tell someone a message.

    D) None of the above.

Answer: B) Construct meaning from a code.

ENCODE- to change a message into symbols. For example, readers encode oral language into writing.

96) **Dictionary study:**
    (Average Rigor) (Skill 5.3)

    A) can begin in grades 1 or 2.

    B) can begin in pre-K using the lush picture dictionaries.

    C) should start on grade three level.

    D) A and B.

Answer: D) A and B.

Dictionary skills should be taught at an early age to assist students in discovering meaning of words. The use of a dictionary is often used to support the reading of a particular text.

97) **The best ways to select words students need to learn to spell include all of the following except:**
(Rigorous) (Skill 5.4)

A) Misspelled words from student writing

B) Lists of theme words

C) Lists from a spelling textbook

D) Lists of words from content areas

Answer: C) Lists from a spelling textbook

Some of the techniques teachers use to determine the words students need to spell include:

- Lists of misspelled words from student writing
- Lists of theme words
- Lists of words from the content areas
- Word banks

98) **Children "own" words when all of the following happen except:**
(Average Rigor) (Skill 5.4)

A) They find these words on their own.

B) The teacher provides a mandated word list.

C) They use the words in their own writings.

D) The words appear in literature that interests them.

Answer: B) The teacher provides a mandated word list.

When students take ownership of words this generally means that the words are of special significance to the child. This could mean that they use the words frequently in their writing, they appear in favorite books, or they discover the words on their own.

99) "Ballgame" is a _____ word. Its meaning is derived from the combination of "Ball" and "Game":
(Easy) (Skill 5.4)

    A) Contraction.

    B) Compound.

    C) Portmanteau.

    D) Palindrome.

Answer: B) Compound

Compound Words occur when two or more base words are connected to form a new word. The meaning of the new word is in some way connected with that of the base word. Examples are *firefighter, newspaper*, and *pigtail*.

100) The word "bat" is a ___ word for "batter-up":
(Easy) (Skill 5.4)

    A) Suffix.

    B) Prefix.

    C) Root word.

    D) Inflectional ending.

Answer: C) Root word.

This is a word from which another word is developed. The second word can be said to have its "root" in the first, such as *vis, to see,* in visor or vision.

101) Four of Ms. Wolmark's students have lived in other countries. She is particularly pleased to be studying Sumerian proverbs with them as part of the sixth grade unit in analyzing the sayings of other cultures because:
(Rigorous) (Skill 5.5)

   A) This gives her a break from teaching and the children can share sayings from other cultures they and their families have experienced.

   B) This validates the experiences and expertise of ELL learners in her classroom.

   C) This provides her children from the US with a lens on other cultural values.

   D) All of the above.

Answer: D) All of the above.

It is recommended that all teachers of reading and particularly those who are working with ELL students use meaningful, student centered, and culturally customized activities. These activities may include: language games, word walls, and poems. Some of these activities might, if possible, be initiated in the child's first language and then reiterated in English.

102) An effective way to build vocabulary and to make connections with mandated science and mathematics material is to teach Greek and Latin roots using:
(Average Rigor) (Skill 5.5)

   A) Semantic maps.

   B) Hierarchical arrays.

   C) Linear arrays.

   D) Word webs.

Answer: D) Word Webs

For example, during readings on rodents (a favorite of first and second graders), the teacher draws her class's attention to the fact that beavers, gnaw at things with their teeth. She then connects the "dent" root or derivative to the children's lives, other words they are familiar with or experiences. The children then volunteer *"dentist," "dental," "denture."* The teacher begins to place these in a graphic organizer, or word web.

103) A bound morpheme is:
(Easy) (Skill 5.5)

A) A prefix.

B) A contraction.

C) An inflectional ending that can be added to a base word to change its case, gender, number, tense or form.

D) A root word.

Answer: C) An inflectional ending that can be added to a base word to change its case, gender, number, tense or form.

MORPHEMES- the smallest units of meaning in words. There are two types of morphemes; free morphemes, which can stand alone such as *love,* and bound morphemes, which must be attached to another morpheme to carry meaning such as *ed* in *loved.*

104) Teachers should select at least ___ words for pre-reading vocabulary discussion:
(Rigorous) (Skill 5.5)

A) 12.

B) 15.

C) 2-3.

D) 8-10.

Answer: C) 2-3

The number of words that require explicit teaching should only be two or three. If the number is higher than that, the children need guided reading and the text needs to be broken down into smaller sections for teaching. When broken down into smaller sections, each text section should only have two to three words which need explicit teaching.

105) Among the literary strategies that teachers can use to activate prior knowledge are:
(Easy) (Skill 6.1)

A) Predicting and previewing a story.

B) Story mapping.

C) Venn diagramming.

D) Linear arrays.

Answer: A) Predicting and previewing a story.

By predicting the events or preview a story the teacher can help students connect with and not only activate prior knowledge, but build vocabulary as well.

106) A key theorist whose work has helped teacher's document children's oral reading progress throughout the school year is:
(Average Rigor) (Skill 6.1)

A) Jerome Bruner.

B) Daniel J. Chard.

C) J. David Cooper.

D) Marie Clay.

Answer: D. Marie Clay

Understanding the value and importance of the concepts of print for beginning readers developed out of the work of Marie Clay in New Zealand. Assessment of these skills typically occurs in kindergarten and into first grade as necessary.

107) Bill has been called up to the teacher for an individual conference. She asks him to retell one of the books he has listed on his weekly log. He begins and is still talking 7 minutes later. Most probably, Bill:
(Average Rigor) (Skill 6.2)

   A) Told the entire story with all its details and minor characters.

   B) May or may not have really gotten the main points and perspectives of the story.

   C) May have really liked the Story.

   D) None of the above.

Answer: A) Told the entire story all its details and minor characters.

A retell should only take a couple of minutes. In a retell, the student should only relay major event, major characters, and provide a summary of key points.

108) When taking a child's running record, the kinds of self corrections the child makes:
(Average Rigor) (Skill 6.2)

   A) Are not important, but the percentage of accuracy is important.

   B) May show something about which cueing systems the child relies on.

   C) Can be meaningful if analyzed over several records.

   D) Both B and C

Answer: D) Both B and C

A running record provides the teacher with insight into what a child is thinking and how they are approaching a text as they read. Teachers are better able to understand a student's strengths and weaknesses.

109) Once a teacher has carefully recorded and documented a running record:
(Rigorous) (Skill 6.2)

   A) There is nothing further to do as long as the teacher keeps the running record for conferences and documentation of grades.

   B) The teacher should review the running record and other subsequent ones taken for growth over time.

   C) The teacher should differentiate instruction for that particular student as indicated by growth over time and evidence of other needs.

   D) Both b and c

Answer: C) The teacher should differentiate instruction for that particular student as indicated by growth over time and evidence of other needs.

After the completion of a running record, the teacher should analyze the record to determine the next teaching step that should occur for the student.

110) "Sounds right" can sound wrong to:
(Rigorous) (Skill 6.2)

   A) Any reader who is not a fluent or early reader.

   B) AN ELL reader.

   C) A struggling reader.

   D) None of the above.

Answer: B) An ELL reader

The English language contains sounds that are not found in other languages and some letters have more than one sound. Because ELL students are not native to English then many of the words will not sound right.

111) Sometimes children can be asked to demonstrate their understanding of a text in a non-written format. This might include all of the following except:
(Easy) (Skill 6.2)

   A) A story map.

   B) A Venn diagram.

   C) Storyboarding a part of the story with dialogue bubbles.

   D) Retelling or paraphrasing.

Answer: D) Retelling or paraphrasing.

Children are expected and encouraged to tell as much of a story as they can remember. Re-telling is far more extensive than just summarizing. Children should include the beginning, middle and end plot lines and should be able to tell about the book's characters.

112) Norm-referenced tests:
   (Average rigor) (Skill 6.2)

   A) Give information only about the local samples results.

   B) Provide information about the local test takers did compared to a representative sampling of national test takers.

   C) Make no comparisons to national test takers.

   D) None of the above.

Answer: B) Provide information about the local test takers did compared to a representative sampling of national test takers.

Norm-referenced –test in which the children are measured against one another. Scores on this test are reported in percentiles. Each percentile indicates the percent of the testing population whose scores were lower than or the same as a particular child's score. Percentile is defined as a score on a scale of 100 showing the percentage of a distribution that is equal to it or below it.

113) The reliability of a test is measured by:
(Rigorous) (Skill 6.3)

A) The number of children who can pass it.

B) The number of children who fail it.

C) The degree to which it measures what it is supposed to measure over time.

D) None of the above

Answer: C. The degree to which it measures what it is supposed to measure over time.

Reliability is the consistency of the test. This is measured by whether the test will indicate the same score for the child who takes it more than once.

114) A quartile on a test is:
(Average Rigor) (Skill 6.3)

A) A quarter of the grades grouped.

B) The division of the percentiles into four segments each of which is called a quartile.

C) 25 of the tests scored.

D) B and C

Answer: B) The division of the percentile into four segment each of which is called a quartile.

One of four segments of a distribution that has been divided into quarters. For example, the second-from-the-bottom quartile of an income distribution is those whose income exceeds the incomes of from 25% to 50% of the population.

115) Validity in assessment means:
(Rigorous) (Skill 6.3)

A) The test went off without any previewing of the questions or leaks on its contents.

B) The majority of test takers passed.

C) The correct time was allowed for the children to complete the test.

D) The test assessed what it was supposed to assess and measure.

Answer: D. The test assessed what it was supposed to assess and measure

Validity is how well a test measures what it is supposed to measure. Teacher made tests are therefore not generally extremely valid, although they may be an appropriate measure for the validity of the concept the teacher wants to assess for his/her own children's achievement.

116) "Bias" in testing occurs when:
(Rigorous) (Skill 6.3)

A) The assessment instrument is not an objective, fair and impartial one for a given cultural, ethnic, or special needs participant.

B) The testing administrator is biased.

C) The same test is given with no time considerations or provisions for those in need of more time or those who have handicapping conditions.

D) All of the above

Answer: D. All of the above.

Bias in testing occurs when the information within the test or the information required to respond to a multiple choice question or constructed response (essay question on the test) is information that is not available to some test takers who come from a different cultural, ethnic, linguistic or socio-economic background than do the majority of the test takers.

117) Communication with parents needs to occur:
(Easy) (Skill 6.4)

   A) at the end of each grading period only.

   B) several times during the grading period.

   C) at the end of the school year.

   D) It is not important to communicate with parents.

Answer: B) several times during the grading period

Teachers should communicate with parents many times during the school year, not only during the two times parent-teacher conferences are typically held. Sending home good news is especially welcome and may build rapport that the teacher can later call on if s/he needs to contact parents with a request to work together on constructive change. "A," though it sounds correct, misses the opportunity of more-frequent communication for building alliances with parents. "C" is woefully inadequate. "D" should not even be considered as a possible answer. Parents and teachers are intimate partners in children's education.

118) Tasks a reading specialist can use to determine student's level of comprehension include:
(Rigorous) (Skill 6.5)

   A) Listening to passages.

   B) Oral Reading

   C) Written Response

   D) All of the above.

Answer: D) All of the above.

In the diagnosis of reading difficulties, the specialist should use tools which measure the child's listening comprehension, oral reading skills, silent reading skills, and his/her ability to respond to reading in written form.

119) To keep abreast of reading trends and research, a reading specialist should subscribe to which of the following periodicals:
(Average Rigor) (Skill 7.2)

A) *The Reading Teacher*

B) *Educational Leadership*

C) *Reading Research Quarterly*

D) All of the above

Answer: D) All of the above

All of the journals listed are key resources to any teacher that teaches reading skills.

120) A strategy is:
(Average Rigor) (Skill 7.3)

A) A practice or routine the teacher can continually refer to.

B) A practice or routine a child can continually refer to or use.

C) A sheet or template for a practice the child can continually fill out.

D) All of the above.

Answer: D) All of the above

All of the answers refer to types of strategies.

TEACHER CERTIFICATION STUDY GUIDE

121) **To assist in the integration of various cultures within the reading program, it helps to employ a variety of strategies including:**
    (Rigorous) (Skill 7.4)

    A) Reading Workshop

    B) Writing Workshop

    C) Responding

    D) All of the above

Answer: D) All of the above.

Teachers have a critical role to play in encouraging multicultural experiences. They have an opportunity to incorporate activities that reflect our nation's increasing diversity and allow students to share their similarities, develop a positive cultural identity, and appreciate the unique contributions of all cultures. The best way to incorporate multicultural literature depicting African-American, Asian, Arabic, Native American, and Hispanic heritage is to integrate it into the established reading program rather than as a separate or distinct area of study.

122) **The phrase "begin with the end in mind" when planning instruction implies teachers need to start the planning process with which of the following at the forefront:**
    (Rigorous) (Skill 7.5)

    A) Assessment

    B) Goals

    C) Objectives

    D) Procedures

Answer: A) Assessment

By employing "assessment for learning" teachers can assess the students before instruction to find out exactly where their deficiencies lie and gear the instruction toward them.

123) To enhance reading instruction it is recommended that schools to provide at least how many minutes of silent reading per day? *(Average Rigor) (Skill 7.6)*

A) 10

B) 15

C) 30

D) 60

Answer: B) 15

It is recommended that students spend at least 15 minutes each day in silent reading.

124) **Reading specialists play a key role in the enhancement of reading instruction within a school. Which of the following demonstrates ways in which this can occur?**
(Average Rigor) (Skill 7.7)

A) Working with groups of students

B) Track student progress in reading

C) Establish reading enrichment programs.

D) All of the above.

Answer: D) All of the above

As a reading specialist within a school, one of the duties entails serving as a resource for the rest of the teachers. There are several ways that this job can be accomplished, such as:

- Working with teachers in the classroom to organize the classroom setting
- Working with small groups of students in the classroom
- Helping organize professional development in the field of reading
- Preparing the Individual Program Plans for students needing extra reading assistance
- Creating inclusive classrooms
- Helping the teachers with learning about and employing different learning theories and ways students learn in the classroom
- Performing the testing on students to determine their reading levels for guided reading
- Tracking the progress of students in reading
- Determining strategies to help students develop as readers
- Identifying the individual needs of students with reading difficulties or those that need more challenges
- Analyzing the assessments and evaluations to provide assistance to the teachers in reporting to parents
- Establishing enrichment programs for students identified as reading beyond grade level

125) Collaboration is a key part of reading instruction. To foster a collaborative environment within a school which of the following factors is key?
(Average Rigor) (Skill 7.8)

A) Working individually to assess classroom teacher's progress

B) Allow time to visit other schools

C) Allow time to visit other classrooms

D) Both B and C

Answer: D) Both B and C

Providing time for teachers to get together to plan instructional activities geared towards reading contributes to a spirit of collaboration in the school. One way to accomplish this is to provide the teachers with time to visit other schools and observe what is happening in another classroom in the district. Teachers within the same division or teachers of one grade in the school can get together on a regular basis to discuss how they are teaching various concepts and to discuss how to best help students that are struggling with reading.

TEACHER CERTIFICATION STUDY GUIDE

Constructed Response Questions

Constructed Response Question One

Jean is a first year teacher who is taking over the classroom of a thirty-year veteran teacher who is retiring. Jean goes in to meet with the teacher. The teacher, Ms. Banks, talks about the importance of teaching the young first graders the concepts of print.

She gives Jean a list of these concepts and suggests that Jean create some assessment format so that she can be certain that all of her first graders learn these concepts. She also tells Jean that she will be volunteering her time in a neighborhood preschool program close to her home and so she will be taking her private books and materials with her. She suggests that Jean go over the list of concepts of print and consider the needs of her class as she prepares for teaching this crucial set of skills. Before Jean leaves the classroom, Ms. Banks tells her that the kindergarten teacher has let her know that three children who will be in her class next year are from ELL backgrounds where their families are not involved in oral story telling or reading from native language texts.

Ms. Banks' concepts of print list:

- STARTS ON LEFT

- GOES FROM LEFT TO RIGHT

- RETURN SWEEP

- MATCHES WORDS BY POINTING

- POINTS TO JUST ONE WORD

- POINTS TO FIRST AND LAST WORD

- POINTS TO 1 LETTER

- POINTS TO FIRST AND LAST LETTER

- PARTS of the BOOK: Cover, Title Page, Dedication page, Author and Illustrator

Jean thanks Ms. Banks for all of this help and asks if she can send Ms. Banks some of her teaching ideas for Concepts of Print and the ways she plans to differentiate instruction for her ELL students before the end of the year. Ms. Banks smiles and says she feels good to know that her classroom will be taken over by Jean. She promises to review Jean's response.

READING

Constructed Response Answer One

First, as far as assessment for the key skills of concepts of print, I have decided that it is very important that I have a record of when and how well each of my students masters these concepts. After much thought, I realized that I will be keeping assessment notebooks for all of my students as part of my general reading and teaching. Therefore, I plan to print out all the key concepts of print on an 8" x 11" piece of paper in a grid format. This sheet will be included with other assessment grids for each individual child.

After conferencing with the child and I determine the child has demonstrated mastery of a particular concept, I will check it off on the grid and date that mastery. If I have other comments to make about the child's level of mastery or fluency, I will make an anecdotal notation about the child as well. I think that this will guarantee that I have a detailed checklist record and anecdotal record of all my children's individual progress on concepts of print.

I plan to use Big Books and many of the latest picture books, including Caldecott award winners in demonstrating and sharing with children many of the concepts of print. I will do much of my instruction mini-lessons. In fact I intend to use some of my own favorite alphabet books to introduce these conventions. With a book like Clare Beaton's, *Zoe and her Zebra*, I can easily and naturally cover the title page, cover, illustrator, and also manage to engage the children in the use of repetitive language.

Once I have shared that delightful book with the children as a read-aloud, we will be able to return to it again and use the repetitive language of it in its big book format to demonstrate for the children how they can point under each word as if there is a button to push. I can also demonstrate for the children how they should start at the top of the text and move from left to right. I will model going back to the left and under the previous line in a return weep.

After modeling this as part of the mini-lesson, the children can be divided in small groups or pairs and take other Big Books and practice the "point under each word" and the "return sweep" as part of "shared reading" or buddy reading. I should be able to identify some highly proficient readers who will be happy to serve as 'buddy" reader/tutors for the ELL children. I will ask that these "buddies" take time in small groups to work on another book from the alphabet book collection to share with the class as a whole. The use of the alphabet books also helps me to get some time in on the alphabetic principle.

I will also do a classroom writing workshop using the original alphabet book I use for the read-aloud, say *Zoe and Her Zebra* as a model for creating our own story. Perhaps we will call it *Barry and his Boxer*. In this way we will have a concrete literary product that demonstrates the children's mastery of and fluency in the concepts of print as they create an "in style of" story about a peer using illustrations, title page, dedication page, numbering of pages, back and front cover and other concepts of print.

I think that using individualized assessments, a group/class collaborative writing project, and an anchor alphabet book will help me successfully teach the concepts of print and address the needs of my ELL learners as well.

Constructed Response Question Two

Marianne has been selected as one of a team of teachers who will start teaching in a brand new school building that has been under construction for several years. While Marianne, a grade three teacher, is thrilled to be moving into new facilities, she is a bit overwhelmed to have to "set up her room" all over again at the new site. Her administrator, Mr. Adams, tells her that there are five new teachers with no previous experience teaching primary school age children who will be on staff. He tells her that these educators could really use help setting up their classrooms.

Marianne smiles and decides that she would very much like to use her set-up of her own grade three classroom as a workshop and demonstration for setting up a literacy teaching environment for these new staff members. Mr. Adams thinks that is a great idea and asks Marianne for an agenda and for a general description of what she will cover in her three hour workshop so that he can give it to the district office.

Marianne is happy to comply because she realizes that she will be assisting new colleagues and getting ten helping hands to help her set up all the materials she has accumulated over a twenty-year career.

Constructed Response Answer Two

The concept of sharing with new colleagues how to set up a classroom is very exciting to me. I know, based on my experiences, how crucial a well-planned and conceptualized space is for young learners' literacy learning. Therefore this is an agenda for what I will cover in my three hour in service session for my new colleagues.

First, I will discuss how whatever the size of the classroom space, it must be sectioned off into the following areas: a meeting area, with a sofa or "soft" setting; a chair, easel and basket to store book bags; a conference table; children's tables; and bin/basket main area for trade books; and another space for computers.

I may even give out a diagram of my classroom from my old school and some pictures. We will discuss collaboratively how I will set up my own new space as well as how they will want to set up their own spaces to allow for different uses of space within their own classrooms.

I will get into the issue of whether or not they want to have a traditional desk or use smaller tables for everyone. I think that they will need time to consider their own teaching styles in this regard. All teachers need to set up a space where they can easily confer with children and have access to individual assessment notebooks, reading folders (plus poetry/spelling, reading response, and handwriting notebooks) for all their students. I intend to show them how to prepare these folders for each child and how to store them so they can get to them when they need to make additional annotations for each child. Given the fact that I am working with new colleagues, I suspect that this will take at least an hour and a half of our time. I am also going to model for them a weekly reading log.

Most important of all, I am going to spend the major amount of time talking to them about the book bins as I place mine around the classroom. I will show them how to label the books using the Fountas and Pinnell levels and how to arrange the book bins with the spines out so that the children can see the books. Together we will examine how the bookcases should be close to the walls and the expository books should be separated from the narrative texts. I will also get together my audio-cassettes and book sets so that they can see how I set up my read-along center for all my children. I will share some dual language tapes I use with ELL students as well. I have some extra "author's hats" and author's chair slipcovers I will share with them.

I also intend to show them how to select Big Books for the easel display and anchor books to be shown there as well. By the way, I will also coach them how to write away for supplies and how to store supplies in common areas so that some children are not missing necessary materials for class activities.

Even though we are focusing on literacy, I am going to show them where to store mathematics materials, other texts, and art supplies. I will end the session by making sure that they know where to place their chart wall and the word wall. If I have time, I will sit down with each of them and start them on the word wall and some key charts for their first day. They will leave my room with an actual experience of setting up a literacy environment, plus viable teaching and reading suggestions for the first day. Most importantly, I will be available for an in-school classroom consultation, if necessary.

Tips and Reflections for tackling the Constructed Response Questions:

- Use as many phrases and words from the question as possible in your response.

- Be specific. Mention specific books, authors, theorists, and strategies you have studied. Even though this is a test about the teaching of reading, make specific use of children's trade books and literature if appropriate.

- Use as many details as you are given in the question to make your response. Write no more than 5-7 moderately brief paragraphs. The more you write, the larger the margin for error. Check your spelling, grammar and check to see that you answered everything that was asked, but no more than what was asked. Be positive and proactive about your ability to respond to whichever situation is presented.

- Stick with strategies, teaching ideas, and methods that are tried and true.

- Reread your writing at least twice for spelling and grammatical errors.

Additional Professional Citations

Block, Cathy Collins. (2002). *Comprehension Instruction: Research Based Practices.* New York: The Guilford Press.

Calkins, Lucy McCormick. (2001). *The Art of Teaching Reading.* New York: Longman.

Cambourne, Briane. (2002). "Conditions for Literacy Learning." *The Reading Teacher,* 55, (8): 758-62.

Cambourne, Briane. (1993). *The Whole Story: Natural Learning and the Acquisition of Literacy in the Classroom.* Auckland, NZ: Ashton, Scholastic.

Cunningham, Patricia M. (2000). *Phonics They Use: Words for Reading and Writing.* 3rd Edition. New York: Addison Wesley Longman.

Evidence Based Reading Instruction. (2002) Articles from International Reading Association. Newark, Delaware: International Reading Association.

Hoyt, Linda. (2002). *Make It Real: Strategies for Success with Informational Texts.* Portsmouth, NH: Heinemann.

Kimball-Lopez, Kimberley. (1999). *Connecting with Traditional Literature.* Boston: Allyn and Bacon.

Moustafa, Margaret. (1997). *Beyond Traditional Phonics.* Portsmouth, NH: Heinemann.

Owocki, Gretchen. (2003). *Strategic Instructions for K-3 Students.* Portsmouth, NH: Heinemann.

Owacki, G, and Y. Goodman. (2002). *Kidwatching: Documenting Children's Literacy Development.* Portsmouth, NH: Heinemann.

Quindlen, Anna. (1998). *How Reading Changed My Life.* New York: Ballantine Books, 1998.

Routman, Regie. (2000). *Conversations.* Portsmouth, NH: Heinemann.

Schultz, C. (2000). *How Partner Reading Fosters Literacy Development in First Grade Students.* Action Research project, Saginaw Valley State University, University Center, Michigan.

Short, K., J. Harste and C. Burke. (1996). *Creating Classrooms for Authors and Inquirers.* Portsmouth, NH: Heinemann.

Trelease, Jim. (2001). *The Read-Aloud Handbook*. 4th Ed. New York: Penguin.

Wilde, Sandra. (2000). *Miscue Analysis Made Easy: Building on Student Strengths.* Portsmouth, NH: Heinemann.

Wilde, Sandra. (2000). *Reading Made Easy*. Portsmouth, NH: Heinemann.

XAMonline, INC. 21 Orient Ave. Melrose, MA 02176
Toll Free number 800-509-4128
TO ORDER Fax 781-662-9268 OR www.XAMonline.com

PRAXIS SERIES   - PRAXIS - 2009

PO#   Store/School:

Address:

City, State Zip

Credit card number _____-_____-_____-_____   expiration_____

EMAIL _____

PHONE   **FAX**

13# ISBN 2007	TITLE	Qty	Retail	Total
978-1-60787-043-2	Art Sample Test 10133			
978-1-60787-031-9	Biology 20231, 20232, 20235			
978-1-58197-691-5	Chemistry 20241 20242, 20245			
978-1-60787-046-3	Earth and Space Sciences 20571			
978-1-60787-033-3	Special Education: Knowledge-Based Core Principles 20351			
978-1-60787-037-1	Special Education: Teaching Students with Behavioral Disorders/Emotional Disturbance 0371			
978-1-60787-035-7	PRAXIS Early Childhood/Education of Young Children 020, 022			
978-1-60787-041-8	Educational Leadership- Administration and Supervision 0410			
978-1-60787-048-7	Elementary Education 0011, 0012, 0014, 0016			
978-1-60787-044-9	English Language, Literature, and Composition 10041			
978-1-60787-053-1	French Sample Test 0173			
978-1-60787-042-5	Fundamental Subjects 0511			
978-1-60787-032-6	School Guidance & Counseling 20420			
978-1-58197-268-9	General Science 10435			
978-1-60787-039-5	Library Media Specialist 0310			
978-1-58197-658-8	Mathematics 10061, 20063			
978-1-58197-269-6	Middle School English Language Arts 10049			
978-1-58197-343-3	Middle School Mathematics 20069			
978-1-58197-263-4	Middle School Social Studies 0089			
978-1-60787-040-1	Physical Education 10091			
978-1-60787-047-0	Physics 0265			
978-1-60787-038-8	ParaPro Assessment 0755			
978-1-60787-036-4	PPST I: Basic Skills 0710, 0720, 0730			
978-1-60787-054-8	Government/Poltical Science 10930			
978-1-58197-577-2	Principals of Learning and Teaching 30521, 30522, 30523,			
978-1-60787-034-0	Reading 0200, 0201, 0202			
978-1-58197-696-0	Social Studies 10081			
978-1-58197-718-9	Spanish 10191, 30194			
	SUBTOTAL		Ship	$8.25
	FOR PRODUCT PRICES VISIT WWW.XAMONLINE.COM		**TOTAL**	

CPSIA information can be obtained at www.ICGtesting.com
Printed in the USA
LVOW021910040112

262375LV00003B/20/P

9 781607 870340